The Renewal of Trinitarian Theology

THEMES, PATTERNS & EXPLORATIONS

Roderick T. Leupp

IVP Academic

An imprint of InterVarsity Press
Downers Grove, Illinois

InterVarsity Press
P.O. Box 1400, Downers Grove, IL 60515-1426
World Wide Web: www.ivpress.com
E-mail: email@ivpress.com

InterVarsity Press® is the book-publishing division of InterVarsity Christian Fellowship/USA®, a student movement active on campus at hundreds of universities, colleges and schools of nursing in the United States of America, and a member movement of the International Fellowship of Evangelical Students. For information about local and regional activities, write Public Relations Dept., InterVarsity Christian Fellowship/USA, 6400 Schroeder Rd., P.O. Box 7895, Madison, WI 53707-7895, or visit the IVCF website at <www.intervarsity.org>.

Scripture quotations, unless otherwise noted, are from the New Revised Standard Version of the Bible, copyright 1989 by the Division of Christian Education of the National Council of Churches of Christ in the USA. Used by permission. All rights reserved.

The hymn on pp. 124-25, "Who Is She?" by Brian Wren, is © 1986 Hope Publishing Co., Carol Stream, IL 60188. All rights reserved. Used by permission.

The excerpt from "Midpoint" is from Collected Poems: 1953-1993 by John Updike, copyright © 1993 by John Updike. Used by permission of Alfred A. Knopf, a division of Random House, Inc.

The lines from "if everything happens that can't be done," copyright 1944, © 1972, 1991 by the Trustees for the E. E. Cummings Trust, are from Complete Poems: 1904-1962 by E. E. Cummings, edited by George J. Firmage. Used by permission of Liveright Publishing Corporation.

Design: Cindy Kiple

Images: green leaves: Image Source/Getty Images
        icon of the Trinity: Sophie Hacker/Getty Images

ISBN 978-0-8308-2889-0

Printed in the United States of America ∞

Library of Congress Cataloging-in-Publication Data

Leupp, Roderick T., 1953-
   The renewal of trinitarian theology: themes, patterns and
explorations / Roderick T. Leupp.
      p. cm.
   Includes bibliographical references and indexes.
   ISBN 978-0-8308-2889-0 (pbk.: alk paper)
   1. Trinity. 2. Theology, Doctrinal. I. Title.
BT111.3L485 2008
231'.044—dc22

                                                                            2008022669

P 29 28 27 26 25 24 23 22 21 20 19 18 17 16 15 14 13 12 11 10 9 8 7 6 5 4 3 2 1

Y 33 32 31 30 29 28 27 26 25 24 23 22 21 20 19 18 17 16 15 14 13 12 11 10 09 08

To my beautiful daughter Rebecca Louise Leupp

Absent in her presence

Present in her absence

Contents

Introduction

The Shape and Integrity of Trinitarian Theology

From the singing of "Holy, Holy, Holy" to being baptized in the threefold name of Father, Son and Holy Spirit, virtually all Christians know that when they confess faith in God, it is the triune God. A theologically dedicated and literate pastor may even offer up a prayer to God the Father through God the Son in the enablement of God the Spirit, knowing full well it is not three prayers being prayed, not three sets of divine ears listening, but one prayer to one God. Youthful joiners of the church will be led through their trinitarian paces much as primary grade students struggle to master the intricacies of English grammar.

Even those who make no Christian confession or who oppose the claims of the gospel will typically know something about the Trinity, if only that they think it nonsense that one God could yet present himself in three distinct but inseparable ways. The doctrine of the Trinity, in short, is of interest to those both within and without the Christian circle, and those who may not be sure where they really are.

Different times, seasons, events and occasions seem to call forth different emphases in Christian theology. Today, front and center, is

the triunity of God. This book is about this centrality. It is an introduction to the renewal of trinitarian theology.

To mention only the most obvious questions, Is the doctrine of the
Trinity available to human knowing exclusively and only as revelation? If the triune God can be known only through revelation, will
God as one-in-three or God as three-in-one make the strongest initial
impression? If knowing the triune God is a holy oscillation between
the one and the three, the three and the one, must we always begin
with the one?

If it is only through primal revelation that God as triune may be known,
can this knowledge be corroborated, demonstrated or even proven in
what we see and know and intuit in the everyday world? Is it to deepen
or cheapen God's triunity if hints of it are somehow strewn throughout
the world? Will we finally agree with the theological language of Paul
Molnar, who contends that "although we obviously have no alternative
but to understand God in the categories available to us in our human
experience, it is not anything within our experience or inherent in those
categories that prescribes who God is *in se* [within the divine self] and *ad
extra* [as known in the world]."[1]

Before the dominance of electronic mail, and for some today in spite
of it, could the simple act of writing, sealing and sending a letter bear
an understated witness to God's triunity? There are three—the author
of the letter, the letter itself, the recipient—but these three make no
sense when abstracted from the unity of the whole event. Dorothy Sayers expands and clarifies this basic insight, likening the doctrine of the
Trinity to writing a book, or any creative act at all, including painting
and sculpture. Any artist approaches the artistic calling with an idea in
mind. What is going to be created? The *what* of the original vision must
be *fleshed out* in the originating creative act. Given this creativity, *how*
is it going to be received in the world? Does this work of art have any
staying power once the artist launches it? Sayers refers to these three intertwined realities as Idea, Activity and Power, as the creative outburst
and its fruit return in some fashion to the creator. If you ask the author
which is "the real book," Sayers believes that the author would be hard
pressed to say, "because these things are essentially inseparable. Each

---

[1]Paul D. Molnar, *Divine Freedom and the Doctrine of the Immanent Trinity* (London: T & T
Clark, 2005), p. ix.

of them is the complete book separately; yet in the complete book all of them exist together."[2]

Trinitarian metaphors and remembrances can be multiplied almost without end, to the point of edification for some and distraction for others. Some of these are by now virtually enshrined in catechetical instruction: the Trinity "proven" by water existing in the three conditions of liquid, solid and gas; an egg's shell, white and yolk bestowing a breakfast homily. It takes no great theological imagination to see oneness flowering into threeness and triplicity converging to unity here, there and everywhere. Would these trinitarian images be convincing or, if not that, at least inviting?

- three trunks growing together to form one tree
- two men walking as one and huddled under a single umbrella
- knife, fork, spoon—all dedicated to the singular quest for food
- three young girls, arms linked, falling over backward in one motion
- three boys, on the porch together, all eating green apples and sharing common talk
- three squirrels frolicking on the same tree branch

To some observers, then, there may be a hidden trinitarian hand in nearly everything. This hiddenness may often rise to conscious view and intelligible articulation. When one of today's leading rock stars, Bono of the group U2, commends the Beatles' "intoxicating mix of melody, harmony and rhythm" and concludes that their mastery of these three dynamics is the greatest balance "that has ever been, before or since,"[3] one may revel in yet another demonstration of God's triunity in a most unlikely place.

Or maybe not. Early Christian sensibilities were formed not so much by a vivid imagination, finding clues to the Trinity everywhere, as by a constant yet growing awareness that

> when the fullness of time had come, God sent his Son, born of a woman, born under the law, in order to redeem those who were under the law, so that we might receive adoption as children. And because you are children, God has sent the Spirit of his Son into our hears, crying "Abba! Father!" (Gal 4:4-6)

---

[2]Dorothy Sayers, *The Mind of the Maker* (San Francisco: HarperSanFrancisco, 1979), p. 41.
[3]Anthony DeCurtis, "Bono," *Rolling Stone*, November 15, 2007, p. 62.

The Christian calling is not to ingenious speculation about how God can be three and yet one, one and yet three, but is rather a firm adherence to the truth of the incarnation, and a glad acceptance of the benefits of the Father's eternal Word appearing in flesh in Jesus Christ, and a sturdy resolve to transform the world in the power of the Holy Spirit.

Yet the singular story of the gospel is played out by three Actors who are themselves the beginning and the ending of salvation history. In the apostle Peter's witness to this history, God the Father chooses and calls and the Holy Spirit sanctifies those who are so called and chose obedience to Jesus Christ, and "to be sprinkled with his blood" (1 Pet 1:2). Because the story is one, "themselves" is not the only way to describe the Christian God, who is also himself or Godself. To give God his full voice, his being three-in-one and one-in-three may not be an easy or simple thing.

Of what consequence is this perplexing back and forth between the three and the one, the one and the three, for Christian faith and practice? for Christian ethics, worship and spirituality? for political life and cultural achievement? for historical progress and technological refinement? for how the sacred world and the secular realm by turns and degrees overlap, interpenetrate and oppose each other?

Must there be representatively, if not explicitly, trinitarian answers and solutions to these arduous questions and the ten thousand related ones? A trinitarian politics, for example, beginning in dialogue and ending in consensus, is obviously superior to an unbending, autocratic regime and may even be better than some forms of democracy.

It would be more true to see the triune God as setting the mood, the tone and the agenda not only for theology but for politics, the arts and culture, than to see trinitarian theology as perpetually rising to the challenge of another crisis, issue or social dislocation. In the beginning is the Word, the eternal Word of God the Father, dwelling among us in Jesus Christ and remaining among us in the Holy Spirit. Social trends wax and wane, but God as triune endures. His endurance is a supple, not a sedentary, one, a covenanted faithfulness of creation, renewal and consummation.

WHY A TRINITARIAN REVIVAL NOW?

To what may we attribute today's renewal of trinitarian theology? It is probably impossible to pinpoint exactly when it began, although early influential books include *The Trinity* (1967; ET 1970) by the Roman Catholic Karl Rahner, and *The Crucified God* (1972; ET 1974) and *The Trinity and the Kingdom* (1980; ET 1981) by Jürgen Moltmann. All of these works are indebted to Karl Barth's *Doctrine of the Word of God*, the first half-volume of his monumental *Church Dogmatics*, first translated into English in 1936, with a revised translation appearing in 1975. Editors Thomas F. Torrance and George W. Bromiley declare that for Barth "the doctrine of the Trinity itself belongs to the very basis of the Christian faith and constitutes the fundamental grammar of dogmatic theology."[4]

Christoph Schwöbel helpfully supplies several reasons why God's tri-unity is central to today's theological outlook and constructive efforts.

1. Increased contacts between Eastern and Western Christians, one result of ecumenical awareness and exchange, have sharpened queries about the person of the Holy Spirit and "therefore the significance of the Trinitarian conception of personhood in general."[5] This has specific reference to the contentious doctrine of the *filioque*, the insistence of Western theology that God the Spirit proceeds with one breath from both the Father and the Son. Eastern Christians have seen the Spirit's procession as originating from God the Father through God the Son, arguing (rightly, in the opinion of many Western theologians) that the double procession of the West in effect introduces two principles of origination into God, whereas ultimately there can only be one, namely God the Father. In the traditional language the Father is not superior to Son and Spirit, but "first among equals" because, after all, there can be by definition no degrees of divinity within the fellowship of the triune God.

The early church, after a gigantic struggle, finally ascribed person-hood to the Holy Spirit. The Spirit was coequal, coeternal, codivine with Father and Son. No longer just the inspiration of the prophets or Scripture-writers, not just the wherewithal of early charismatics, the Holy Spirit came to be fully vested in all the qualities of divinity. It is this triunely realized personhood, what it is and how humans can come to replicate it, that drives much of today's Trinity talk.

---

[4]Thomas F. Torrance and George W. Bromiley, in Karl Barth, *Church Dogmatics* 1/1, trans. G. W. Bromiley (Edinburgh: T & T Clark, 1975), p. ix. (Hereafter abbreviated *CD*.)

[5]Christoph Schwöbel, "The Renaissance of Trinitarian Theology: Reasons, Problems, and Tasks," in *Trinitarian Theology Today*, ed. Christoph Schwöbel (Edinburgh: T & T Clark, 1995), p. 4.

The trinitarian grasp of personhood is therefore a leading test case for the overall relevance of trinitarian theology. People are today preoccupied with the question of "who am I?" more than with "who is God?" If trinitarian theology is to engage with the deepest human aspirations and the sharpest human contradictions, it will have to be at the point of providing a model for what it means to be human in today's world. With every conceivable human psychology, to say nothing of economic strategy and sociological theory, postulating a view of the human, what can trinitarian theology add to the conversation?

2. Western trinitarian formulations are usually indebted to the groundbreaking work of Augustine, and this indebtedness has come in for reexamination. Must progress in Western trinitarian theology be measured only by faithfulness to Augustine? Schwöbel suggests that Augustine's analogy of love, which was later developed by the medieval theologian Richard of Saint Victor, may be the way ahead.[6] There is great power and beauty in saying that God is the Lover, God is the Beloved, and God is Love itself, three impulses of one great surge of love. This is not to elevate love above God but only to say that love's full span can only be calibrated triunely.

3. The perceived irrelevance of the doctrine of the Trinity for practical Christian life, voiced by many but best of all by Karl Rahner, hits home existentially. Rahner's assessment, often imitated but never surpassed, bears repeating here:

> Despite their orthodox confession of the Trinity, Christians are, in their practical life, almost mere "monotheists." We must be willing to admit that, should the doctrine of the Trinity have to be dropped as false, the major part of religious literature could well remain virtually unchanged.[7]

There seems to be at this point a fundamental disconnect between Christian theology and devotional exercise. Conceptually, as Schwöbel notes, the triune reality "must be conceived as the gateway through which the theological exposition of all that can be said about God in Christian theology must pass."[8] True enough. The doctrine of the Trinity is not so much exclusionary, about what is admitted to and what is

---

[6]Ibid., p. 5.
[7]Karl Rahner, *The Trinity*, trans. Joseph Donceel (New York: Crossroad, 1997), pp. 10-11.
[8]Schwöbel, "Renaissance of Trinitarian Theology," p. 6.

prohibited from Christian theology, as it is exemplary, the meticulous and loving maintenance of the entire theological vineyard. The trinitarian impress must be found wherever theological truth is proclaimed, because, to a greater degree than with any other theological formulation, the doctrine of the Trinity is that wherein all Christian teaching finds its reason to be.

But if a gateway, it would be a shabby gateway opening onto a rutted and pocked landscape if only the cognitive and the intellectual are nourished. Recent trinitarian renewal has agreed that this doctrine must address the entirety of the human condition, since it presumes to describe the whole of God.

4. What Ted Peters has called "Rahner's Rule" states theologically what Rahner had intuited spiritually.[9] Rahner's dictum that "The 'economic' Trinity is the 'immanent' Trinity and the 'immanent' Trinity is the 'economic' Trinity" teaches that God cannot be divided into one God consumed with his own interiority, and a second God of outgoing charity, creativity and redemptive tenacity.[10] God as two will not do in classical trinitarian confession. Rahner's insight that God in himself is at the same time God for the world has led, says Schwöbel, to "almost unanimous agreement that immanent and economic Trinity must be viewed as essentially related."[11] To point out the clear relationship between the economic and the immanent Trinity is not the end of the conversation but only its beginning. Precisely how is the economic Trinity related to the immanent? If finally they are the same, which must be true, does it matter with which Trinity the theological task begins? Is there a give-and-take between the immanent Trinity and the economic after the fashion of the one-and-the-three and the three-and-the-one?

For those who may still doubt that the doctrine of the Trinity is truly biblical theology, the fact that the economic Trinity is none other than the Trinity of salvation history shows the biblical rootedness of this teaching.

---

[9]Ted Peters, *God as Trinity: Relationality and Temporality in Divine Life* (Louisville: Westminster/John Knox Press, 1993), pp. 96-103. Peters first laid forth the rule in "Trinity Talk, Part I," *Dialog* 26 (1987): 46, as noted in Stanley J. Grenz and Roger E. Olson, *20th Century Theology: God & the World in a Transitional Age* (Downers Grove, Ill.: InterVarsity Press, 1992), p. 358 n 51.

[10]Rahner, *Trinity*, p. 22.

[11]Schwöbel, "Renaissance of Trinitarian Theology," p. 7.

5. Philosophical theism, which argued that God could not suffer and therefore avoided the messiness of human travail, has been weighed and found wanting. Centuries of sharpened philosophical reasoning could not rescue this God, however culturally familiar this view of the divine may be and however defended by a certain type of common sense. A God who is changeless, timeless, absolute, austere and omnipotent—in other words the God of traditional theism—is conceivably an icon of social stability and moral suasion. But this God of theism is a desiccated, colorless God propped up by Greek philosophy and not at all the robust God we meet in the pages of Scripture. To conclude that God is "impassible," meaning incapable of suffering or being acted upon, is for Robert Jenson "the central and least biblical concept of late Hellenic theology."[12]

The pillars of Western thought and even civilization that are upheld by the God of theism create an unlivable space. "We cannot believe if we have conceptualized God in existentially repugnant ways," writes Clark Pinnock, one voice among many who say that theism is simply unbiblical, regardless of how well it may be attested philosophically.[13] The theology of hope pioneered by Jürgen Moltmann and Wolfhart Pannenberg has been heralded as the theological reason for the collapse of Eastern bloc communism. In a similar vein, trinitarian theology has dismantled the wall of theism by exposing its spiritual vacuity and intellectual irrelevance.

6. The question of God is never a question to be asked in disregard of the world as it is and as it should become. As Moltmann has shown, theological ideas inevitably have political, social and therefore moral consequences.[14] There is a direct line of descent, believes Moltmann, from the unyielding God of philosophical theism to the entrenched patriarchalism of our time. The principle of triunity frees both God and humanity. It may also free theology, or at least proposes a theological reexamination of such central doctrines as creation, human nature, incarnation, salvation and ecclesiology.

---

[12]Robert W. Jenson, *The Triune Identity: God According to the Gospel* (Philadelphia: Fortress Press, 1982), p. 63.

[13]Clark Pinnock, "Systematic Theology," in Clark Pinnock et al., *The Openness of God: A Biblical Challenge to the Traditional Understanding of God* (Downers Grove, Ill.: InterVarsity Press, 1994), p. 102.

[14]Jürgen Moltmann, *History and the Triune God: Contributions to Trinitarian Theology,* trans. John Bowden (New York: Crossroad, 1992), pp. 1-18.

Theological science must necessarily interact with the human sciences that survey nature and society. Religion, society, nature and science can be divided intellectually, but not in real life. John Thompson summarizes this issue in asking, "Is God as triune not only the source of our salvation but also the ground and paradigm of true social life and liberation?"[15]

7. Thompson enumerates an additional reason that supports the existential relevance of the doctrine of the Trinity. Of course the mystery of the Trinity is not a mystery for its own sake of mysteriousness but for the sake of human salvation and creation's renewal.[16] The broad outline and basic persuasion of Moltmann's "Trinitarian theology of the cross"[17] has won wide acceptance, since "the cross opens a pathway for all the suffering of the world to be taken into the very being of God,"[18] where it can be redeemed. Catherine Mowry LaCugna believes that "the mystery of God can be thought of only in terms of the mystery of grace and redemption."[19]

There may be an appealing symmetry in these seven reasons for today's trinitarian renewal, one for each day of the theological week. However, by now we know that trinitarian theology always says "unity" in the same breath as "plurality," and hence these seven reasons necessarily seek their own commonality, their point of mutual regard.

That point is simply this: renewed classicism, refreshed orthodoxy, reclamation of what has always been. The triune God is coming around again because in fact this God has never left.

DEFINING TRINITARIAN THEOLOGY

If the whole of Christian theology can be likened to an archery target, round in shape with concentric rings drawing ever-tighter circles toward the center, trinitarian theology is the center point. That is a given. Many theological exercises fall outside of the explicitly trinitarian, and yet no

---

[15]John Thompson, *Modern Trinitarian Perspectives* (New York: Oxford University Press, 1994), p. 3.

[16]Ibid., p. vi.

[17]Jürgen Moltmann, *The Crucified God,* trans. R. A. Wilson and John Bowden (New York: Harper & Row, 1974), pp. 235-49.

[18]Elizabeth A. Johnson, *Consider Jesus: Waves of Renewal in Christology* (New York: Crossroad, 1990), p. 121.

[19]Catherine Mowry LaCugna, *God for Us: The Trinity & Christian Life* (San Francisco: HarperSanFrancisco, 1991), p. 2.

realm of Christian theology can remain Christian without constant contact with the Christian understanding of God, which is of course the Trinity. The circumference of the target, the border that gives it shape and integrity, is also God the Father, God the Son and God the Holy Spirit. No part of theological endeavor remains untouched by the questions and proposals arising from today's resurgent interest in the doctrine of the Trinity. "Trinitarian theology," so Schwöbel correctly knows, "therefore appears to be a summary label for doing theology that affects all aspects of the enterprise of doing theology in its various disciplines."[20]

Summation is at the same time the summit. The doctrine of the Trinity is rightly the summit and apex of all Christian theology. In the past, this has often meant that the Trinity is rare air, abstruse territory that is unscaled and even unknown except by theological professionals. In contrast, today's trinitarian theology is equal-opportunity theology. It is not necessarily user-friendly theology, if by that is meant a breezy and overly familiar way with God. Martin Luther knew that it is not we who presume to handle God but rather God handles us. But current trinitarian theology is open to all who approach God with reverence, commitment and patience. A trenchant summation does not appear magically at the end but is implied at every juncture by the flow of the story. Trinitarian theology implicates itself all along the way of Christian theology. There is nothing Christian that is not at the same time trinitarian.

The triune premise can therefore be nothing less than a centering and virtually a defining condition of the entire gamut of Christian theology. The American Lutheran theologian Robert Jenson is exactly correct in writing that "the doctrine of the Trinity is no one teaching or homogeneous set of teachings, as is, for example, the doctrine of justification by faith alone. It is a complex of expressions of various forms and various relations to the identification of God."[21] Jenson properly notes the multiplicity of trinitarian discourse. Even if one pushes the summit-of-theology metaphor to its extremity, the doctrine of the Trinity is not an isolated palace at the top of the heap. It is made of the same stuff as is the entire mountain. If Christian theology's deepest fathoming of the

---

[20]Schwöbel, "Renaissance of Trinitarian Theology," p. 1.
[21]Robert W. Jenson, "The Triune God," in *Christian Dogmatics*, ed. Carl E. Braaten and Robert W. Jenson (Philadelphia: Fortress, 1984), 1:84.

triune God is that this God is no solitary God,[22] then no doctrine of the Trinity can itself replicate the isolation that has already been excluded from God's essential nature. Paul Metzger is therefore correct to note that "there is no one way of doing Trinitarian theology, but rather, a variety of ways."[23] The fact that every summit can be gained in a variety of ways does not destroy the view from the top. Trinitarian theology, if many-splendored, is yet not diverse to the point of dissipation. The center holds in God as three-in-one, one-in-three.

Theology is often described as a reflective rather than an immediate activity. First we worship, tremble and quake before the sacred, and only then—if then—do we take a reflective pause. Every prayer certainly has theological meaning and structure, but we hope that the one who prays desires only to exult, thank and petition God, not to ponder the syntax and organization of ideas. That may come later. The one who prays may later ask: Did I truly pray *to* the Father, *through* the Son, *in* the Spirit? But prayer is its own immersion, just as acting creates its own aesthetics. An actor who so concentrated on the method and craft of acting in the midst of the performance might be technically marvelous but aesthetically absent. The praise and worship of God likewise are ends in themselves, to glorify and adore God.

In answer to the question "What is the point of trinitarian theology," Jenson admits that theology is a "second-level discourse," but not initially so. Trinitarian theology is initially "the first-level act of calling on God by the triune name, and of making prayers and sacrifices that follow the triune logic and use the triune rhetoric. And in this mode, trinitarian theology does not have a point, it is the point."[24]

Let Jenson's meaning be clear. He is not denying the reflective quality of trinitarian theology. But he is asserting an enriched and expanded definition of theology that allows triunity free play from first to last. The gasp uttered when entering a cathedral may be more than aesthetic recognition. God may be in the gasp. Absence of breath may mean presence of Holy Spirit. Trinitarian theology cannot flourish as a second-

---

[22]Robert L. Wilken, *Remembering the Christian Past* (Grand Rapids: Eerdmans, 1995), pp. 63-93.

[23]Paul Louis Metzger, "What Difference Does the Trinity Make?" in *Trinitarian Soundings in Systematic Theology,* ed. Paul Louis Metzger (New York: T & T Clark, 2005), p. 6.

[24]Robert W. Jenson, "What Is the Point of Trinitarian Theology?" in *Trinitarian Theology Today,* ed. Christoph Schwöbel (Edinburgh: T & T Clark, 1995), p. 31.

level discourse unless rooted in first-order immediacy. This is what Jenson means.

A family enjoying a midsummer's picnic in a mountain meadow may hint at the generous promises upheld by trinitarian theology. This picnic demands practicality, from planning the menu to driving to the site to protecting against marauding ants. This picnic demands exertion, as the family hikes from the parking lot to the meadow and as solitude and respite from pressing care is sought. Yet practicality and exertion equal the joy of contemplation as the family considers the peaks above, still glaciered in the heat of August.

Trinitarian theology is practical. It instructs in the way of Christian salvation and is a shorthand of the gospel. Trinitarian theology is also demanding, calling forth the strict exertions of thought and the purposeful resolve of action. Above all, trinitarian theology glows in its own beauty. Practicality and exertion are caught up into pure delight.

1

Surveying the
Trinitarian Landscape

Throughout the vast midsection of the United States, many states claim to represent the vital essence of all American life. This peculiar gospel is propagated by that humblest of means, the license plate. "The Heart of It All" declares one such plate; "Native America" is a second. One state located hundreds of miles from the country's geographical center nonetheless boasts of being "The Crossroads of America."

However these states' advertisements may be judged, in the realm of Christian theology there is and can be only one center. That is the doctrine of the Trinity. If a universe may be defined as innumerable realities shaped by and answering to a primary organizing principle, then the Christian conviction of God as triune is the center of the theological universe.

Universality is seldom if ever at the same time uniformity, even as God as triune is a richer God than a God of naked monotheism. The theological universe anchored by the triune God is a richly populated one. Christology, pneumatology, ecclesiology and sacramental theology are only some of the more obvious inhabitants of this universe.

When the ancient Christian tradition tried to capture the Trinity metaphorically, it turned not to legalistic, forensic or juridical metaphors but organic ones. Forensic ways may suffice for certain approaches to the atonement, but not for the Trinity. Christian wisdom has not seen fit to describe God the Father as a presiding judge, with God the Son as the lead defense attorney and God the Spirit as his second.

Instead, the triune God is the trunk, the branch and the shoot, three impulses of one growth. A mountain lake releasing a single cascading stream whose course eventually becomes a waterfall makes the same point. One water in three presentations. Or, in a symbol that probably crosses the line into modalism, the heresy that fails to distinguish Father from Son from Spirit sufficiently, the Trinity is the one sun giving forth continual streams of heat and light.[1]

Not all word pictures are acceptable to trinitarian orthodoxy. In fact Gregory of Nazianzus (329-389), one of the Cappadocian Fathers of the fourth century, explicitly excluded metaphors that harkened back to the old pagan degrees of divinity: "To compose the Trinity of Great and Greater and Greatest, as if of Light and Beam and Sun . . . makes a 'ladder of deity' that will not bring us into heaven but out of it."[2] That Gregory excludes this particular luminous metaphor from true trinitarian witness serves to remind us that not all metaphors are capable of carrying this profound truth. In fact it is the truth of God's triunity that lends such credence as any metaphoric approach to God may bear. For obviously it is not for the sake of the metaphor that the Trinity exists but rather exactly the reverse.

Standing atop the Empire State Building, holding fast to the observation deck, one is engulfed by a sea of skyscrapers, especially looking to the north. Each building has its own peculiar identity, its identifying corporate logo, its undeniable reason to be. Yet all of the buildings visible from that privileged perch cohere only as part of the borough of Manhattan. Their street addresses and telephone exchanges identify them as Manhattan, not Staten Island or the Bronx.

The doctrine of the Trinity dominates the panorama of Christian theology in the same way that the Empire State Building fixes the attention of anyone viewing midtown Manhattan from afar. The many other com-

---

[1]Robert W. Jenson defines modalism as "the teaching that God himself is above time and [above] the distinctions of Father, Son, and Spirit but appears successively in these roles to create, redeem, and sanctify" (*The Triune Identity: God According to the Gospel* [Philadelphia: Fortress Press, 1982], p. 65).

[2]Gregory of Nazianzus, quoted in ibid., p. 90.

ponents of Christian theology, such as those previously noted, are legitimated and made possible by the centering realization that God is three-in-one, and, just as importantly, one-in-three. How this can be true is the task of the trinitarian theologian. The doctrine of the Trinity, the goal and sweep of this theological reflection, is always a captive to enabling grace. The undoubted mental rigors of trinitarian theology never forget that theology sings as well as cogitates, and prays as well as deduces.

A PERENNIAL PUZZLER?

Remembering events sixty-five years past, the psychologist Carl Jung was still ruminating on the Trinity. In his autobiographical *Memories, Dreams, Reflections*, Jung recounted how he had sought an answer to this most vexed theological question from his Protestant parson father. The youthful Carl was "fascinated" by this teaching "because of its inner contradiction."[3] This tantalizing puzzle evinced "a oneness which was simultaneously a threeness."[4] But Jung was to be disappointed, for not only did his father make no attempt to explain the doctrine of the Trinity, the elder Jung admitted "I really understand nothing of it myself."[5]

It cannot be known if an adequate answer from Pastor Jung would have saved his brilliant son for Christian orthodoxy. While Carl believed that God was "an annihilating fire and an indescribable grace," the language of mystics early and late, he was never a conventional Christian.[6]

Carl Jung's experience is certainly not unique. Many great minds and capacious hearts have given up on Christianity because of the supposed obtuseness of the Trinity. The wit of Dorothy Sayers will speak to many, concluding that any real meeting with the doctrine of the Trinity may well lead beyond befuddlement to something worse: "Whether the theologian extols it [the doctrine of the Trinity] as the splendor of the light invisible or the skeptic derides it as a horror of great darkness, there is a general conspiracy to assume that its effect upon those who contemplate it is blindness, either by absence or excess of light."[7]

---

[3]Carl G. Jung, *Memories, Dreams, Reflections*, ed. Aniela Jaffe, trans. Richard and Clara Winston (New York: Pantheon Books, 1961), p. 53.

[4]Ibid., p. 52. Anthony Kelly examines the psychological ramifications of the doctrine of the Trinity, with special reference to Carl Jung, in *The Trinity of Love: A Theology of the Christian God* (Wilmington, Del.: Michael Glazier, 1989), pp. 209-15.

[5]Ibid., p. 53.

[6]Ibid., p. 56.

[7]Dorothy Sayers, *The Mind of the Maker* (San Francisco: HarperSanFrancisco, 1979), p. 35.

The critics and even the pundits must be given their due. Those who are more perplexed than edified serve the apologetic purpose of challenging Christians to become fully cognizant that the Trinity cannot be simply dogmatically asserted in a dismissive way. The epigram remains true: the Trinity is mystery, but not mystification. But if the doctrine of the Trinity sticks in the craw of the short-sighted and the hyper-rational as a frustrating confusion, it still remains the perennial Christian theology. Here *perennial* means evergreen, never failing to hold a bloom, rich in a complex yet unifying way, fecund.

If there is one common thread tying together much of today's trinitarian theology, it is that this teaching is a practical one and has always been a practical doctrine. Catherine Mowry LaCugna states simply that "the doctrine of the Trinity is in fact the most practical of all doctrines."[8] By practical LaCugna chiefly means that God as triune is God's relational arc and bond with all of creation, God for us in salvation history. Stephen Seamands concludes that, really, the doctrine of the Trinity is a doctrine for all seasons: "The Trinity is a solution that makes so many perplexing issues intelligible."[9]

Centuries of smoke and dust come off the Sistine Chapel's ceiling to reveal Michelangelo's true brilliance. Theologians and art restorationists have at least this much in common: they both desire that the original be seen for what it is. God has never been confused about his own identity, and to that extent God does not need to be restored. Yet the serene beauty of God's triunity has often been misunderstood and, what is worst of all, ignored.

Two Types of Trinitarian Theology?

Are there two types of trinitarian theology? At the existential and the practical level no, because God's triunity cannot be pitted against itself in a competitive way, but at the conceptual level yes.

The first type, which might be called *essentialist* or even *exemplary*, is more narrowly drawn and focused than is the second. Virtually every book-length treatment of the doctrine of God will have a chapter devoted

---

[8]Catherine Mowry LaCugna, "The Practical Trinity," *Christian Century*, July 15-22, 1992, p. 679.

[9]Stephen Seamands, *Ministry in the Image of God: The Trinitarian Shape of Christian Service* (Downers Grove, Ill.: InterVarsity Press, 2005), p. 11.

to the question of the Trinity. Donald G. Bloesch's *God the Almighty* and Thomas C. Oden's *The Living God* are examples.[10] The relationship between the immanent Trinity (also known as the ontological or the essential Trinity) and the economic Trinity will be discussed, as will the shared reality of oneness and threeness.[11] The biblical foundations and the historical development of the doctrine may be analyzed. Diagrams may guide the perplexed. Here the Trinity is the apex of Christian reflection, and while the nature and the character of God may well be described in many other ways, the doctrine of the Trinity cannot be surpassed.

The second type could be called the *representative* or the *participative* approach. It recognizes that any doctrine of God will necessarily impact every theological idea because the approach to God is absolutely fundamental. To speak of a triune premise that influences, for example, one's approach to the doctrine of salvation, theology of culture or eschatology is to acknowledge the second type of trinitarian theology.

The two types are not exactly synonymous with the concentrated (type one) and the diffuse (type two), or the specific (type one) and the general (type two), but those descriptors at least hint in the right direction. Perhaps the relationship between the two types is something like that between an artist's acknowledged masterpiece (the essentialist or exemplary approach) and the sketches and doodles (the representative or the participative approach) that may have led up to that masterpiece. One cannot stretch that analogy too far because today's thinking about the triune God reaches for and realizes both the masterpiece and the doodle. The pencil sketch or doodle is not a theological second thought or castaway, but is rather the assurance that there is no theological place, however studied or casual, where the trinitarian perspective is not welcome and indeed necessary.

---

[10]Donald G. Bloesch, *God the Almighty: Power, Wisdom, Love, Holiness* (Downers Grove, Ill.: InterVarsity Press, 1995); Thomas C. Oden, *The Living God*, Systematic Theology: Volume One (San Francisco: Harper & Row, 1987).

[11]Catherine Mowry LaCugna defines the immanent Trinity as "the divine persons with respect to one another." See her "Important Terms" in Karl Rahner, *The Trinity*, trans. Joseph Donceel (New York: Crossroad, 1997), p. 2. S. Mark Heim takes us within the ontological Trinity, describing it as "the actual triune persons whose communion in God is the divine life itself" (*The Depth of the Riches: A Trinitarian Theology of Religious Ends* [Grand Rapids: Eerdmans, 2001], p. 126). LaCugna's definition of the economic Trinity is "the divine persons as they are revealed and act in salvation history" (LaCugna, "Important Terms," p. 1). Heim's definition is "an understanding of the triune persons as varying external faces of God's action in the world" (*Depth of the Riches*, p. 126).

Recalling that in the introduction trinitarian theology was described as "a summary label," the current resurgence may begin with the essentialist trinitarian theology, or the doctrine of the Trinity *as such*, but it does not end there. Today's trinitarian theologians recognize that God's triunity implicates itself every place where theological analysis unfolds.

A tour around Washington, D.C., bears impressive witness to the monuments democracy has raised. Because democracy cannot be locally confined, in seeing the Lincoln Memorial or the Jefferson Memorial one may see the essence of democracy, but not its full expanse. Mount Rushmore, the Statue of Liberty, Ellis Island and the St. Louis Arch are equally eloquent. If essentialist trinitarian theology is like a visit to the nation's capital, then a tour around the United States deepens and validates what one has first learned there.

Some may see the essentialist trinitarian theology as playing in the major leagues of Christian theology, whereas the representative or participatory is somehow second tier. This is ill-advised. From the standpoint of the true baseball fan, equal pleasure can be had in both realms. Some may even prefer the minor leagues for their warmth and proximity to the players. Who can, after all, get the autograph of a real major leaguer? The two types of trinitarian theology need each other, much as the major and minor leagues do.

TALKING ABOUT A REVELATION

> *Surely some revelation is at hand.*
> (William Butler Yeats, "The Second Coming")

Grammarians and other protectors of the common good sometimes fuss about how unique *unique* really is. Dare anyone attach a mere modifier like totally, absolutely, inescapably or unsurpassably to *unique?* Is what is unique always its own validation, its own justification, its own criterion for inclusion?

A grammatical entry into trinitarian theology is not accidental but instructive. Grammar enables speech. Grammar proposes and indeed guards what is possible with speech and defeats the absurd. As Stephen Seamands notes, articulate speech and understanding are possible without a deep knowledge of that language's grammar, yet surely there is a high correlation between linguistic utility and grammatical mastery. Seamands states that "knowledge of trinitarian grammar is important. Without it we can't fathom the richness or depth of the Christian understanding of God, nor can we communicate it effectively to others."[12]

There are many ways, limited only by the ingenuity of the theologian, of organizing and propagating Christian theology. Any one of the ten or twelve commonly accepted focal points or loci of Christian theology could serve, if not as explicit launching pad, then at least as the major rudder guiding this particular theological project.[13] Not surprisingly, sometimes a constructive Christian theology will organize itself around the thrice-told rhythm of God's triunity. One such volume is H. Ray Dunning's *Grace, Faith, and Holiness*, whose three main sections explicate doctrines connected to God the Sovereign, God the Savior and God the Spirit.[14]

To say that the doctrine of the Trinity is central is clearly not to say that it is everything, and yet the Trinity is the fullest doctrinal canopy there could possibly be. Traditionally, for example, there have been three or four main approaches to the theology of the atonement, which are to one degree or other mutually exclusive, and three main eschatological persuasions, which again cannot easily coexist, but when it comes to God, Trinity is the introduction that contains the seeds of its own conclusion.[15] God's triunity is primary and in that sense definitive. Of course, a doctrine as deeply anchored as God's triunity, as well fleshed out by Christian Scripture and tradition, will necessarily bend and stretch one way for one theological tradition or emphasis, and another way for another.

---

[12]Seamands, *Ministry in the Image of God*, p. 11.

[13]*Christian Dogmatics*, 2 vols., ed. Carl E. Braaten and Robert W. Jenson (Philadelphia: Fortress, 1984) list twelve such loci: prolegomena or introduction, the Triune God, the knowledge of God, the creation, sin and evil, the person of Jesus Christ, the work of Christ, the Holy Spirit, the church, the means of grace, Christian life and eschatology.

[14]H. Ray Dunning, *Grace, Faith, and Holiness* (Kansas City: Beacon Hill, 1988).

[15]The classic study, detailing three types of atonement theology, is Gustaf Aulén, *Christus Victor: An Historical Study of the Three Main Types of the Idea of Atonement*, trans. A. G. Hebert (New York: Macmillan, 1954). The three are the Classic or Christus Victor, the Merit or Satisfaction, and the Moral Influence or Liberal. See Thomas C. Oden, *The Word of Life*, Systematic Theology: Volume Two (San Francisco: Harper & Row, 1989), pp. 412-13, for a chart comparing and illustrating these three plus a fourth, the Rectoral ("making right"), Governance theory.

For example, the two great trinitarian analogies are the psychological and the social.[16] The psychological teases out God's unity more than God's threefoldness and sees the very capacities of the human mind—memory, will, understanding—as a undeniable witness to the Trinity. A human mind that cannot functionally integrate these three into one is a mind absent and apart. This was Augustine's great insight. Dorothy Sayers, an Augustinian for a modern day, found within the psychological analogy "a trinity of sight." This must be "the form seen, the act of vision, and the mental attention which correlates the two. These three, though separable in theory, are inseparably present whenever you use your sight."[17]

When three distinct humans are seen to share one common essence (Peter, Mary and John), or when one person exercises his or her humanity in three complementary ways (e.g., as spouse, parent, sibling), then the social analogy is nigh. This analogy welcomes God's threeness, whereas the psychological arises more naturally from God's oneness. Each analogy is powerful. Neither is freestanding. Both are necessary. Yet some historical eras may call forth one more than the other. Fractious as today's living can be, the social analogy may have the greater urgency. The inherent flexibility and adaptability of trinitarian theology shows that it is liberating, not calcifying.

Before he was a great fantasy novelist J. R. R. Tolkien was a gifted linguist. But for his prodigious gifts as a linguist—fluency in classical Greek and Latin, Old Norse, Old English, medieval Welsh, Anglo Saxon and Gothic, an ancient form of German—*The Lord of the Rings* might never have seen the light of day. For his masterwork he concocted a new language, "High Elvish," with even a new alphabet. He once remarked that "I wrote *Lord of the Rings* to provide a world for the language. . . . I should have preferred to write the entire book in Elvish."[18]

The triune God did not invent a new language called "Trinitarian." Rather, this God is this language. If the truth of such a language be granted, then only God can call forth from "Trinitarian" its full range of meanings, can set its linguistic conventions, can revel in its vernacu-

---

[16]Roderick T. Leupp, *Knowing the Name of God* (Downers Grove, Ill.: InterVarsity Press, 1996), pp. 101-2 (psychological analogy and social analogy), pp. 75-76 (social analogy).

[17]Sayers, *Mind of the Maker*, p. 36.

[18]J. R. R. Tolkien, quoted in "Literary and Historical Notes," on National Public Radio's *The Writer's Almanac with Garrison Keillor*, January 3, 2006 <http::://writersalmanac.publicradio.org/programs/2006/01/02>.

lar splendor; and yet the invitation to Christian discipleship is at the same time immersion in learning this new language of faith. Michael Downey writes that "when we are at home with the faith and practice of the church, Trinity is the language spoken, the language of the house."[19] Fluency leads to sharing in God's very essence, to the privilege of becoming "participants of the divine nature" (2 Pet 1:4).

God's graceful intervention in a human life works to free that life from awkward dependence on a "trinitarian phrase book"—in other words, working toward a thorough knowledge of the triune God as only an intellectual spectacle, yet missing his ecstatic presence within the heart and through creation. To know the triune God, to welcome and live the triune life within is not to speak like a professional theologian, not to master technical jargon appropriate for the seminar room or academic conference. S. Mark Heim is correct that "Christians may be thoroughly trinitarian without using any technical language."[20] Of course, technical language in the right hands—whether the poet, the preacher, the novelist, the theologian, the painter—will undoubtedly ease the way for every Christian to live a "thoroughly trinitarian" life. To ascend a moonlit hill in the presence of a professional astronomer, for whom an exacting explanation of heaven's wonders is second nature, is not to ruin the experience but only to cast it in a different, possibly truer, light.

If we may speak of an economic Trinity and an immanent Trinity, there may also be two trinitarian grammars corresponding to these, which are of course not alien to one another but implied each within the other. Today's trinitarian renewal consistently speaks in the economic grammar of God's relatedness to his creation. We know God because God has chosen to reveal himself. Seamands's summary statement is therefore appropriate and edifying: "As the Christian grammar, trinitarian doctrine enables us to speak rightly about the God who is revealed in Scripture as Father, Son and Holy Spirit. In fact, it is this doctrine that makes the Christian understanding of God distinctly Christian and not merely theistic."[21]

---

[19]Michael Downey, *Altogether Gift: A Trinitarian Spirituality* (Maryknoll, N.Y.: Orbis, 2000), p. 46.

[20]Heim, *Depth of the Riches*, p. 131.

[21]Seamands, *Ministry in the Image of God*, p. 11.

Theologically, the most potent word in Seamands's statement is of course *revealed* or *revelation*. It is with the question of revelation that much contemporary trinitarian theology begins. Many agree that the very headwaters of the doctrine of the Trinity are in the Son's declaration of his unity with the Father, best expressed in John 10:30: "The Father and I are one." This mutual knowing is sealed by the Holy Spirit, who joins Son to Father. Because God's triunity is not self-possessed but given to the world through outpoured love, we may speak of revelation, God's initiative of grace.

Revelation is a theological word in ways that cognate words such as *disclosure*, *unveiling* and *exposition* are not. *Manifestation* comes part of the theological way to *revelation*, but not the entire distance. Specialized terms such as *theophany*, an appearance of God, or *epiphany*, more broadly meant to include not only God but someone's moment of ecstatic personal awareness, are great and telling words, but not employed as often as *revelation*. Call them poetic takes on revelation.

Henry van Dyke's exultation that "hearts unfold like flowers before thee" begins with theophany and ends in epiphany.[22] No realm, zone or sphere is finally absent from epiphany. I agree with Michael Downey's summation: "Human life, all of it, is the precinct of epiphany—of God's showing, of God's constant speaking and breathing."[23] This is the progress of the soul in acknowledging God's great gift, theophany, whose open-flowered return to God is like unto epiphany, the soul's finding its true life exclusively in God. The total effect is revelatory.

The Christian understanding of revelation is that it is God's gift, not God's obligation. Within the human heart, to say nothing of social structures and the march of human history, there is nothing inherently "revelation-worthy" or "revelation-causing" to force God's hand. Eberhard Jüngel writes that "The God who can reveal himself is not obliged to reveal himself."[24] When God comes revealingly, a good but not necessarily safe God is announced. This is Mr. Beaver's commendation of Aslan the Lion, who in C. S. Lewis's Chronicles of Narnia represents Jesus Christ.[25]

---

[22]Henry van Dyke, "Joyful, Joyful, We Adore Thee" (1907).

[23]Downey, *Altogether Gift*, p. 35.

[24]Eberhard Jüngel, *God's Being Is in Becoming: The Trinitarian Being of God in the Theology of Karl* Barth, trans. John Webster (Grand Rapids: Eerdmans, 2001), p. 31.

[25]C. S. Lewis, *The Lion, the Witch and the Wardrobe* (New York: Macmillan, 1950), p. 64.

Karl Barth believed in a God who is good but dangerous. Barth (1886-1968) is the chief instigator of and inspiration for today's trinitarian renewal, at least among Protestant theologians. Barth, who loved the music of Mozart and announced that upon arriving in heaven he would eschew the theologians' corner and head straight for Mozart entertaining the angels, himself helped to shape a great artist, the writer John Updike.[26] If a novelist can be a Barthian, Updike is. In the front papers of *Roger's Version* he quotes Barth's late-career essay "The Humanity of God": "What if the result of the new hymn to the majesty of God should be a new confirmation of the hopelessness of all human activity?"[27] For Barth, that God revealed himself fully in Jesus Christ is God's majesty. The doctrine of the Trinity is the theological capture and explanation of this majesty. Human activity could never arrive at this mystery through its own devices.

"Midpoint," Updike's long and presumably autobiographical poem, offers this encomium of Barth and his legacy:

Praise *Barth*, who told how saving Faith can flow
From Terror's oscillating Yes and No.

Is the triune God really a holy Terror as Updike claims? Does Barth throw his full theological weight behind this Terror? Later in "Midpoint" Updike cautions:

Beware false Gods: the Infallible Man,
The flawless formula, the Five-Year Plan.[28]

This is a poetic rendering of Barth's well-known attack upon theological liberalism. Instead, Barth offered up a dialectical theology, which Updike describes as the "oscillating Yes and No."

Before humanity can hear God's good news of redemption in Jesus Christ, humanity must take full stock of its own sorry lot. Human preening can never discover God's triunity; this can only be given in revelation. Thus must God's no be fully felt before God's yes can be

---

[26]John Updike contributed the foreword to *Wolfgang Amadeus Mozart* by Karl Barth, trans. Clarence K. Pott (Grand Rapids: Eerdmans, 1986). See Updike's book review, "To the Tram Halt Together," in his *Hugging the Shore: Essays and Criticism* (New York: Alfred A. Knopf, 1983), pp. 825-36, where his preference is clearly Barth (*His Life from Letters and Autobiographical Texts* by Eberhard Busch) over Paul Tillich (*His Life and Thought: Volume I: Life*, by Wilhelm and Marion Pauck).

[27]John Updike, *Roger's Version* (New York: Knopf, 1986), p. ix.

[28]John Updike, "Midpoint," *Collected Poems 1953-1993* (New York: Knopf, 1994), pp. 96, 99.

heard and received. The German theologian Otto Weber, himself a Barthian, writes that "the Church's Doctrine of the Trinity has its basis, its point of departure, and its object in revelation. It cannot seek to explain revelation. Its sole task can be to interpret revelation on the basis of its being an event and of that event itself."[29]

The event of revelation is Jesus Christ. Theological liberalism sought to isolate and then to elucidate a kind of humanistic God of good and genial feelings. This God was an ethical God, at times a God of the least common denominator and above all else a civil God. But this God is not the triune God, as Gregory Jones explains: "To begin with a general account of the attributes of 'godness' (i.e., to provide a general description of God) and then subsequently to 'fill in' and 'complicate' that simple description by consideration of God's Trinity, is to misunderstand the Christian doctrine of the Triune God."[30] God's triunity does not evolve from the general to the specific. It cannot be constructed, imagined, envisioned or fancied, but only known through God's self-initiated self-disclosure.

One recurrent strategy of the dialectical theology is to place before the seeker the "either-or." Barth learned this technique from the Danish theologian Søren Kierkegaard (1813-1855). The winnowing and at times withering light of the "either-or" demands decision. Either human pride or divine worship. The cultured speculations of liberalism could always discover one more ingenious way God could be contrived or explained along a bland continuum of human progress. There might be as many gods as there are seekers after the divine. The end of this is to arrive not at the God of the Bible but rather, to use John Macquarrie's piquant word, a "godling" or, in Robert Jenson's diminutive, a "godlet."[31]

Kierkegaard and Barth's "either-or" shouts *no!* to these humane approaches to God. Barth believes that "the root of the doctrine of the Trinity lies in revelation, and that it can lie only in this if it is not to become at once the doctrine of another and alien god, of one of the gods, the man-gods, of this aeon, if it is not to be a myth."[32] This is the only choice

---

[29]Otto Weber, *Foundations of Dogmatics*, trans. Darrell L. Guder (Grand Rapids: Eerdmans, 1981), 1:363.

[30]L. Gregory Jones, *Transformed Judgment: Toward a Trinitarian Account of the Moral Life* (Notre Dame, Ind.: University of Notre Dame Press, 1990), p. 88.

[31]Jenson, *Triune Identity*, p. 26.

[32]Karl Barth, *Church Dogmatics* 1/1, trans. G. W. Bromiley (Edinburgh: T & T Clark, 1975), p. 346.

Barth will allow: *either* human-concocted myth *or* the revealed truth of the holy One.

The freedom of God to be God is a hallmark of Barth's theology. God freely gives of his mystery because his nature is to give. In the opinion of Jürgen Moltmann, "If one takes Barth at his word, then everything has its hidden beginning in the mystery of the immanent Trinity."[33] But from these hidden beginnings grow the roots of God's creation, the redemption that is offered in Jesus Christ, and the consummation of all things in God. The fact that "in revelation God really does come forth out of His mystery" must be for Barth a paradox and even a miracle.[34] The grain of sand around which the doctrine of the Trinity forms is the lordship of Jesus Christ. "The doctrine of the Trinity is simply a development of the knowledge that Jesus is the Christ or the Lord," Barth claims.[35]

This lordship is not Jesus' alone, but one he shares with the Father and the Spirit, so that, really, there is a "threefold yet single lordship."[36] Barth's Trinity is of God as Revealer (Father), Revelation (Son) and Revealedness (Holy Spirit). The Father is characterized by the hiddenness of self-veiling and is known for his holiness. Here Barth follows Martin Luther, who believed, as Robert Jenson explains, that "the true God's majesty is precisely his hiddenness."[37] It is his self-unveiling that marks God the Son, whose way, above all, is to show mercy. God the Spirit's quality is self-impartation, by which the world is bathed in love.[38]

In the grammar of God's triunity, then, the Trinity is really and truly the *tri-iteration* of God, which is another way of saying Revealer, Revelation, Revealedness. Barth's simple insight is that God as Trinity perfectly and completely corresponds to himself. Eberhard Jüngel uses this concept to great advantage in explicating Barth's trinitarian thinking. From first to last Barth's trinitarianism accents the freedom of God. It is God who speaks, God who enables us to hear. John Webster explains that "the whole scope of the event of divine communication, from its

---

[33]Jürgen Moltmann, *History and the Triune God: Contributions to Trinitarian Theology*, trans. John Bowden (New York: Crossroad, 1992), p. 130.

[34]Barth, *CD* 1/1, p. 331.

[35]Ibid., p. 334.

[36]Ibid.

[37]Jenson, *Triune Identity*, p. 27.

[38]Barth, *CD* 1/1, p. 381.

inception through its enactment to its effective presence in the human realm, is a free divine activity."[39]

In the life of Jesus Christ, this tri-iteration is seen with perfect clarity in his baptism. It is here, for Barth, that "everything, the voice from heaven, the incarnate One, and the gift from above, are all the work of the one God, Father, Son and Spirit."[40] God's tri-iteration is nothing less than "the thrice single voice of the Father, the Son, and the Spirit."[41]

Gerard Manley Hopkins, in his poem "Margaret Clitheroe," hints at Barth's tri-iteration:

> She caught the crying of those Three,
> The Immortals of the eternal ring,
> The Utterer, Uttered, Uttering.[42]

Barth is of course no believer in three Gods, no tritheist. It may not be quite truthful to the triune persons to describe them as "Immortals," as if each divine voice, impervious to the ravages of time, somehow found its own level and range. No, as stated previously, God's voice is not three, nor yet one unmodulated drone, but "thrice single." It is Hopkins's third line that best captures Barth's tri-iterative view of God. Grammatically, the same point can be made in Barth's insistence that the triune God is, in Jüngel's paraphrase, "subject, predicate and object of the event of revelation."[43]

Are There Trinitarian Footprints?

Could the winter fun of crafting a snowman be implicit witness to the Trinity? Rolling three progressively smaller balls of snow, positioning them one atop the other and hoping that passing motorists might have the Trinity in mind? The attempt to find analogies and illustrations of the Trinity in nature is known as the *vestigium Trinitatis* or the vestiges of the Trinity. Vestiges means footprints. Is it not the case that in his eternal wisdom God has elected to implant within nature manifold demonstrations of his very character and essence? Making a snowman

---

[39]John Webster, "Translator's Introduction," in Jüngel, *God's Being Is in Becoming*, p. xiv.
[40]Barth, *CD* 1/1, p. 362.
[41]Ibid., p. 347.
[42]Gerard Manley Hopkins, "Margaret Clitheroe," quoted in R. D. Williams, "Barth on the Triune God," in *Karl Barth: Studies of His Theological Methods*, ed. S. W. Sykes (Oxford: Clarendon, 1979), p. 147.
[43]Jüngel, *God's Being Is in Becoming*, p. 28.

is child's play compared with the much more sophisticated attempts theologians have made in this regard. Jüngel points to the "great variety of attempts [that] have been made to show a similarity between certain structures of created reality and the structure of the being of God conceived as Trinity."[44]

Augustine believed in the *vestigium trinitatis*, as already evidenced in the earlier recounting of the psychological analogy of the Trinity. The master of Christian psychology, Augustine reasoned that if God had not impressed his very triunity upon the human mind, where else might it be found? But Barth rejected all natural demonstrations of God's triunity. The *vestigium trinitatis* is futile, wrong-headed and unavailing. For Barth this move crosses the line from interpretation to illustration. Revelation can only be *interpreted*; it cannot be *illustrated*.[45]

Here is how Barth differentiates between these two concepts, which are sometimes thought to be nearly synonymous: "Interpretation means saying *the same thing* in other words. Illustration means saying the same thing *in other words*."[46] Is this as self-evident to others as it is to Barth? One responsible interpreter of Barth is Alan Torrance. For him, what Barth means by interpretation is "testimony to one reality with which there are no parallelisms but which may be articulated (or, rather, which may articulate itself) in a whole variety of different ways." If the interpreter is disallowed from using conceptual parallels because none exists, not so for the illustrator. Illustration employs "conceptual parallelisms" and thereby reduces "theological affirmation to conceptual expression." Torrance characterizes Barth's distinction between interpretation and illustration as being "slightly abstruse." However, Torrance concludes that "it is precisely this dynamic which must characterize the theological enterprise."[47]

Barth's view of revelation is a reality complete unto itself. The solid centrality of its suasion does not need to back down. Revelation's confidence in its own integrity allows for its *sameness* to be uttered in other words, but these other words enhance the sameness. Illustration frays, if not compromises, meaning by refracting sameness into *other words*.

---

[44]Ibid., p. 17.

[45]Ibid., p. 24.

[46]Barth, *CD* 1/1, p. 345, quoted in Jüngel, *God's Being Is in Becoming*, p. 25.

[47]Alan J. Torrance, *Persons in Communion: Trinitarian Description and Human Participation* (Edinburgh: T & T Clark, 1996), p. 204.

However innocent may be its start, the dilution inherent in illustration may swell into outright adulteration. "Revelation," Barth states, "will submit only to interpretation and not to illustration." The attempt to illustrate revelation is to "set a second thing alongside" of revelation. To illustrate revelation focuses our attention away from it and toward the illustration. In the end "we no longer trust revelation in respect of its self-evidential force."[48]

This distinction between interpretation and illustration may seem only a clever linguistic sleight of hand to the detractors of Barth. He once again presents his readers with the either-or of accepting or rejecting revelation. Revelation is *Dei loquentis persona* or nothing less than God speaking in person.[49] David Cunningham, one such detractor, is puzzled by how "revelation seems to be personified and given a will of its own that allows it somehow to operate without the help of language, and to 'capture' language in ways which evade the wills of the human beings who use this language."[50] Barth, according to Jüngel, teaches that God's speech is not personified, not attached from without, but is rather the *personal* speech of Jesus Christ.[51]

Because Barth cautioned against the use of illustrative analogies, one must be careful. But perhaps the following analogy is not wide of the mark. Imagine an airborne pilot over the remote South Seas. Engine lights warn of impending disaster. The pilot parachutes to an island he thinks must be uninhabited. But he is wrong. Soon natives appear. They seem friendly. How can they communicate about the pilot's basic needs of clean water, edible food and rest? Do they puzzle it out with wild gesticulations until something finally clicks?

Imagine that the pilot has parachuted into the Island of God. He brings with himself nothing worthy of receiving anything of value from the islanders. But yet the islanders are kind and see to his material and physical needs. How can this be? The errant pilot can receive these gifts only as profound graces and endowments. The pilot cannot impose his language on the islanders but can only receive with gratitude the native

---

[48]Barth, *CD* 1/1, p. 345.
[49]Ibid., p. 304, quoted in Jüngel, *God's Being Is in Becoming*, p. 27.
[50]David Cunningham, *These Three Are One: The Practice of Trinitarian Theology* (Oxford: Blackwell, 1998), p. 195 n. 41, quoted in "Translator's Introduction" in Jüngel, *God's Being Is in Becoming*, p. xiv n. 5.
[51]Jüngel, "Translator's Introduction," in *God's Being Is in Becoming*, p. xiv n. 5.

tongue. Revelation is like this native tongue in the South Seas. Revelation brings with it the conditions of its own understanding. Understanding could not be achieved by some sort of mixture of the two speeches, the pilot's and the islanders'. The pilot can be rescued only through accepting the islanders' speech and all of its provisions.

Barth's trinitarianism can be summarized under three main points, according to Carl Braaten and Robert Jenson. In Barth's explication the Trinity is, first, "the God identified by the biblical narratives" and "is Christianity's identification of which God it worships."[52] Otto Weber asserts that the God of the Bible is "not a solitary God. He is not a lifeless God. He is not a God who is wrapped up in himself."[53] Barth agrees with this.

In contrast to Friedrich Schleiermacher (1768-1834), who ended his influential work *The Christian Faith* with a brief exposition of the Trinity that is more an afterthought than a culmination, Barth's monumental *Church Dogmatics* takes the Trinity as "prolegomena" for all that will come after. Barth's locomotive trinitarianism is thus in direct contrast with the caboose trinitarianism of Schleiermacher. Jüngel explains why Barth's prioritizing of the Trinity is of such great importance, not only for Barth's own work but for all theological work. "The placing of the doctrine of the Trinity at the beginning of the *Church Dogmatics* is therefore a hermeneutical decision of the greatest relevance because, on the one hand, the whole *Church Dogmatics* finds its hermeneutical foundation here, and, on the other hand, with this decision hermeneutics itself finds its own starting-point."[54] Hermeneutics is the art and science of interpretation. Jüngel is simply saying that for Barth, God's triunity is God's understanding of himself, and must therefore be the stepping-off point for all theology. It is hence the case that "the doctrine of the Trinity is the interpretation of the self-interpretation of God."[55]

Second, there can be no gap between *who* God is in himself and *how* and *what* God reveals himself to be. The essence or the *who* of God may be ontologically *prior* to the *how* and *what*, because in a sense God simply *is* before God *acts* in salvation history. God's freedom to be God as

---

[52]Carl E. Braaten and Robert W. Jenson, eds., *A Map of Twentieth-Century Theology: Readings from Karl Barth to Radical Pluralism* (Minneapolis: Fortress, 1995), p. 180.

[53]Weber, *Foundations of Dogmatics*, 1:358.

[54]Jüngel, *God's Being Is in Becoming*, p. 17.

[55]Ibid., p. 29.

God sees fit must always be preserved. God has chosen to exercise his sovereign freedom toward humanity in the incarnation of Jesus Christ. For Paul Molnar, a latter-day Barthian, "the strength of trinitarian theology" is displayed in "the fact that Jesus Christ is the eternally begotten Son of the Father and that this takes place in the unity of the Holy Spirit."[56] God chooses to exercise the *who* of his freedom toward the *how* and *what* of salvation history. Third, Barth's trinitarianism makes its presence felt through the entire course of his theological work. His doctrine of creation, for example, emphasizes both the unity of the creation and the fact that the primal love between Father and Son exemplifies and demonstrates the love between the Father and humankind.[57]

To Clarify Karl Barth

The Trinity is for Karl Barth a self-directed and self-propelled God. God's dynamism and power come from within, and are thrice articulated as Father, Son and Holy Spirit. Not all theologians have lined up behind Barth to congratulate him on his theological accomplishment. Jürgen Moltmann derides what he calls Barth's "monarchian doctrine of the Trinity," claiming that however potent may be this God, he is not relationally available.[58] Barth's view therefore slights the "personal encounter of the Father who loves the Son, the Son who prays to the Father and the Spirit which confesses the Father and the Son."[59] Moltmann's reservations are in line with an older criticism of Barth, by Walter Russell Bowie, that Barth's theology squeezes warmth and life from God, that his theology ossifies into "the chilled idea that God is not within the real life [people] have to lead."[60]

---

[56]Paul D. Molnar, *Divine Freedom and the Doctrine of the Immanent Trinity* (London: T & T Clark, 2005), p. 330.

[57]Braaten and Jenson, *A Map of Twentieth-Century Theology*, p. 180. Other treatments of Barth's trinitarian theology are found in Richard H. Roberts, *A Theology on Its Way? Essays on Karl Barth* (Edinburgh: T & T Clark, 1991), pp. 81-93, and R. D. Williams, "Barth on the Triune God," in *Karl Barth: Studies of His Theological Methods*, ed. S. W. Sykes (Oxford: Clarendon, 1979), pp. 147-93. A book-length treatment is by Eberhard Jüngel, *God's Being Is in Becoming. The Doctrine of the Trinity: God's Being Is in Becoming*, trans. Horton Harris (Grand Rapids: Eerdmans, 1976), is an earlier edition of this work.

[58]Moltmann, *History and the Triune God*, p. 131.

[59]Ibid., quoting the German theologian Edmund Schlink.

[60]Walter Russell Bowie, *Jesus and the Trinity* (New York: Abingdon, 1960), p. 102.

We have seen already that Barth is uncomfortable in the presence of the *vestigium trinitatis*, which he views as a poor and presumptuous substitution for the reality of God's revelation. In fact the true *vestigium trinitatis* "is the form assumed by God in revelation."[61] The sovereign God, in what came almost to be a theological cliché, must be the "Wholly Other," a sentiment shared by his theological comrade-in-arms Emil Brunner. God, stated Brunner, "reveals himself as the unheard-of, unrecognized mysterious person, who cannot be discovered anywhere in the world."[62] Barth and Brunner alike are enamored of the paradoxical language wherein God is at one and the same time hidden and revealed.

However stark and unapproachable Barth's view of revelation may seem, it is the only proper starting place for the Trinity. The natural theology prized by the philosophically astute is for Barth a curse. Instead, he writes,

> We do not know what we are saying when we call God Father and Son. We can say it only in such a way that on our lips and in our concepts it is untruth. For us the truth we are expressing when we call God Father and Son is hidden and unsearchable. . . . Nevertheless, in naming God thus we are expressing the truth, His truth.[63]

It cannot have escaped notice how often Barth uses the language of speech and aurality in this passage: saying, lips, expressing, the call, naming. Hearing is the dominant theological sense for Barth. The ear may be the safer theological sense, as the eye is singled out for its tendency to wander into untoward desire (1 Jn 2:16). The Trinity and God's tri-iteration stirs up aural connections and reverberations, but is chary of visual intimations.

If tri-iteration is an apt concept for Barth's doctrine of the Trinity, then a paraphrase that clarifies and analytically draws out the center of Barth's meaning will aid our understanding. Happily, Barth has found his paraphraser or clarifier in his student Eberhard Jüngel, who in fact names his small and dense book *God's Being Is in Becoming* a paraphrase.

---

[61]Barth, *CD* 1/1, p. 339.
[62]Emil Brunner, *The Theology of Crisis* (New York: Charles Scribner's, 1935), p. 33, quoted in Bowie, *Jesus and the Trinity*, pp. 101-2.
[63]Barth, *CD* 1/1, p. 433.

Jüngel's book is certainly not Barth lite or a Barth digest. It is definitely not Barth made easy. But it is Barth made cogent and Barth identified for the theological claims he made. More than that cannot be asked of anyone who paraphrases. On his own terms Jüngel is a brilliant theologian. He would have to be to understand Barth well enough to mount such a successful paraphrase.

Barth probably did not know of the English poet William Cowper (1731-1800), but especially the second couplet of a verse of "God Moves in a Mysterious Way" is vintage Barth:

> Blind unbelief is sure to err
> And scan His work in vain;
> God is His own interpreter,
> And He will make it plain.[64]

In this verse, at least, Cowper is a Barthian before Barth. Not even the most sympathetic scan of the created world will necessarily yield clues as to the divine mystery, absent the God who is his own and perforce the world's only standard of interpretation. As Jüngel compactly puts it, "as *interpreter* of himself, God corresponds to his own being."[65] Anyone with an immersion experience in crosscultural dynamics understands how crucial interpretation is. People from divergent cultural locations can never occupy an identical interpretive space, try as they might. Jüngel is saying that in the triune God's self-knowing, this God is nothing less than the only One in the universe with perfect self-understanding.

Each of the five words in the English title of Jüngel's book, *God's Being Is in Becoming*, is a pregnant word, and none of these five words can stand alone from the other four.[66] Within God, being and becoming are not fighting with each other for supremacy, nor yet is God's becoming the manner in which God's being strives to realize some real or perceived shortfall or lacuna within the divine character.

Some have read the entire history of Western philosophy as a conflict between, or at the least a conversation regarding, being and becoming. The ancient Greeks typically stressed the constant reliability of being over the alleged fickleness of becoming. Modern views known as pro-

---

[64]William Cowper, "God Moves in a Mysterious Way" (1774).

[65]Jüngel, *God's Being Is in Becoming*, p. 36.

[66]The German title is *Gottes Sein ist im Werden*, so that John Webster's translation is at once accurate and poetic.

cess philosophy and theology have picked up the becoming end of the stick. It is the "creative advance into novelty" that stirs the cosmic drink, and this especially applies to God. Alfred North Whitehead consigns those stuck in the being paradigm to obscurantism. "The pure conservative is fighting against the essence of the universe" he believes.[67]

But Barth is not interested in this philosophical issue. Jüngel correctly notes that Barth's trinitarian theology is both antimetaphysical and antimythological.[68] It is antimetaphysical because revelation does not depend on any philosophical validation. To try to demonstrate the truth of the triune premise from the history of religion is to slide to the mythological or at best to a noble principle that may be beautiful and well-regarded, but that is not revelatory.[69]

We must look elsewhere than metaphysics or myth to arrive at trinitarian truth. Instead, writes Jüngel, we must "think of the being of God as event."[70] What does Barth understand by event? There could never be two divine events, one where God relates exclusively to the divine self and a second event of outreach to the world in creation and redemption. The one triune event who is God is God's self-communication to humanity wherein "*all* three divine modes of being are at work," as Jüngel summarizes.[71] The works of Father, Son and Holy Spirit in the world are indivisible, as stated by the ancient provision of trinitarian theology *opera trinitatis ad extra sunt indivisa*, meaning simply that the external works of the Trinity in creation and redemption cannot be divided.[72] The seamless quality of how God works in the world arises from God's own internal relatedness, known as *perichoresis*, which Barth describes as working in this way: "the divine modes of being mutually condition and permeate one another so completely that one is always in the other two and the other two in the one."[73] We will discuss perichoresis in much greater detail in chapter two.

---

[67]Alfred North Whitehead, *Adventures of Ideas* (New York: Macmillan, 1933), p. 354, quoted in John B. Cobb Jr. and David Ray Griffin, *Process Theology: An Introduction Exposition* (Philadelphia: Westminster Press, 1976), p. 59.

[68]Jüngel, *God's Being Is in Becoming*, p. 42.

[69]Barth, *CD* 1/1, p. 342.

[70]Jüngel, *God's Being Is in Becoming*, p. 42.

[71]Ibid., p. 44.

[72]Ibid.

[73]Barth, *CD* 1/1, p. 370, quoted in ibid., p. 45.

The filmmaker and writer Woody Allen has been known to host elaborate New York City parties on New Year's Eve, in spacious accommodations. The guest list from entertainment, music and the arts would keep paparazzi busy for as long as they cared to pop their flashbulbs. Whether because of his real or imagined shyness, or some other reason, Woody does not really patronize his own event, retreating to the upper reaches of the party space and sequestering himself in a bedroom. A God who would plan, orchestrate and even launch a grand spectacle and yet withhold the one thing that animates the party—his own being—is a very sorry God. And this God is not Barth's God.

God's presence makes the party. In a sense, God's presence is itself enough to make the party, because the staging of the event discloses no gap or divine deficit. Here Jüngel clarifies that "as event, God's being *is* his own decision."[74] Here we see that God's very act of decision—the dynamism of his becoming—itself constitutes his being. Decision is crucial for Barth. Decision may also be inscrutable. God does what God does—because God does what he does.

With anyone else, such power of decision would be frighteningly despotic. But because it may be said of no one else that this being lives in perfect self-correspondence, God as Trinity can be trusted. Jüngel explains that, for Barth, "God's being *ad extra corresponds* essentially to his being *ad intra* in which it has its basis and prototype."[75] These Latin phrases are not theological mumbo jumbo. *Ad extra* is the works of God, especially in creation, redemption and consummation. For those with eyes to see, *ad extra* is everywhere. What God does in the world arises from God's triune life *ad intra*, God's life within. This relationship between God's inner life and outward works is symmetrical, mutually enriching, noncompetitive and progressive. The divine plenitude begins within and overflows. Kathryn Tanner makes this point: "God is different from the world in virtue of the fullness of God's trinitarian life, but it is this very fullness that enables God to overflow in goodness to us."[76]

God as event shows himself to be at the same time "our *God*" and "*our* God." There may be a logical priority to the first of these, because in all

---

[74]Ibid., p. 81.
[75]Ibid., p. 36.
[76]Kathryn Tanner, *Jesus, Humanity and the Trinity: A Brief Systematic Theology* (Minneapolis: Fortress, 2001), p. 13.

three of God's modes of being God is "equal to Himself, one and the same Lord."[77] But finally God is God for the sakes of those to whom he unites himself. As *our* God, Barth writes, "He can meet us and unite Himself to us, because He is God in His three modes of being as Father, Son and Spirit, because creation, reconciliation and redemption, the whole being, speech and action in which He wills to be our God, have their basis and prototype in His own essence, in His own being as God."[78]

So Barth's God, if not a three-player weave or variations on the triangle offense favored by some basketball teams, is a God in motion, a God in a hurry even, if not a frantic or frazzled God. This God suffers, and in this suffering gives himself away but does not give himself up.[79] Something very much like this happens in C. S. Lewis's *The Lion, the Witch and the Wardrobe*, when Aslan the lion gives himself away to the White Witch but never gives himself up to her schemes and degradations. After Aslan's summit with the White Witch, which he has convened to win back the soul of the errant Son of Adam Edmund, Aslan declares to all gathered, and especially to Edmund's brother and sisters Peter, Lucy and Susan: "I have settled the matter. She has renounced the claim on your brother's blood."[80]

This reality of divine suffering is never out of Jüngel's view; in the book's forward he exclaims that "the God whose being is in becoming can die as a human being," stating not a hypothetical imperative but a visceral reality.[81] God's willingness to suffer is, once again, not a foreign incursion, not a circumstantial oddity that assails the divine life for a moment and then recedes. It is *who God is.* "Even in suffering," says Jüngel, "God's being *remains* a being in *act*, a being in *becoming*. God persists in the historicality of his being."[82] This is Barth's counterproposal to metaphysics and myth: God's *historicality*. The triune God engages with human history. That is the meaning of creation, reconciliation and redemption.

Barth's view of how and why God suffers sustains the trinitarian critique of traditional theism. The received theistic wisdom is that God

---

[77]Barth, *CD* 1/1, p. 383, quoted in Jüngel, *God's Being Is in Becoming*, p. 35.
[78]Ibid.
[79]Jüngel, *God's Being Is in Becoming*, p. 102.
[80]Lewis, *Lion, the Witch and the Wardrobe*, p. 115.
[81]Jüngel, *God's Being Is in Becoming*, p. xxv.
[82]Ibid., p. 102.

cannot suffer, that faced with the choice between expressing genuine pathos and keeping inviolate the divine perfections, God always chooses the latter. God's suffering is for Barth so far from an inherent contradiction that it is the truest proof of God's divinity. "Barth takes the passion of God very seriously,"[83] so that for Barth "The Almighty exists and acts and speaks here in the form of One who is weak and impotent, the eternal as One who is temporal and perishing. . . . The One who lives for ever has fallen a prey to death. The Creator is subjected to and overcome by the onslaught of that which is not."[84]

POETICIZING THE TRINITY

John Updike once said that of all the traditional arts—painting, sculpture, dance, acting and so forth—it is only with *writing* that an amateur may surprise the world with a fresh expression emerging straight from the writer's mind without the cultivation of thousands and thousands of hours of practice. A housewife writes a blockbuster. This simply does not happen in other artistic realms. By analogy, perhaps, some of the greatest contributors to trinitarian theology are not necessarily professional theologians and not always even members of the clergy. A good case in point is Dorothy L. Sayers, best known as a playwright and writer of detective stories. Her 1941 book *The Mind of the Maker* is in some ways a vigorous restatement of the psychological analogy of the Trinity, but not only that. The scope of her book is not merely the creative act, within whose enchantments she finds evidence of the Trinity, but the very structure of the universe.

Sayers's small and stimulating book was rightly hailed in its time as "the most brilliant and stimulating work of lay theology in our day." To say in the next breath that it is "one of the boldest efforts to comprehend the Christian affirmation of the Trinity ever penned" seems a bit ambitious, putting Sayers in the company of those she generously quotes, such as Augustine and Thomas Aquinas.[85] At the very least, though, Sayers deserves a hearing as an attractive writer and a resourceful thinker. The stated purpose of her book is the sheer exposition of the dynamics of

---

[83]Ibid., p. 99.
[84]Ibid., quoting Barth, *CD* 4/1, p. 176.
[85]Henry P. Van Dusen, "The Trinity in Experience and Theology," *Theology Today* 15 (1958): 382.

creativity as these reveal the mind of God, which are also taken to be "true statements about the mind of the human maker." While she expresses "no personal opinion about their theological truth," it is hard to escape the intuition that for Sayers this is very truth indeed.[86] Her theological opinions may not be front and center throughout, but it remains true, in the words of another, that "they do not have to be mentioned in order to be apparent."[87]

Sayers's work may be largely overlooked today, making, for example, no appearance in Stanley Grenz's exhaustive treatment of recent trinitarian theology.[88] At its appearance *The Mind of the Maker* drew notice as "a very illuminating aid to the understanding of the faith" and an "extraordinarily interesting study."[89]

Is the recent neglect of Sayers's insights into the Trinity justified? Is her work one of the main roads of trinitarian reflection or a clever and maybe forgettable bypass? Cyril C. Richardson finds two basic strategies for explicating God's triunity. The primary thrust, whose recent champion is Karl Barth, is "the Trinity of revelation." Another strategy involves surveying "the modes of God's activity" to find within these modes a reliable witness to the Trinity.[90] This second option has been voiced by the Cappadocian father Gregory of Nyssa (c. 335-c. 395). Any given activity God might choose to undertake—creation, providential oversight, redemption—is one to which each triune person makes his signal contribution. But of course the result is not three more-or-less random acts struggling toward coherence. Gregory saw "a unity in Father, Son and Holy Spirit," and beheld the Father as Origination, the Son as Actualization and the Spirit as Power.[91] In Richardson's summative comment, "the one result can be viewed as the concurrence of their different actions: the Father supplies the source, the Son the actualization, the Spirit the perfection."[92]

---

[86]Sayers, *Mind of the Maker*, p. xiv.

[87]Madeleine L'Engle, introduction to Sayers, *Mind of the Maker*, p. xvi.

[88]Stanley J. Grenz, *Rediscovering the Triune God: The Trinity in Contemporary Theology* (Minneapolis: Fortress, 2004).

[89]Leonard Hodgson, *The Doctrine of the Trinity* (New York: Charles Scribner's, 1944), p. 230; Claude Welch, *In This Name: The Doctrine of the Trinity in Contemporary Theology* (New York: Charles Scribner's, 1952), p. 85.

[90]Cyril C. Richardson, *The Doctrine of the Trinity* (New York: Abingdon, 1958), p. 133.

[91]Ibid.

[92]Ibid., p. 134.

Richardson sees Sayers as a latter-day revisiting of Gregory's program. The one divine activity that Sayers sees as representing all of the others is creativity. Together, Barth and Sayers cover the waterfront of trinitarian methodology. Their respective starting points do not so much overlap as juxtapose. They are not mutually exclusive or inherently contradictory one to the other, but ill at ease in each other's company. To borrow terms usually associated with the study of Jesus Christ, or christology, Barth's trinitarianism is "from above" while Sayers's is "from below," because Sayers begins with the human act of creativity and by analogy ascribes this to God. Barth, by contrast, finds revelation to be without any human comparisons. Ted Peters is correct to summarize Barth's approach as seeking "a guarantee that in the very structure of divine revelation itself the threefoldness of the divine reality is uncovered."[93]

Sayers is not hostile to the claims of divine revelation. The appendix to *The Mind of the Maker* lists, "for handy reference," "relevant portions" of the Apostles' Creed, the Nicene Creed and the Athanasian Creed. Since her book is an extended unpacking of what these creeds teach, she must "explicitly affirm the revelational basis for the doctrine [of the Trinity]."[94] Yet her chosen means of affirmation, the creativity which throbs in the mind of the artist as analogous to "the Mind of the Maker," is un-Barthian. For Barth, strictly speaking, revelation can have no analogies. That is why he rejected the *vestigium trinitatis*.

Not so Sayers. She does not mention the humble, everyday word pictures sometimes used to teach the Trinity to children: the three-leaf clover; water that exists in the three forms of liquid, solid, vapor; a pie with bottom crust, filling, top crust; an egg with its shell, yoke, and white. But she does protest that regarding the Godhead or the Trinity, "the emphasis is always placed on the mystery and uniqueness of the structure," when the true accent, siding with Augustine, ought rather to be placed on the Trinity's being "a homely and intimate thing."[95]

To call something homely and intimate is not at the same time to slide into the familiarity that, says the aphorism, breeds contempt. An-

---

[93]Ted Peters, *God as Trinity: Relationality and Temporality in Divine Life* (Louisville: Westminster/John Knox Press, 1993), p. 211 n. 12.
[94]Welch, *In This Name*, p. 91.
[95]Sayers, *Mind of the Maker*, p. 214.

ticipating the contemporary spirituality that claims to find "wonder in the ordinary" and "epiphanies at breakfast," Sayers invites us to consider our pet dog. If we can look "behind the appealing eyes and the wagging tail" we will behold "a mystery as inscrutable as the mystery of the Trinity."[96] To say this is not to elevate dogness to divinity or to devalue the divine to the canine, but merely to say that the only possible thinking available to the human mind is the analogical. It is Sayers's philosophical bedrock that "all language about everything is analogical; we think in a series of metaphors. We can explain nothing in terms of itself, but only in terms of other things."[97] Just here we see again the contrast to Barth, whose conclusion was exactly that revelation is its own explanation.

I have already suggested that Sayers's approach to the Trinity is one that is mainly "from below," her chosen vessel for investigating the Trinity being the creativity of the artist. Her book is hence "an argument from the trinitarianism of finite creativity to a Divine Trinity," in Claude Welch's opinion.[98] In her own words, Sayers finds that trinitarian doctrine "is a plain *a posteriori* induction from human experience," which is not the same as to contend that the idea of the Trinity is somehow a human creation arising *strictly* from human endeavor.[99] Sayers is *not* saying that each human being may discover within his or her own consciousness some latent, inchoate concept of the three-in-one, which when seen through the lens of creativity and multiplied, clarified, magnified eventually becomes the triune God of Christian confession. Such a claim is, after all, heresy, the presumption that the idea of the Trinity is somehow within every person as standard operating equipment of what it means to be human. This is to model the Trinity on a human scale rather than receiving as grace-endowed the reality of God's triunity.

God's creativity is not modeled on human creativity, but the reverse is true. For someone to discover this creativity within, and refine its enactments, is only to discover God's implanted gift. Even so, Sayers can say that "between the mind of the maker and the Mind of his

---

[96]Ibid., p. 23.
[97]Ibid.
[98]Welch, *In This Name*, p. 86.
[99]Sayers, *Mind of the Maker*, p. 183.

Maker, [there is] a difference, not of category, but only of quality and degree."[100] God's mind is not a mind apart, a mind to be understood only on its own terms, but a mind separated from the human mind only by quality and degree. To develop and even perfect the creative urge is to become more godlike. This conclusion is conceivably one starting point for the finding of religious truth and scientific truth within each other. Sayers is clearly a bridge-builder, not an erector of fortresses. Nothing would please Sayers more than that the artist, the theologian and the scientist could all speak the same language. The eventuality of this would prove Sayers's general thesis of a convergent moving "towards a synthesis of experience."[101]

Sayers is not the sort of classic theological liberal Barth contested against, but even so her finding a rather facile bridge to trinitarian complexity through human creativity is contrary to the spirit of Barth. The Trinity of revelation is never an induction from human experience. It is an unexpected and ultimately undeserved gift of grace.

The easy congruity Sayers finds between the human and the divine Creator, whose minds "are formed on the same pattern," is, as I have suggested, a kind of revitalization of the psychological analogy of the Trinity.[102] At slight variance from her mentor Augustine, whose emphasis fell most naturally on a single mind contemplating its interlaced functions of memory, will and understanding, Sayers analyzes the three trajectories of creativity—Idea, Energy, Power—whose threeness dissolves into oneness as one intuits the full splendor of the creative act.

In what may whimsically be called the "librarians' proof of the Trinity," Sayers finds the book as thought, the book as written, the book as read to sum up all that this doctrine intends to say.[103] In her unique language, which has echoes in Gregory of Nyssa, Idea, Energy, Power correlate to this literary tri-unity, or in the time-honored expressions Father, Son, Holy Spirit. Sayers argues for the universal appeal of this metaphor. Everyone is at least potentially creative, such that creativity is "something perfectly familiar to our experience."[104] The inherent elasticity of Idea, Energy, Power may inspire ongoing trinitarian reflection.

---

[100]Ibid., p. 182.
[101]Ibid., p. 31.
[102]Ibid., p. 213.
[103]Ibid., pp. 113-15.
[104]Ibid., p. 122.

The common feminist refiguring of Father, Son, Holy Spirit as Creator, Redeemer, Sustainer is not a good fit with Sayers's trinity, because she obviously spreads creativity among all three divine persons. A better fit is to speak of God the Father as "primordial" being, God the Son as "expressive" being, and the Holy Spirit as "unitive" being, as the philosophical theologian John Macquarrie does.[105]

The future of trinitarian theology likely belongs more to the heirs of Barth than to Sayers. The bedrock of revelation never gives way, but the anchor of Sayers's proposal, creativity, "cannot be neatly organized in the abstractions of Idea, Energy, and Power. These are only three factors in an infinitely complex series of events, capacities, and relationships."[106] In making this comment Cyril Richardson, who is himself no friend of orthodox trinitarianism, says that Sayers is merely multiplying theological rabbits, and that finally she can exercise no control over Idea, Energy, Power.

Sayers rightly says that trinitarian doctrine is not mythological. For her it is analogical.[107] A third, and better, possibility to which she inadequately attends is simple in its power of explanation. Trinitarian theology is biblical.

THE DOCTRINE OF THE TRINITY: ALLUSIVELY

The doctrine of the Trinity is like an art museum, perhaps especially an urban museum with a distinguished collection. What prompts anyone—from a casual passerby to a graduate student in art history—to patronize this museum, to ponder, however brief or extended a time, the museum's collection? Before there is analysis or dissection of the worth of this or that painting, there is sheer wonder that art this good could be contained within four walls.

The Christian who approaches the Trinity, or who rather is drawn into this mystery, may at the outset agree with Henri de Lubac, who names the Trinity as a

> sealed mystery. We do not always know how to embrace the most pregnant truth, which must slowly produce its fruit within us. Impatient

---

[105]John Macquarrie, *Principles of Christian Theology*, 2nd ed. (New York: Scribner's, 1977), pp. 198-201.
[106]Richardson, *Doctrine of the Trinity*, p. 139.
[107]Sayers, *Mind of the Maker*, p. 123.

as we are, we would like to understand immediately, or rather, in our shortsighted pragmatism, if we are not shown practical applications for it right away, we declare it to be abstract, unassimilable, "unrealistic," an "empty shell," a hollow theory with which there would be no point in burdening ourselves.[108]

But a dedicated patron will not long hence be transfixed by the theological beauty and rapt by the compulsion to worship this three-in-one God.

> Holy, holy, holy is the LORD of hosts;
> the whole earth is full of his glory. (Is 6:3)

Curators and art historians may fuss over what to include in any given exhibit, what to leave in, what to leave out. These labors are akin to the theological wisdom that distilled trinitarian theology from its first formulations into its received orthodoxy, which might then, in service to the church and humankind, be subtly shifted for new times and places. But it is the patrons, the people streaming through the doors, who have kept the museum open. The common Christian confessor and even at times the merely curious onlookers are the final test of trinitarian relevance.

What art on what walls will these believers see? How many trinitarian masterpieces are there? Trinitarian theology is of course not only art, if by that we mean an appeal to devotional and emotional sensibilities; it is also science. The greatest minds in Christian history have gathered around this mystery.

Regular museum-goers have often seen day-trippers careening about with portable listening devices, taking in the guided lecture from the presumed expert. There is a certain utility to hearing what the learned have to say about great art. But the real patron eventually desires his or her own counsel, a reckoning that is surely leavened by the wisdom of others, but not its mere duplication. The savvy art lover understands that one tour is never enough and that the moment of greatest recognition may come hours or even days later.

When we come to our theological senses, we will arrive at Catherine LaCugna's insight that "God's economy is not the austere distribution

---

[108]Henri de Lubac, *The Christian Faith: An Essay on the Structure of the Apostles' Creed* (San Francisco: Ignatius Press, 1986), pp. 11-12, quoted in Catherine Mowry LaCugna, *God For Us: The Trinity & Christian Life* (San Francisco: HarperSanFrancisco, 1991), p. 379.

of meager resources but lavish grace, a glorious inheritance, bestowed in prodigal good pleasure, foreordained to be consummated."[109] God's economy, we recall, is "the wellspring of trinitarian faith."[110] It is not too much to say that God the Holy Spirit is our only true and gentle guide.

---

[109]LaCugna, *God for Us*, p. 377.
[110]Ibid.

2

The Divine Revolution Touches the Human

Theological doctrines are not like sleeping dogs, lazing, dozing and languishing in the noonday sun. While doctrines do not have lives of their own, apart from being proclaimed from pulpits and sang in pews, doctrines are propulsive and energized in motion. The trinitarian reclamation of our time is no accident; it arose through the realized intuition that theological work has no reason to be apart from the Trinity.

Grounding and leading this resurgence is the economic Trinity, or rather the claim that all investigations into God's triunity have their proper beginning here. Michael Downey speaks for many others when he writes:

> All theology, indeed, all Christian faith and practice, has to start with the economic Trinity, with the naming of Father, Son and Spirit in the scriptures. The answer to theology's single most important question—Who is God?—emerges by looking to God's grand economy of redemption through Word and Spirit in history, and then reads this back into the mystery of God as Love itself.[1]

---

[1]Michael Downey, *Altogether Gift: A Trinitarian Spirituality* (Maryknoll, N.Y.: Orbis, 2000), p. 52.

This encompassing and very nearly definitive statement on behalf of the economic Trinity validates the practicality of the doctrine. A God who is known in isolation from the press and crush of human history is a God who is not worth knowing, as Jürgen Moltmann states: "We cannot say of God who he is of himself and in himself; we can only say who he is for us in the history of Christ which reaches us in our history."[2] The crucial phrase here is "in our history." However, it is not human history that somehow humbles and brings the history of God within its compass. That would be the proverbial tail wagging the dog. It must rather be the case that God's trinitarian history, which Moltmann here names "the history of Christ," is given precisely *to* human history to redeem that history.

The Trinity names a God who builds a house fit for human dwelling, and it is the economic Trinity who brings this to pass. *Economic* is a word of utility, not a flight of speculation. *Economic* is a constructive, evident, almost palpable word. It is a word that walks before it soars. Catherine Mowry LaCugna, a noteworthy champion of the economic Trinity, locates it as referring to

> the three "faces" or manifestations of God's activity in the world, correlated with the names, Father, Son, and Spirit. In particular, economic Trinity denotes the missions, the being sent by God, of Son and Spirit in the work of redemption and deification. These missions bring about communion between God and humankind.[3]

If the economic Trinity is the "faces" God presents to the world, what is behind these faces? Surely not, as in *The Wizard of Oz* motion picture, the humbug of a man found out when Toto the dog tugs at the curtain, showing the so-called wizard behind the on-screen fulminations. No, behind the evident "faces" is the immanent Trinity, who is also variously known as the essential or even the ontological Trinity. The immanent Trinity, says LaCugna, "points to the life and work of God in the economy, but from an 'immanent' point of view."[4] Talk of the immanent Trinity is the attempt to fathom what kind of God

---

[2]Jürgen Moltmann, *The Crucified God*, trans. R. A. Wilson and John Bowden (New York: Harper & Row, 1974), p. 238.
[3]Catherine Mowry LaCugna, *God for Us: The Trinity & Christian Life* (San Francisco: HarperSanFrancisco, 1991), p. 211.
[4]Ibid.

would engage himself in creation, redemption and the in-gathering of all realities to himself.

Clearly, one is not forced to choose between the economic Trinity and the immanent Trinity, as one might choose between marrying one of two equally desirable twin siblings. In an earlier theological time the study and indeed the worship of God within himself, the pure divine essence as such, was held as the pinnacle of theological reflection, such that the immanent Trinity very nearly seemed the only Trinity. The finer theological distinctions of God within God's own self wrought over the centuries eventually reached the dead-end of irrelevance. Economic trinitarianism, not neglecting the older emphasis on the immanent Trinity but rescuing it from obscurity, has moved the entire trinitarian conversation forward.

Geoffrey Wainwright demonstrates how keeping our theological eyes and ears open can indeed open to a ravishing immanent sky:

> To the extent that God engages himself with the world, it is legitimate to read back from his presence and action into his very being. If he appears to engage himself with the world in different ways [for example as Father, Son and Spirit], it will to that extent be legitimate to trace a certain plurality into God himself. If the "economy" is read and experienced in a trinitarian way, then there is so much grounding for "immanent trinitarianism," though it must be remembered that the best traditional trinitarianism has always been sensitive to its own inadequacy in the face of the unfathomable God.[5]

There are hence not two trinities, as we observed already in chapter one, not one trinity of practical application and a second of studied and austere distance, rapt in its own contemplation. There can be only *one* Trinity. Explaining Karl Rahner's equating of the economic and immanent Trinity, LaCugna states that

> the identity of the economic and immanent Trinity therefore means that what God has revealed and given in Christ and the Spirit is the reality of God as God is from all eternity. What is given in the economy of salvation, in other words, is the mystery of God which exists from all eternity as triune.[6]

---

[5]Geoffrey Wainwright, *Doxology: The Praise of God in Worship, Doctrine, and Life* (New York: Oxford University Press, 1980), p. 100.
[6]LaCugna, *God for Us*, p. 212.

The anchoring of virtually all trinitarian sensibilities in the economic Trinity, and the further description of the immanent Trinity in economic terms, has seemed to some theologians a disservice to and surely a dilution of God's profundity and depth. This has seemed to functionalize God overmuch. Can the economic Trinity really bear all of this ontological weight? Is overloading the economic Trinity akin to one too many circus riders heaped on a high-wire bicycle? Eventually, the whole affair crashes into the safety net.

LaCugna and others like her would counter that the immanent Trinity is in fact that safety net, that layer of assurance allowing Father, Son and Spirit, if we may ridiculously picture them astride that high-wire bicycle, to do what they do. Furthermore, LaCugna knows that

> the distinction between economic and immanent Trinity is strictly conceptual, not ontological. There are not two trinities, the Trinity of experience and a transeconomic Trinity. There is one God, one divine self-communication, manifested in the one economy of creation, redemption, and consummation.[7]

Is this "strictly conceptual" distinction between the economic and the immanent Trinity at the same time a distinction without a difference? Or is the very identity of God at risk if what is practical is *always* of first consequence, and that which supports the practical valued only because it can manifest itself as practicality? Must not God first *be* before God can *perform?* Contemporary trinitarian theology understands the need to preserve the integrity of God's being, but at times the balance seems misplaced, as if the immanent Trinity is merely an afterthought, theological window dressing for the intellectually curious.

If *economic* is a building word, what better example of the economic Trinity than building a house? It was my recent privileged experience to be on site for dozens of hours as a television reality series worked its magic on a previously forlorn patch of Oklahoma landscape. *Voila!* In those dozens of hours, or less, a stunningly beautiful house, almost a minimansion, was erected through the kind ministrations of the *Extreme Makeover: Home Edition* TV show. The widow of a recently departed Baptist pastor stepped suddenly from the shambling modesty of a double-wide trailer to a splendid living with her five at-home children.

---

[7]Ibid.

The house may have gone up overnight, but there was nothing heedless, careless or calculating about its rising. Forthcoming home inspections mandated by the construction's haste will likely turn up nothing untoward or slapdash or dangerous. The volunteers who erected the house were not slackers but masters. The months-long planning regimen was failsafe, excruciatingly detailed, a triumph of logistics and efficiency. The blueprints are solid, maybe even works of art.

It does not take a genius to connect the theological dots. The immanent Trinity may stand for the brains behind this house-building operation. What motivated the craftsmen to rise above mediocrity to a stellar performance, the hand that realized the blueprints, the conceptual leap that truly brought the project to reality—all of these factors and dozens of related others are like the immanent Trinity.

Perhaps a master builder cannot *not* build. There may be an internal compulsion. When we observe the fruit of that genius, we may marvel at the genius but never forget the fruit. If the economic Trinity is the divine fruit, God's eternal fecundity on display for all to see, then this fruit can only blossom forth from who God truly is, the immanent Trinity. Regardless of where one begins—with the fruit or with the impulse to grow—the only possible ending is the one Trinity.

The economic and the immanent Trinity is not "Two Easy Pieces for Theology and Contemplation." The correct verb must be *is*, for to say the economic and the immanent Trinity *are* only confuses the issue by implying *two trinities*. If not "Two Easy Pieces," then perhaps a grand symphony in two movements. This symphony is none the less complex and beautiful for its being able to be heard, for its gift to humankind, for the God so signified is entirely worthy of adoration and worship.

Identifying the economic and the immanent Trinity, and averring their final coalescence into one Trinity, was never meant to be a formulaic simplification. The conceptual neatness of two trinities who are really one Trinity must never eclipse the pervasive mystery that attends all trinitarian talk. God's mystery is not diminished as that mystery is passed from Father to Son to Holy Spirit. For in reality that mystery is not so much passed *between* Father to Son to Spirit as it is shared *among* Father and Son and Spirit. God's mystery is more a circulating wholeness than it is a smooth linear progression.

The temptation to see the immanent Trinity as complex and the economic Trinity as simple must be resisted. God's work in the world, the province of the economic Trinity, may be every bit as complex and variegated as God's inner sanctum. Because there is only one Trinity, the differentiations one may draw between the economic and the immanent Trinity are not such as may finally divide the one Trinity into two. The rather more "visible" work accomplished by the economic Trinity is in total keeping with who God is. For Michael Downey, God's "selfgiving is at the very heart of who God is. The incomprehensibility of God lies in the utter gratuity of life and love, in God's constant coming as gift. God is inexhaustible Gift, Given and Gift/ing in and through love. This is who God is and how God is."[8] The "who" and the "how" of God might be other ways of saying, respectively, immanent Trinity and economic Trinity. God's "whoness" is not a mystery unto itself, a puzzle known only to itself. *Who* God is necessarily goes forth into the world as *how* God acts in the world. Neither *who* nor *how* is complete without the other.

Having admitted that, pondering the inner-trinitarian relations found in the immanent Trinity may invite the sort of humble silence that is relatively easier to dispel when contemplating the economic Trinity. The paradox of knowing but finally not knowing is more sharply drawn with the immanent Trinity. Gary Badcock's acknowledgment of this is exactly correct: "The task of developing a theology of the inner-trinitarian relations from the economy therefore has to reckon seriously with the paradox that an adequate doctrine of the immanent Trinity is only possible when an apophatic reticence about it is embraced."[9]

An apophatic approach to Christian spirituality and trinitarian theology may be construed more broadly or more narrowly. Badcock's speaking of "apophatic reticence" regarding our knowledge of the immanent Trinity is the broader usage. It invites the cautious respect that always reins itself in whenever one is tempted toward the presumption of knowing too much.

But the narrower take on apophasis will not allow even this circumspect caution. "Only what God is not," in the words of T. F. Tor-

---

[8]Downey, *Altogether Gift*, p. 43.
[9]Gary D. Badcock, *Light of Truth & Fire of Love: A Theology of the Holy Spirit* (Grand Rapids: Eerdmans, 1997), p. 255.

rance, must content the rigorously apophatic theologian.[10] Poetically and hymnically, the first two lines of a classic hymn speak of God apophatically:

Immortal, invisible, God only wise,
In light inaccessible hid from our eyes.

Torrance notes that both Gregory of Nazianzus and John Calvin found a relentless apophaticism to be a futile and dead theological end. Gregory concluded that in reality one can never say what God is not without some prior and positive knowledge of what and who God is.[11] Can one explain the concept of dryness without prior recourse to water and moisture? Not likely. So also with God. The hymn writer Walter Chalmers Smith understood this also, and concludes his first verse by moving from the silence of God's inaccessibility to the relatively more open theater of the praise of God:

Most blessed, most glorious, the Ancient of Days
Almighty, victorious, thy great name we praise.[12]

To turn an apophatic lens on the immanent Trinity is only to deepen the mystery of God's triune character and to agree with Badcock as to "the ultimately apophatic character of the immanent Trinity."[13] Yet the undoubted respect God commands in both the economic and the immanent Trinity is not a "lights out" approach ending in the not knowing of God at all. Confidently, Torrance claims that in Jesus Christ God is "making himself accessible to us and giving us entry into the inner fellowship of God's Life by allowing us to share in God's own eternal Spirit."[14] The whole of this is nothing less than "the greatest *revolution in our knowledge of God*."[15] For Torrance, the Jewish faith or Greek philosophy or indeed any non-Christian religion falls outside of this revolution and is in fact hostile to the "scandal of particularity" of God's coming to us in Jesus Christ. One might almost conclude that at its farthest stretch, if vacated from a trinitarian context, the

---

[10]Thomas F. Torrance, *Trinitarian Perspectives: Toward Doctrinal Agreement* (Edinburgh: T & T Clark, 1994), p. 37.
[11]Ibid.
[12]Walter Chalmers Smith, "Immortal, Invisible, God Only Wise" (1876).
[13]Badcock, *Light of Truth & Fire of Love*, p. 255.
[14]Torrance, *Trinitarian Perspectives*, p. 1.
[15]Ibid.

apophatic approach to God is not Christian at all because, in place of God's revelation in Jesus Christ, the apophatic offers only this, in Torrance's words: "God remains ultimately unknowable, the nameless, the incomprehensible One, who cannot be known in himself or conceived in his inner life."[16]

If, however, the apophatic is continually governed by the *homoousion*, the reality that God the Son is coeternal and coequal with God the Father, Torrance is willing not only to retain the language of the apophatic but even to recommend it. If the "apophatic knowledge" of God is carefully qualified in a trinitarian way, it even points to the soul's communion with God that is *theosis*. For Torrance, then, this apophasis signifies the

> positive ineffability of God who in making himself known through the Son and in the Spirit reveals that he infinitely transcends the grasp of our minds, but who through the Son and in the Spirit lifts us up to the level of participation in God where we are opened out for union and communion with him far beyond the limits of our creaturely existence— which is another way of describing *theosis*.[17]

THE FREEDOM OF THE TRIUNE GOD

The solid theological consensus that begins trinitarian theology in the economy of God does not always end in the embrace of Karl Rahner's dictum that identifies the economic Trinity and the immanent Trinity. In Paul Molnar's recent and, by most accounts, definitive investigation of contemporary trinitarian theology, the title says it all: *Divine Freedom and the Doctrine of the Immanent Trinity*. Molnar's exacting and rigorous discussion aims to protect God's freedom against any conceivable encroachment, forfeiture or diminution. If we as humans experience God's freedom palpably in the economic Trinity, we must never mistake *our experience* of God's freedom for God's *experiencing his own freedom*, the freedom of the immanent Trinity. By definition God's freedom answers only to itself, and God's freedom is to be trusted. While the doorway to the immanent Trinity is the economic Trinity, so that for Molnar "we must adhere to the economic Trinity for

---

[16]Ibid.
[17]Ibid., p. 87.

our information about the immanent Trinity," there can be no simple equation of the economic and the immanent Trinity. "Theologians should neither separate nor confuse the immanent and the economic Trinity," Molnar concludes.[18]

To separate the economic from the immanent Trinity is a theological disaster. There cannot be two trinities. Furthermore, how God is in the economy is not at variance with how God is immanently. Here Molnar agrees with T. F. Torrance, whose theology Molnar describes as insisting "that what God is toward us he is in himself, and that precisely is one God who is equally divine as Father, Son and Spirit *ad intra* [within himself] and *ad extra* [toward the world]. On this fact rests the validity of the incarnation, reconciliation and redemption."[19] To err in theological beginnings, misstating the doctrine of the Trinity, can thus be the ruination of nearly everything to follow, especially in the christological doctrines of incarnation and redemption.

To take up Molnar's other qualifier, what happens theologically when the economic and the immanent Trinity are *confused*? What happens is this: the theological priority of grounding human freedom in divine freedom is dramatically overturned. Then, divine freedom is placed at the service of human freedom, which violates God's sovereignty. Positively, to esteem and value the freedom of the immanent Trinity properly is for Molnar to affirm "that God has in fact exercised his transcendent freedom to be for us specifically in Christ and the Spirit."[20] Negatively, if God's freedom must answer to human freedom, then the entire project and task of Christian theology is overthrown. Faith seeking understanding, a tried and proven theological method, is corrupted into understanding seeking faith.[21]

Throughout Molnar's exposition his purposes are very clear, if sometimes heatedly expressed, and his resolution firm. The truth of the Christian gospel can and must be deeply rooted within us, for this is the end for which the Word became flesh, but this truth *never arises within us*. It is given from without, through revelation. Following Barth, Molnar asserts that "revelation is not the projection of human experience

---

[18]Paul D. Molnar, *Divine Freedom and the Doctrine of the Immanent Trinity* (London: T & T Clark, 2005), p. 312.
[19]Ibid., p. 322.
[20]Ibid., p. 312.
[21]Ibid.

into God, but the action of God naming himself to us and including us in a genuine relationship with himself by faith and grace."[22] In completely trinitarian language, Molnar believes "that knowledge of God takes place from Jesus Christ through the power of his Holy Spirit and consequently it must be sought in and from a center outside us, that is, from a center in God acting for us. It must be sought and found objectively in Christ and subjectively through the Holy Spirit."[23]

The endless questing of the twentieth-century spirit, which will only deepen in the new century, has for Molnar sought answers within the confines of its own ecstasy. What the human spirit discovers there is not God in Christ but rather self in the world. *Are You Experienced?* is the title Jimi Hendrix gave to a collection of songs hailed as one of the greatest of all rock 'n' roll albums. "It's a collection of free feeling and imagination," Hendrix said of his work. "Imagination is very important."[24] Imagination cannot be less important for the Christian than for anyone else. The incarnation of the Word of God in human flesh means that of all people the Christian must be the most possessed of a lively imagination. However, for Molnar, the freedom of the Christian imagination has no legitimate foundation but the freedom of the immanent Trinity.

If it is true, and it must be, "that God sets the terms for theological insight," then to start at any other place than God's freedom is to court disaster.[25] Of the many theologians who come under Molnar's withering criticism, none feels it as sharply as Karl Rahner. It is not so much Rahner's equating of the economic and immanent Trinity that provokes Molnar as it is Rahner's operational theological method. If God's freedom in both the economy of salvation and God's immanence is regarded and upheld, then we can accept Rahner's conclusion that the immanent and the economic Trinity are the same.

Rahner appeals to transcendental experience, beginning his theological investigations more with the question of "who am I as a transcendent self capable of knowing God?" rather than by pondering who God is in himself. This very nearly invalidates his famous trinitarian maxim.

---

[22]Ibid., p. 21.
[23]Ibid., p. 126.
[24]Jimi Hendrix, quoted in *Rolling Stone: The 500 Greatest Albums of All Time*, ed. Joe Levy (New York: Wenner, 2005), p. 34.
[25]Molnar, *Divine Freedom*, p. 313.

Because we are human and not divine, we have no choice "but to understand God in the categories available to us in our human experience," as Molnar explains in his book's preface.[26] But this does not allow us to create God in *our* own image, to project our all-too-limited, all-too-human experiences upon God. This is Rahner's great mistake.

Rahner's method, in Molnar's indictment, "leads him to make the experience of self the foundation, norm and source of understanding God, revelation and grace."[27] While Rahner's anthropological bearings do turn to the demonstrably theological, Molnar does not believe Rahner can ever overcome his faulty methodology. As Molnar describes Rahner's approach, "whenever one recognizes a supreme one transcending the many, whatever name is given to this reality,"[28] there one has intuited God's oneness. For Karl Barth, by contrast, God's oneness can be known to us only in Jesus Christ through the direction of the Holy Spirit.[29]

As a result, Rahner's christology is doomed to one or even both of the ancient heresies of the Ebionite (undervaluing Christ's divinity) and Docetic (disregarding Christ's humanity) christologies.[30] As great a trinitarian theologian as Rahner aspires to be, his theology yet illustrates what goes wrong when the freedom of the immanent Trinity is slighted or confused with human freedom. Rahner's slippery slope may and typically does lead to these four negative indicators, as set forth by Molnar: (1) God becomes dependent on human history rather than the reverse; (2) the truth of christology is inverted, suggesting that it is the humanity and not the divinity of Jesus Christ that reveals God; (3) the Holy Spirit and the human spirit become a hopeless muddle, with no hope of discerning where the holy ends and the human begins or vice versa; (4) when theological reflection begins in human experiences of self-transcendence, those experiences determine theological truth rather than Jesus Christ as the object of faith.[31]

Divine Freedom and the Doctrine of the Immanent Trinity, Molnar's synthesizing analysis of more than a half-century of trinitarian theol-

---

[26]Ibid., p. ix.
[27]Ibid., p. 108.
[28]Ibid., p. 160.
[29]Ibid.
[30]Ibid., p. 50.
[31]Ibid., p. 311-12.

ogy, illustrates and possibly proves the old baseball adage that good pitching beats good hitting (in broader sports lingo, a good defense beats a good offense). For Molnar's thinking and writing are primarily defensive, warning of the dangers of neglecting the divine freedom. Stanley Grenz finds Molnar's main contention to be "that a return to the immanent Trinity is crucial to the task of recognizing, upholding, and respecting God's freedom."[32] As certain as is Grenz's description of what Molnar is about, it yet provokes of Molnar a further question: what exactly does he mean by divine freedom?

He believes that all theologians must respect the sanctity of the immanent Trinity. He agrees with Karl Rahner that no good can possibly come from what Rahner called "wild conceptual acrobatics" into God's immanent hiddenness.[33] Molnar's advice that the economic Trinity leads us to the immanent Trinity must conclude that our beholding of this magnificent freedom is in and of itself sufficient. Furthermore, the contemplation of the divine freedom is itself an opening to God's revelation through Jesus Christ in the power of the Holy Spirit, in other words a return to the economy.

Immigrants to the United States of one hundred years ago and more rode the ocean waves to the harbor of New York. If the entire immigration experience may be hastily likened to the beautiful leading of the economic Trinity to the immanent Trinity and back again, then let the ocean crossing—the close quarters, the second thoughts, the homesickness, the diseases—stand for the economy of salvation. Was the zeal for freedom squeezed out during the Atlantic crossing? Hardly. After all of that, what immigrant could not but rejoice in the august serenity of Lady Liberty bidding an American welcome to each and to all?

Let the Statue of Liberty stand for the immanent Trinity. As much as the immigrant may have wished to explore from base to tip this marvelous monument to liberty, which after all is why the immigrant forsook the old world for the new, the ship steams straight for Ellis Island, where the immigrant is once again thrust into the actuality, the economy, of the immigration process: the health screenings, the checking of documents, the hoisting of personal cargo, the refinding of family. Even

---

[32]Stanley J. Grenz, *Rediscovering the Triune God: The Trinity in Contemporary Theology* (Minneapolis: Fortress, 2004), pp. 200-201.
[33]Molnar, *Divine Freedom*, p. 312.

if the immigrant never does get a personal landing on Liberty Island, the symbolic heft of Lady Liberty will never leave the immigrant's consciousness. The stockyards of the Midwest or the tenements of New York's Lower East Side will stretch the economy of immigration in new and often unforeseen directions, but whatever is good can be traced to and validated by the immanent and abiding truth of Lady Liberty.

Nicene Trinitarianism for a New Day

Paul Molnar is himself blessed by the humility that must attend any deep engagement with God's triunity. He shares this humility with a theologian of marked trinitarian sensibilities, T. F. Torrance, who is widely regarded "as the most significant British academic theologian of the twentieth century."[34] They also share an affinity for the trinitarian theology of Athanasius (c. 296-373), the bishop of Alexandria and "greatest and most consistent theological opponent of Arianism," the christological heresy denying the full deity of the Logos who came into flesh in Jesus Christ.[35]

Torrance's lengthy career has significantly engaged trinitarian themes throughout its unfolding. He is found to be in the company of Athanasius, Calvin and Barth, his entire project being "shaped at the outset by the reality of the triune God," for one commentator.[36] Torrance referred to his theology as "deeply Nicene and doxological . . . with its immediate focus on Jesus Christ as Mediator, and its ultimate focus on the Holy Trinity."[37] A trio of books relatively late in Torrance's writing life summarize his mature trinitarian theology. *The Trinitarian Faith* (1988) is a detailed explication of the Niceno-Constantinopolitan creed of 381, this creed appearing in calligraphy at the front of the book. This book aspires to make known "the evangelical theology of the ancient Catholic church" as its subtitles attest. The subtitle of his 1994 collection of essays, *Trinitarian Perspectives*, is also consequential, it being "toward doctrinal agreement." This book aims toward an ecumenical consen-

---

[34]Alister E. McGrath, *Thomas F. Torrance: An Intellectual Biography* (Edinburgh: T & T Clark, 1999), p. xi, quoted in Grenz, *Rediscovering the Triune God*, p. 202.

[35]*The Oxford Dictionary of the Christian Church*, 2nd ed., s.v. "Athanasius."

[36]Robert J. Palma, "Thomas F. Torrance's Reformed Theology," *Reformed Review* 38, no. 1 (1984): 13, quoted in Grenz, *Rediscovering the Triune God*, p. 206.

[37]R. D. Kernoha, "Tom Torrance: The Man and the Reputation," *Life and Work* 32, no. 5 (1976): 14, quoted in Grenz, *Rediscovering the Triune God*, p. 206.

sus on the doctrine of the Trinity, especially regarding Torrance's own Reformed tradition and Eastern Orthodoxy. Finally, in 1996 Torrance published the most systematic of the three trinitarian works, *The Christian Doctrine of God: One Being Three Persons.*

Torrance most often interacts with the theology of Athanasius in these three volumes, even more than with his professor Karl Barth, whose *Church Dogmatics* Torrance helped to translate and edit. At Torrance's own half-century mark, in 1963, the icon of Saint Athanasius was presented to him as a gift, and its loveliness is reproduced as a color plate in the front of *The Trinitarian Faith.*

One of Athanasius's first theological principles, if not in fact the preeminent one, is: "It would be more godly and true to signify God from the Son and call him Father, than to name God from his works and call him Unoriginate."[38] Both Molnar and Torrance quote this; for them it is less the conclusion of a long chain of theological argumentation than it is the presupposition for the construction of a trinitarian theology. To signify God as Unoriginate is no better than the God of various philosophical systems, but to own God as Father of Jesus Christ is to think and confess biblically.

"If theological truth is now perfect in Trinity," the great Nicene theologian continues, "then this is the true and only divine worship, and this is its beauty and truth, it must always have been so."[39] This reverent tone from Athanasius accords well with Torrance's belief that the triune God "is more to be adored than expressed."[40] Yet Athanasius's trinitarian theology is not only devotionally sensitive. It is also conceptually rigorous. In that regard Torrance has met his soul mate, for Torrance's theological method is a hand-in-glove fit with that of Athanasius, who would see himself in Torrance's commendation of the best theological method: "Piety and precision, godliness and exactness belong together, and condition one another, for knowledge of God arises and takes shape in our mind under the determination of his revealed nature, and is maintained in the experience of worship, prayer, holiness and godliness."[41]

---

[38]Athanasius, quoted in Molnar, *Divine Freedom*, p. 324, and Thomas F. Torrance, *The Christian Doctrine of God, One Being Three Persons* (Edinburgh: T & T Clark, 1996), p. 117.

[39]Athanasius, quoted in Torrance, *Trinitarian Perspectives*, pp. 7, 137.

[40]T. F. Torrance, *The Trinitarian Faith: The Evangelical Theology of the Ancient Catholic Church* (Edinburgh: T & T Clark, 1988), p. 46.

[41]Ibid., p. 54.

Can one enter the door of God's triunity equally well through the door marked "one" as through the door marked "three"? In a literal sense this figure of speech is an abuse of classical trinitarian language, because of course there cannot be two doors into the knowing of God, but only one, the door of God's gracious bestowal in Jesus Christ. More simply put, is it God's unity or God's Trinity that first attracts us? Is the answer to this question even theologically significant?

Both John Calvin, who cited this statement in his *Institutes of the Christian Religion*, and Torrance, who notes this citation, agree with this justly famous utterance of Gregory of Nazianzus: "I cannot think of the One without immediately being surrounded by the radiance of the Three; nor can I discern the Three without at once being carried back to the One."[42] Note that Gregory begins with the One, and from the One experiences the Three, and back again.

During more than three decades of enjoyable if sporadic ocean-front sojourning in a vacation home, the muffled but still muscular ocean's roar was a more effective sleep inducement than any pill could be. Let this surf's speech stand for the One toward whom Gregory is intuitively drawn. Yet, even when they are out of sight, as drowsiness dropped into restful sleep, the sky and the sand can never be out of mind. Surf, sky and sand may not be a trinity, yet may serve as a humble illustration of how the contemplation of the One (the ocean's roar) necessarily draws someone into "the radiance of the Three."

Gregory's timeless statement is everything good trinitarian theology is called to be. The "I" of Gregory's self-consciousness is not a self-determined "I" in the sense of René Descartes's "I think therefore I am." Rather Gregory's "I" is immediately given over to the God whom Torrance identifies as "the ineffable I AM of the One Ever-living God."[43] Gregory's language is not that of philosophical speculation, not that of mystical absorption, but that of ecstatic adoration. He has given over his human will to the will of the Holy Spirit, by whom Gregory is carried back and forth between the One and the Three.

If one needs a point of entry into the Trinity, then Gregory's solution is one for all time, perpetually relevant. Torrance knows this. He writes:

---

[42]Gregory of Nazianzus, quoted in Torrance, *Trinitarian Perspectives*, p. 55.
[43]Torrance, *Trinitarian Perspectives*, p. 142.

> In a faithful account of the doctrine of the Holy Trinity our thought
> cannot but engage in a deep circular movement from Unity to Trin-
> ity and from Trinity to Unity, for we are unable to speak of the whole
> Triunity without already speaking of the three particular Persons of
> the Trinity or to speak of any of the three Persons without presuming
> knowledge of the whole Triunity, for God is God only as he is Father,
> Son and Holy Spirit.[44]

Torrance looks over his shoulder as he writes this. His approach to
the Trinity is not the narrowing and individuating "my thought" but
rather the "our thought" of heritage and tradition. The "deep circular
movement" he commends is a movement calibrated in centuries, not
weekends. It resists flighty theological trends and abides instead in deep
rhythms. Torrance values the practitioners of Greek patristic theology,
such as Athanasius and Gregory of Nazianzus, for their "godliness and
accuracy, worship and precision,"[45] four qualities that clearly name Torrance's own theological priorities also.

In the face of today's fractious life there endures a deep hunger for
the unifying and in-gathering One. The famous *Shema* of Israel is never
far from human consciousness, however wildly plural our lives have
become: "Hear, O Israel: the LORD our God, the LORD is One" (Deut
6:4 NIV). The way a widow answers her telephone says as much. Living alone, her children at a distance, she yet answers: "Williams family, Joanne speaking" (not her real name). The lone widow is drawn to
the memory, still very much alive in her mind and heart, of the *entire
family*, subsuming her own aloneness under the one. The absence of
the husband has not and cannot destroy the unity of the family. The
intuitive flow of Mrs. Williams toward the one is like the trinitarian
theologian who must first speak of the unity, of the One-in-Three, and
only then of the triunity, the Three-in-One.

This was also the strategy of Athanasius. If we define the term with
care, Athanasius was a *Monarchian*. The customary textbook definition of a Monarchian is someone who so elevates the Father over the
Son and the Holy Spirit as to deny full divinity to any but God the Father. Athanasius did not subscribe to this view, which in fact is heresy.
The Greek patristic theology of which Athanasius is a leading represen-

---

[44]Torrance, *Christian Doctrine of God*, p. 27.
[45]Ibid., p. 128.

tative typically began trinitarian thinking with God the Father as the fountain of divinity. Extreme care was always exercised so as not to suggest any degrees of divinity within the Godhead. Gregory of Nazianzus is highly aware of how even a single misplaced word may defeat the full deity of Son and Holy Spirit: "I should like to call the Father the greater, because from him flows both the equality and being of the equals, but I am afraid to use the word origin *[arche]* lest I should make him the origin of inferiors."[46] If the Father is the principle of origination within the Godhead, he is not superior to the Son and the Holy Spirit, who must be considered as "whole God" and "whole from whole."[47] Athanasius cited no less an authority than Jesus Christ himself for the full, complete equal divinity of the three persons: "The Lord taught the perfection of the Holy Trinity as an indivisible and single Godhead."[48]

If Athanasius is not a Monarchian of the heretical, subordinationist stripe, in what sense may he be named thus? Torrance notes that it is to Athanasius that we may trace "the normative emphasis on One God in Three Persons rather than Three Persons in One God."[49] Torrance's "deep circular movement" begins with Athanasius's emphasis on God's unity. In heretical hands, the monarchy is strictly limited to God the Father, with the Son and the Spirit forced to play subsidiary and possibly even bit parts. No such heresy befalls Athanasius, for a Godhead of only the Father is not at all the biblical Trinity. When Athanasius writes that "there is one Form of Godhead which is also in the Word," he is asserting that the Godhead is fully expressed in the Father and equally so in Son and Spirit.[50] This means, in Torrance's words, that "the Monarchy is not to be thought of as limited to one Person—the One Monarchy is the Trinity in Unity and the Unity in Trinity."[51] If the dominant strategy of Greek patristic theology is, in Torrance's words, "that the unity of God is ensured by tracing it back to the Father as the one underived Person," this is not to dismiss the Son and the Holy Spirit as inferior.[52] As Gregory

---

[46]Gregory of Nazianzus *Oratio* 40.43, quoted in Colin E. Gunton, *The Promise of Trinitarian Theology* (Edinburgh: T & T Clark, 1993), p. 167, where Gunton thanks Torrance for pointing this text out to him.

[47]Torrance, *Trinitarian Perspectives*, p. 136.

[48]Athanasius *Ad Serapionem*, quoted in Torrance, *Trinitarian Perspectives*, p. 137.

[49]Torrance, *Trinitarian Perspectives*, p. 137.

[50]Athanasius *Contra Arianos*, 3.15, quoted in Torrance, *Trinitarian Perspectives*, p. 137.

[51]Torrance, *Trinitarian Perspectives*, p. 138.

[52]Ibid.

of Nazianzus expressed it: "And One is not more and Another less God, nor is One before and Another after. . . . But differentiated as the Persons are, the entire undivided Godhead is One in Each Person, and there is one mingling of Light, as it were of three suns joined to each other."[53]

How are T. F. Torrance and Paul Molnar to be compared? It must be initially agreed that of the two, Molnar is more interested in and possibly adept at the art of the comparison. Most of the contents of *Divine Freedom and the Doctrine of the Immanent Trinity* first appeared in print as technical articles in various theological journals, and Molnar's typical strategy is comparative. Molnar's "gold standard" for trinitarian theology remains Karl Barth, against whom the likes of Karl Rahner and even Jürgen Moltmann are compared unfavorably. Being a true Barthian, Molnar esteems Torrance also, and in his book's comparative analysis of Torrance and Rahner the latter is found wanting in comparison with the long-time Edinburgh theologian.

If Molnar's theology is more contemporarily focused, Torrance is very comfortable with the entire sweep of historical trinitarian theology. His slim volume, *Trinitarian Perspectives*, is also a collection of articles, but engages a wider realm of trinitarian thought than does Molnar. John Calvin's doctrine of the holy Trinity is thoroughly unpacked. As noted earlier, since this volume of essays seeks to move "toward doctrinal agreement," Torrance also includes valuable ecumenical probes toward Christian consensus, especially between his own Reformed tradition and the Orthodox theologians among whom Torrance is so much at home. Toward the close of Torrance's "Commentary on the Agreed Statement on the Holy Spirit," he offers this wonderful statement:

> We cannot know what God is in his One Being, for as such the Being of God is utterly beyond all finite comprehension; nor can we ever know how God is One Being, Three Persons, for that is beyond all finite explanation. But we may know who God is, for he has made himself personally known to us through the Incarnation of his Son, and the Communion of the Holy Spirit.[54]

Although Paul Molnar's style is much more polemical and even combative than is Torrance's, and although Molnar set himself a different

---

[53]Gregory of Nazianzus *Oratio* 31.14, quoted in Torrance, *Trinitarian Perspectives*, p. 138.
[54]Torrance, *Trinitarian Perspectives*, p. 142.

theological task—to protest against the dangerous dilution of the freedom of the immanent Trinity—it can still be said that he and Torrance end in the same neighborhood, if perhaps not under the same roof. Torrance's wisdom, "that God is ineffable does not mean that he is unintelligible," is also for Molnar the truth of gospel.[55] For both of them the gospel is given in Jesus Christ and never of human instrumentality. Thus is God's freedom known.

THE DANCING GOD WHO WOULD BE KNOWN

Of the many words that might modify and describe the noun *theology*, today's multireligious context surely demands that *Christian* be the modifier of first recourse. There might, after all, be Buddhist or Islamic or Hindu theology. Indeed the word *theology* predates the explicitly Christian appropriation of it. But following close on the heels of *Christian* theology must certainly be *trinitarian* theology. While it is redundant to say "Christian trinitarian theology," any theology that is Christian must at the same time be trinitarian, unless its promulgators fall into dire contradiction. Anyone promoting a Christian theology that is not defensibly trinitarian to the marrow has a lot of explaining to do. Many of the root components of a fully articulated Christian theology that formerly may have shown little interest in the Trinity—for example christology, ecclesiology, sacramental theology, pneumatology, even evangelism—are by now fully cognizant of the interpretive dynamics of the Trinity. So any given Christian theology may continue to be, for example, a Wesleyan, a Lutheran, a Roman Catholic, an ecumenical, a Pentecostal, a postmodern, a Calvinian or scores of other modifiers, but any theology that deserts or slights the trinitarian mandate is suspect.

Every theology necessarily offers a theology of salvation or reclamation, the formulation and figuring of which is known as soteriology. Although he is before our focal contemporary period, the Danish Lutheran theologian Søren Kierkegaard (1813-1855), offers up this lovely prayer that is at once fully trinitarian and graciously endowed with the fruits of salvation:

> Father in Heaven! To Thee the congregation often makes its petition for all who are sick and sorrowful, and when someone amongst us lies ill,

---

[55]Torrance, *The Trinitarian Faith*, p. 214.

alas, of mortal sickness the congregation sometimes desires a special petition; grant that we may each one of us become in good time aware what sickness it is which is the sickness unto death, and aware that we are all of us suffering from this sickness. O Lord Jesus Christ, who didst come to earth to heal them that suffer from this sickness, from which, alas, we all suffer, but from which Thou art able to heal only those who are conscious that they are sick in this way; help Thou us in this sickness to hold fast to Thee, to the end that we may be healed of it. O God the Holy Ghost, who comest to help us in this sickness if we honestly desire to be healed; remain with us so that for no single instant we may to our own destruction shun the Physician, but may remain with Him—delivered from sickness. For to be with Him is to be delivered from our sickness, and when we are with Him we are saved from all sickness.[56]

In Kierkegaard's prayer we see not only many features of orthodox trinitarianism, but also note the ease with which a therapeutic approach to salvation, or salvation as healing, may be expressed in a trinitarian way. All prayer, so traditional trinitarian spirituality guides us, is to be addressed *to* God the Father. Jesus Christ as mediator is the one *through* whom prayer is to be made. As mediator, Christ fulfills many roles. In Kierkegaard's prayer, Jesus is especially the physician, the only one who can truly deliver from the universal malady, the sickness unto death. This deliverance is sealed and solidified in the Holy Spirit, whom Kierkegaard names as explicitly *God*, an acclamation which at certain times in the history of the doctrine of the Holy Spirit was not honored. The hovering help offered by God the Holy Ghost is another way of saying all prayer must be *in* the Spirit's utterance.

The Holy Spirit bears witness to who Jesus Christ is and what Jesus Christ accomplishes in his ministry of healing. This bearing witness is one component of the ancient trinitarian teaching of *perichoresis*, a Greek word for which there is no altogether adequate English rendering. One can only bear witness if there is mutual regard flowing from the bearer of witness to the one worthy of the witness, and back again. The continual regard each of the divine persons has for the other two is at the heart of perichoresis. In Jürgen Moltmann's telling phrase, per-

---

[56]Søren Kierkegaard, *The Prayers of Kierkegaard*, ed. Perry D. LeFevre (Chicago: University of Chicago Press, 1956), p. 26.

ichoresis "makes it possible to conceive of a community without uniformity and a personhood without individualism."[57]

Leonardo Boff suggests that perichoresis has two fundamental meanings, which in turn led to two slightly different Latin translations. The first meaning is more solid, even sedentary, "a situation of fact, a static state."[58] Here the three divine persons are situated in the same neighborhood. They live together, even under one roof, not begrudgingly but lovingly.

At a McDonald's restaurant in a crowded country in the developing world, sometimes there were not enough hard, fixed, plastic chairs to go around. One small table to which was attached two rigid chairs as appendages, might need to accommodate strangers across this narrow table if everyone was to be seated. And so a posted sign admonished, "Share a seat, win a friend." The first meaning of perichoresis, rendered in Latin as *circuminsessio*, means "being seated, having its seat in, seat."[59] Unlike the McDonald's repasters, Father, Son and Holy Spirit need no introduction. From all eternity, they have been the closest of friends, for they are one. They have always shared a seat together, so that the McDonald's advisory implies and in fact registers what has always been reality for Father, Son and Holy Spirit.

Circumincessio is the second Latin translation, meaning to "permeate, com-penetrate and interpenetrate."[60] Here the three divine persons are not merely under one roof. They are playing, singing, even telling jokes together. They are doing what all families do, for they are the Primal Family. For Boff this second meaning of perichoresis shades off into koinonia: "a permanent process of active reciprocity, a clasping of two hands: the Persons interpenetrate one another and this process of communing forms their very nature."[61]

If today's devotees of trinitarian theology learn only one technical term, perichoresis should be it. Not only does it go a great distance toward describing the immanent Trinity, it also has implications for per-

---

[57]Jürgen Moltmann, *Experiences in Theology: Ways and Forms of Christian Theology*, trans. Margaret Kohl (Minneapolis: Fortress, 2000), p. 316.

[58]Leonardo Boff, *Trinity and Society*, trans. Paul Burns (Maryknoll, N.Y.: Orbis, 1988), p. 135.

[59]Ibid., p. 136.

[60]William J. Hill, *The Three-Personed God: The Trinity as a Mystery of Salvation* (Washington, D.C.: Catholic University of America Press, 1982), p. 272.

[61]Ibid.

sonal and social ethics, for family life, for politics and even for aesthetics and the theology of Christian worship. It is not exactly known who first used perichoresis, but the Greek theologian John of Damascus (c. 675-c. 749) was an early champion.[62] In somewhat scholastic language, John describes the perichoresis as follows:

> The subsistences dwell and are established firmly in one another. For they are inseparable and cannot part from one another, but keep to their separate courses within one another, without coalescing or mingling, but cleaving to one another. For the Son is in the Father and the Spirit: and the Spirit in the Father and the Son: and the Father in the Son and the Spirit, but there is no coalescence or commingling or confusion.[63]

Later, the Council of Florence (1438-1445) summarized the tradition of perichoresis by stating that "The Father is wholly in the Son and wholly in the Holy Spirit; the Son wholly in the Father and wholly in the Holy Spirit; the Holy Spirit wholly in the Father and wholly in the Son."[64]

For those with a metaphoric bent, there are two images which may help to convey what perichoresis means and how it functions. John of Damascus likens it to "three suns cleaving to each other without separation and giving out light mingled and conjoined in one."[65] In our time, Leonardo Boff sees the mutual interpenetration of Father, Son and Holy Spirit as approximating to

> three fountain jets gushing upward and toward each other, mingling and uniting so as to form a single column of water. Logically, it is not the column that comes first, but the jets. The Persons of the Trinity form the beginning without beginning, simultaneous and co-eternal. The process of self-realization in the Trinity is each Person being able to realize the others.[66]

---

[62]Thomas G. Weinandy gives some of the historical background of the term in *The Father's Spirit of Sonship: Reconceiving the Trinity* (Edinburgh: T & T Clark, 1995), p. 78 n. 41. See also Moltmann, *Experiences in Theology*, p. 316, where he writes that Gregory of Nazianzus was probably the first to use the term. Moltmann notes further than the two New Testament uses of the term, Mt 3:5; 14:35, are not theologically significant, meaning "the world around."

[63]John of Damascus *Exposition of the Orthodox Faith* 1.14, quoted in Millard J. Erickson, *God in Three Persons: A Contemporary Interpretation of the Trinity* (Grand Rapids: Baker, 1995), p. 229.

[64]Quoted in Boff, *Trinity and Society*, p. 135.

[65]John of Damascus *Exposition of the Orthodox Faith* 1.8, quoted in Erickson, *God in Three Persons*, p. 229.

[66]Boff, *Trinity and Society*, p. 128.

Perichoresis then, as Moltmann expresses it, points to "the circulatory character of the eternal divine life. An eternal life process takes place in the triune God through the exchange of energies. The Father exists in the Son, the Son in the Father, and both of them in the Spirit, just as the Spirit exists in both the Father and the Son."[67] Descriptions such as "circulatory" and "the exchange of energies" insure that perichoresis is a dynamic and organic way of construing God's triune life.

Following this organic lead, Millard Erickson suggests that perichoresis is like the three vital organs without which life is impossible: heart, brain, lungs.[68] Erickson knows that no analogy or comparison can be perfect, especially when applied to God. Brain, lungs and heart cannot "interpenetrate" because although no one of them can survive without the other two, they cannot yet be synthesized or amalgamated into one. Erickson's recourse to these three vital organs is probably closer to the psychological analogy of the Trinity than it is to the classic explication of perichoresis. Augustine, it will be recalled, saw the mind's exercise of memory, will and understanding as three yet overwhelmingly one, because each is futile and in fact dead if excised from the other two. Moltmann notes, rightly, that today's climate of trinitarian thinking is interested relatively less in the psychological analogy and relatively more in "the eternal *perichoresis* of Father, Son and Spirit. . . . 'Communion,' 'fellowship,' is the nature and purpose of the triune God."[69]

The idea of perichoresis may be historically attested, theologically sensible and even metaphorically lucid. But is it biblical? It has often been noted that a full-blown doctrine of the Trinity is more of a church doctrine, which gradually grew to maturity in the formative first four centuries, than strictly speaking a doctrine whose complexity was lifted straight from the pages of the Bible. Moltmann agrees with this common assertion, adding that a refined trinitarianism "only arose in the controversies of the early church over the unity of Christ with God himself."[70] But the foundational building blocks for the later sophisti-

---

[67]Jürgen Moltmann, *The Trinity and the Kingdom*, trans. Margaret Kohl (San Francisco: Harper & Row, 1981), pp. 174-75, partially quoted in Erickson, *God in Three Persons*, p. 229.

[68]Erickson, *God in Three Persons*, p. 233.

[69]Jürgen Moltmann, *History and the Triune God: Contributions to Trinitarian Theology*, trans. John Bowden (New York: Crossroad, 1992), p. xii.

[70]Moltmann, *Crucified God*, p. 241.

cation of the doctrine of the Trinity must already be in evidence in the
New Testament. Is this true for perichoresis also?

For Erickson the answer is yes. Erickson seems to follow Moltmann's
suggestion for where to look: in passages that assert the unity of the Son
to his Father. The Gospel of John yields, to Erickson's lights, a rich har-
vest for perichoretic theology. The Son's stated oneness with his Father
can only be true if perichoretically orchestrated by the Holy Spirit (Jn
10:30). In John 14:11 Jesus testifies that "I am in the Father and the Father is in me," a Scripture John Calvin uses to assert that "the Father is
wholly in the Son and the Son is wholly in the Father."[71] This perichoresis
of Father and Son must be true of the Trinity as such, in T. F. Torrance's
elegant analysis, "In the mysterious communion of the eternal Persons in
the Godhead Father, Son and Holy Spirit wholly indwell one another as
one God, without ceasing to be what each personally and distinctively is
in relation to the others, so that the fullness of the Godhead applies unre-
strictedly to each divine Person as well as to all of them together."[72]

This desire for perichoretic union, fully realized only in the Trinity,
extends to humanity, as in John 17:21-22, where in his prayer for his disciples, Jesus offers his own unity with the Father as the promise of human inclusion: "may they also be in us. . . . [S]o that they may be one, as
we are one."[73] Perichoretic blessing strewn and grown throughout the
created world is a much richer concept than "all for one and one for all."
At the demand for true self-sacrifice, is any human being as "other regarding" as before the demand? The obvious limits of self-sacrifice soon
reached by human persons are simply unknown to divine persons.

If the eternal love generated by and shared among Father, Son and
Holy Spirit is truly available for mortal partaking, how different could
the world be? As a modest beginning, Moltmann finds perichoresis to
be healing balm for the male and female knowing of one another. Perichoresis leads to "the mutual fellowship of man and woman." Perichoretic life is "not super- and sub-ordination, but a shared common life
in fellowship that corresponds to the triune God and is the incarnate
promise of his kingdom."[74]

---

[71]John Calvin, *Institutes of the Christian Religion* 1.13.19, quoted in Torrance, *Trinitarian Per-
    spectives*, p. 35.
[72]Torrance, *Trinitarian Perspectives*, pp. 35-36.
[73]Erickson, *God in Three Persons*, pp. 230-31.
[74]Moltmann, *History and the Triune God*, p. 138.

The renewal of trinitarian theology, as in the renewal of any theological trend at all, never happens in a vacuum. There must be wider cultural trends that both answer to and are encouraged by trinitarian refreshment. One such trend is the critique of hierarchy, which of course typically goes hand in hand with the critique of patriarchy. Organic models of reciprocity and symbiotic complexity are proposed in place of patriarchy and hierarchy.

Gargantuan cultural displacement such as the one from hierarchy to an organic model will move ahead only at a glacial speed. It may yet be true that for certain tasks and goals, a more hierarchical arrangement is for the best. The influential management thinker Peter Drucker suggested as much, writing not long before his death that "one hears a great deal today about the 'end of hierarchy.' This is blatant nonsense."[75] Yet those who are looking for a theological and indeed a trinitarian justification for the end of hierarchy will be drawn to perichoresis, since it sounds most clearly the note of mutuality. However, the Eastern Orthodox provenance of perichoretic thinking may call for a second look. For the Orthodox, God the Father remains "first among equals" and "fount of divinity" within the triune God, even in the midst of all of this inner-trinitarian give and take. But this Father is much more like the Father toward whom the prodigal son ran (Lk 15:11-32) than the unbalanced, nearly misanthropic fathers of much feminist critique.

PERICHORETIC LIFE AND HUMAN LIFE

Perichoresis is one of the live points of contact between the doctrine of the Trinity and theological anthropology, which answers the question "who is the human?" As we ponder the triune persons in perpetual motion, wherein each is always and forever on both the giving and the receiving end, the question naturally arises: what does this mean for human knowing, for human becoming? How can the perichoretic approach to personhood guide and in fact transform the "merely" human grasp of personhood?

One of the most complex problems for any trinitarian theology is to define and illuminate how and in what manner each of Father, Son and Spirit can be at one and the same time both a distinguishable person

---

[75]Peter F. Drucker, *Management Challenges for the 21st Century* (New York: HarperBusiness, 1999), p. 11.

and yet fully vested in the one community who is the triune God. If the balance is tipped too far toward distinguishability, then each person frays off into individualism, and we have tritheism. There is tritheism in the air if we describe perichoresis as "three divine selves in perpetual motion." If all differentiation from Father to Son to Spirit collapses, God is monotheistic and modalistic, which boils down to only "human ways of looking at God," which are not after all intrinsic to the very being of God.[76]

What to do? William J. Hill sees the Trinity as demonstrating

> an interpersonal unity. The persons in God thus constitute a divine intersubjectivity: Father, Son and Spirit are three centers of consciousness in community, in mutual communication. The members of the Trinity are now seen as constituting a community of persons in pure reciprocity, as subjects and centers of one divine conscious life.[77]

The divine koinonia that comprises perichoretic life is for Hill made up of "three who are conscious by way of one essential consciousness, constituting a divine reciprocity that is an interpersonal and intersubjective unity."[78] Hill's carefully chosen words make room for both the plural—"centers of consciousness"—and the singular, "one essential consciousness."

It may be somewhat easier to say what this does not mean than what it does mean. Hill is not arguing for what is called a "God beyond or behind God." There is no "one essential consciousness" that is somehow prior to, above, behind or beyond the triune God.

At the close of one second-grade day, as I was retrieving our eight-year-old Emily from the hallway outside of her classroom, three excited little girls were helping Emily hide from her father. Along a side hallway stood a cardboard box that appeared to have been cut to size for a small puppet theater. Three of Emily's friends giggled as they stood in front of her, as she knelt behind them on the carpeted floor. One could easily imagine the Father, Son and Holy Spirit somehow hiding their shared divine essence behind themselves, as Emily's friends were hiding her from her father. One can picture this, but this image violates the integrity of trinitarian theology, for there is no God behind the triune God.

---

[76]Boff, *Trinity and Society*, p. 87.
[77]Hill, *The Three-Personed God: The Trinity as a Mystery of Salvation*, p. 272.
[78]Ibid.

This God is One-in-Three. This God is Three-in-One. The "one essential consciousness" of Hill's description is in fact the perfect melding together of those "three centers of consciousness."

For today's Western culture the proclivity toward rank individualism is one that is dramatically critiqued by the perichoresis of Father, Son and Holy Spirit. To hear *person* today is in most ears to hear "unique individual" or maybe "undiluted singularity." When the poet e. e. cummings enthused that "there is nothing as something as one" he may not have been intending to describe modern consciousness, but in fact he was.[79] Because of its insurmountable individualism, Karl Barth abandoned *person* to describe the three divine persons, using instead the more philosophical but he hoped more accurate "mode of being." Barth agreed with the older theologian F. Diekamp that "in God, as there is one nature, so there is one knowledge, one self-consciousness."[80]

Classical trinitarianism has sometimes struggled to try to assign specific content or even character traits to each of the three divine persons. Some ascriptions are fairly obvious, following the course of salvation history, as for example the saving ability of God the Son and the sanctifying power of God the Holy Spirit. But the bigger question remained: What, if any, qualities did God the Father own as his alone? How about God the Son? Or God the Spirit? Would the presence of too many such traits, parceled off one by one to each of the three divine persons, conspire to defeat the unity of God? Is each person merely a foil for the development of the other two? If so, regardless of how ego-emptying or self-effacing Father, Son and Spirit might be, at some point might not any divine person become an "empty divine suit" or "divine doormat"?

The way forward through this dilemma is made much easier if what is meant by "person" can be made clear. Leonardo Boff provides a very helpful service by giving attention to three different, if subtly overlapping, senses of *person* as these meanings evolved in the history of Christian thought, ending with the focus of this section, personhood realized through perichoresis.

The first meaning of *person* is bequeathed to us from late antiquity. A person is, in Boff's phrase, "an existing subject (subsistant) distinct

---

[79]E. E. Cummings, *Complete Poems: 1904-1962*, ed. George J. Firmage (New York: Liveright, 1991), p. 594.
[80]Karl Barth, *CD* 1/1, p. 358, quoted in Erickson, *God in Three Persons*, p. 231.

from others."[81] If the persons of the Trinity are distinct one from the other, both modalism and what Boff calls "monotheistic unitarianism" are overcome. And yet each Person's uniqueness remains, the exaggeration of which of course leads to tritheism. What helped to defeat tritheism was a combination of these factors: (1) all three persons were judged to be consubstantial and coequal, one with the other. Of none of the three could it be said: "He is more divine than the other two." (2) The Son's being begotten by his Father. (3) The Holy Spirit's proceeding from the Father through the Son (in the Eastern Orthodox tradition). Furthermore, the one principle of origination within God, the Father, helped to insure the Trinity's unity.

But a related problem arose, which has already been hinted at. The persons are distinct, but the qualities and traits to be attributed to each are sketchy, shady, maybe even unknown. "When it is asked three what," Augustine puzzled, "then the great poverty from which our language suffers becomes apparent. But the formula three persons has been coined, not in order to give a complete explanation by means of it, but in order that we might not be obliged to remain silent."[82] The novice trinitarian may take some comfort that even the great Augustine often felt silenced by what he was attempting to discern.

The second meaning of *person* takes us into the deep heart of the Trinity. *Person* here means that which remains after each has given himself to the other two. No one can give everything away, not even Father, Son and Spirit. The act of self-gift is itself a statement of personhood. Boff explains, "So one person exists in and for himself or herself in complete independence of another precisely in the act of bestowing himself or herself completely on another."[83] This logic leads to the familiar trinitarian principle that all is one within God except "the otherness in the relationship by which one Person proceeds from another and so is distinguished from the other."[84] By definition the Son cannot be his own offspring. He is the Father's only begotten Son. To himself, hence, the Son is God. To the Father, the Son is Son, without of course ceasing to be God. The relationships that define Father as Father, Son

---

[81]Boff, *Trinity and Society*, p. 87.
[82]Augustine, quoted in ibid.
[83]Boff, *Trinity and Society*, p. 88.
[84]Ibid.

as Son, and Spirit as Spirit are the only thing that is not freely shared among Father and Son and Spirit.

Human analogies quickly desert us here, because no group of humans enjoys the "pure reciprocity" of the triune persons, to say nothing of "divine intersubjectivity." But can anything be gained from considering the space shuttle *Challenger* astronaut Christa McAuliffe? Assuming, if we can, that astronauts as a whole can be considered a fairly homogenous bunch, with their shared mathematical, scientific and technical backgrounds, how did a high school teacher fit into this august company? Astronaut McAuliffe undoubtedly tried her best to give herself over to the fraternity of astronauts. Regardless of the astronautic communion she was able finally to realize, something significant remained that was uniquely hers. She was a teacher and enjoyed many other distinguishing traits in addition. Her unity with the *Challenger* mission was her credentials as an astronaut; her distinction from the space mission was her being a teacher. If we can configure this little digression to fit into trinitarian reality, it would be that Ms. McAuliffe, like Father, Son and Spirit, gave herself over to the astronautic communion, in the same fashion as Father, Son and Holy Spirit give themselves over to each other. But not everything could be given. Christa remained a teacher even in her self-gift to the other astronauts, much as in the very act of self-gift the Three still retain their own identities.

The second meaning of *person* moves ahead of the first by allowing greater relational movement and consequence among Father, Son and Spirit. And yet "the incommunicability of each in the act of communicating," which marks the second understanding of person, opens the door a crack for the third view of person, which is in keeping with the fully relational quality of modern life.[85] Hence, in Boff's explication, "Being-in-itself is enriched in the encounter with the other, which nourishes reciprocity toward the other."[86]

In the moments before I was baptized, standing in lukewarm water in a place called the crossroads of Asia, I was overcome by emotion as my wife Stephanie strode to the pulpit to read the baptismal Scripture I had chosen. Following the lead of Catherine Mowry LaCugna, I had selected for Stephanie to read Ephesians 1:3-14, named by LaCugna "the shape of

---

[85]Ibid., p. 89.
[86]Ibid.

salvation history."[87] This seemed an appropriate choice in that baptism was a defining moment in my own history of salvation. At the request of the presiding elder I made a statement, part of which, tearfully delivered, was my desire to "understand the mystery of being Asian." I was among Asians, presuming to teach them Christian theology and ethics, including the Trinity.

The wisdom of perichoresis may come more naturally to Asians than to Westerners, as Asians more deeply feel and intuit the centuries-long ties of clan, family, tribe and nation. It may be the special contribution Asian Christians can make to trinitarian theology to stress God's unity. Western Christians will always stand up for how Father, Son and Spirit remain distinguishable even as they are finally inseparable. Boff's concluding note that perichoresis helps us to see that each person is a center of "interiority and freedom" who yet actualizes his freedom "in being always in relation to the other Persons" is exactly appropriate.[88]

The main lineaments of perichoresis have, I hope, been adequately represented. It helps above all to remember that in discussing this intimate doctrine, we are looking at a painting, even a symbolic representation, much more so than examining a minutely detailed photograph. Colin Gunton is doubtless correct in describing perichoresis as "only an analogy."[89] Applied to God, "it implies a total and eternal interanimation of being and energies."[90] In spite of our best human intentions, human aspirations and accomplishments can never fully animate the analogy of perichoresis. Humans can never attain the "pure reciprocity" of William Hill's description of inner-trinitarian life. As assisted by grace, humans can admit, with Gunton, that "we are what we are in perichoretic reciprocity."[91] Popeye may crow "I Yam What I Yam," but at the end of the day even this sailor man realizes that everything he intends to be is somehow entwined with a villain to rehabilitate, Bluto, and a woman's heart to win, Olive Oyl.

---

[87]LaCugna, *God for Us*, p. 21.

[88]Boff, *Trinity and Society*, p. 89. See also Erickson, *God in Three Persons*, pp. 232-33, for his commentary on Boff's three definitions of *person*.

[89]Colin E. Gunton, *The One, the Three and the Many: God, Creation and the Culture of Modernity* (Cambridge: Cambridge University Press, 1993), p. 170.

[90]Ibid.

[91]Ibid.

3

God Suffers for, with and among Us

Visiting the public library, seeking clarity as I completed the master's degree in library science, was almost never boring, and often eye-opening. One particular table, within hearing but out of sight range of my customary perch, hosted citizens of the community who, compared to the general population, were off beat, odd, mentally challenged. Strange pitches and sometimes disquieting sounds temporarily filled the atrium-like space of the central traffic area.

Another sound, the sound of godforsakenness, was just about the only salvageable part of a well-regarded passion play I viewed many times, while working as a temporary usher. The climax of the crucifixion scene was punctuated by *Eloi, Eloi, lema sabachthani* rolling around the sandy hills and the marshy hollows of the central Florida peninsula. Little else of the passion play ever spoke to me. But "My God, my God, why have you forsaken me?" (Mk 15:34) never sounded trite or forced or inconsequential. With palms unpierced and side unspeared, the passion play's phantom crucifixion got whatever emotional color it had from this cry.

The library and the passion play may seem to be worlds apart, but for Jürgen Moltmann they are not. It is for the benefit of those library patrons, who may be more tolerated and ignored by the mainstream community than welcomed and loved, that the crucified Christ cried out. Godforsakenness is clearly not a respecter of persons, but among the less-than-beautiful people it seems to be nearly a birthright.

Today's trinitarian theology expands the traditional Christian signifier "the cross of Christ" to its full-blown aspect as "the cross of the triune God" or a trinitarian theology of the cross. Throughout Moltmann's career, beginning with *The Crucified God* (1972) and present in many of his other works, Moltmann has drawn new meaning from old vessels; the crucifixion has a new vocabulary.[1]

Christian theology and history has deeply and thoroughly plowed the ground of the crucifixion's human benefits. This familiar terrain is by no means any sort of "burned over distinct," because at an elemental level it will always be true, as Philip Melanchthon said:

> To know Christ means to know his benefits. . . . For unless you know why Christ put on flesh and was nailed to the cross, what good will it do you to know merely the history about him? . . . Christ was given us as a remedy and, to use the language of Scripture, a saving remedy (Luke 2:30, 3:6; Acts 28:28).[2]

Moltmann asks a different sort of question. It is logically prior, and even existentially prior, because Christian theology first confesses its belief in and understanding of God before it turns to the human question. He turns theological convention on its head, asking what the crucifixion means for who God is. As Paul Fiddes puts it, for Moltmann "the cross is the event in history which discloses the inner nature of God without reservation. There can be no untouched hinterland in the being of the God who is revealed in the cross."[3] The cross is not just one more star in the constellation of revelation, trying to hold its own among brighter and lesser stars like politics, art, human personality and natural beauty. The cross is uniquely revelatory of the triune God. Here as nowhere else is God to be known in earnest.

---

[1]Jürgen Moltmann, *The Way of Jesus Christ: Christology in Messianic Dimensions*, trans. Margaret Kohl (San Francisco: HarperSanFrancisco, 1990), p. 177, where Moltmann presents Golgotha as a "theodicy trial" and then examines four possible responses to Jesus Christ's cry of dereliction, finally concluding that "Jesus' sufferings are divine sufferings, and God's love is a love that is able to suffer and is prepared to suffer."

[2]Wilhelm Pauck., ed., *Melanchthon and Bucer* (Philadelphia: Westminster Press, 1969), pp. 21-22.

[3]Paul S. Fiddes, *The Creative Suffering of God* (Oxford: Clarendon, 1992), p. 135.

At the start of the twenty-first century Moltmann published *Experiences in Theology*, explaining connections among the events of world politics, history and culture, his own personal life journeys and his resulting theological development. His looking back on nearly thirty years of his own theological history is worth hearing:

> When in 1972 I came to concentrate on the theology of the cross, and wrote *The Crucified God*, I turned the traditional question upside down. The question traditionally asked was the soteriological one: what does the cross of Christ mean for us men and women? My question now was the theological one: what does the cross of the Son of God mean for God himself? And I came face to face with the pain of the Father of Jesus Christ who suffered with him. If Christ dies with the cry of profoundest God-forsakenness, then in God the Father there must be a correspondingly profound experience of forsakenness by the Son. If the Son suffers his death on the cross not just as a human death but also as an eternal death of God-forsakenness, and thus as "the death of God", then—or so we must conclude—the God whom he always called "Abba, dear Father" suffers the death of his Son and the deadly tornness of his own heart and eternal being. The death of the Son of God on the cross reaches deep into the nature of God. . . . Christ's death on the cross is an inner-trinitarian event before it assumes significance for the redemption of the world.[4]

God's suffering is not, then, a merely ephemeral inconvenience or even an unfortunate culmination of circumstances gone beyond God's control. God's suffering is an "inner-trinitarian event" that is who God is and therefore always has been.

It may be too much to claim that Moltmann invented the trinitarian theology of the cross. There are New Testament references to it, of which Moltmann makes full use. At least one pioneer before Moltmann was grabbed by this astonishing theology of the cross. In *The Crucified God* Moltmann quotes from Bernhard Steffen's 1920 work, *The Dogma of the Cross:*

> The scriptural basis for Christian belief in the triune God is not the scanty Trinitarian formulas of the New Testament, but the thoroughgoing, unitary testimony of the cross; and the shortest expression of the

---

[4]Jürgen Moltmann, *Experiences in Theology: Ways and Forms of Christian Theology*, trans. Margaret Kohl (Minneapolis: Fortress, 2000), pp. 304-5.

Trinity is the divine act of the cross, in which the Father allows the Son to sacrifice himself through the Spirit.[5]

Moltmann seconds Steffen's compacting of trinitarian theology down to the event of the cross, knowing that the doctrine of the Trinity "is nothing other than a shorter version of the passion narrative of Christ in its significance for the eschatological freedom of faith and the life of oppressed nature."[6] For both Steffen and Moltmann, *short* does not mean abbreviated, slight or abridged. Still less does it mean "brevity is the soul of wit," as it is hard to imagine the crucifixion as some witty wayside. The cross is "short" for the doctrine of the Trinity in the same way that the Statue of Liberty is short for democratic freedom. More could be said, but whatever else might be said is only footnotes.

A handful of Pauline utterances are Moltmann's building blocks for his trinitarian theology of the cross.[7] In particular, these are:

What then are we to say about these things? If God is for us, who is against us? He who did not withhold his own Son, but gave him up for all of us, will he not with him also give us everything else? (Rom 8:31-32)

For our sake he made him to be sin who knew no sin, so that in him we might become the righteousness of God. (2 Cor 5:21)

Christ redeemed us from the curse of the law by becoming a curse for us—for it is written, "Cursed is everyone who hangs on a tree." (Gal 3:13)

It is no longer I who live, but it is Christ who lives in me. And the life I now live in the flesh I live by faith in the Son of God, who loved me and gave himself for me. (Gal 2:20)

Like the dull thud of the wooden mallet driving iron into wood in the film *The Passion of the Christ*, Moltmann gives these Scriptures their full voice. He does note, carefully, that the word for "deliver up" (Rom 8:32 KJV) has no sweetness. It "has a clearly negative connotation. It means: hand over, give up, deliver, betray, cast out, kill."[8]

---

[5]Bernhard Steffen, quoted in Jürgen Moltmann, *The Crucified God*, trans. R. A. Wilson and John Bowdon (New York: Harper & Row, 1974), p. 241. Also quoted in Eberhard Jüngel, *God as the Mystery of the World*, trans. Darrell Guder (Grand Rapids: Eerdmans, 1983), p. 351.

[6]Moltmann, *Crucified God*, p. 246.

[7]Ibid., pp. 242-44.

[8]Ibid., p. 241.

God the Father is no sadist, even as he is binding over his Son to execution. And God the Son is no passive victim. Jesus Christ may go bleatingly, for he is after all the Lamb slain from the foundation of the world (Rev 13:8), but he goes willingly. In Galatians 2:20 Moltmann sees that "it is not just the Father who delivers Jesus up to die godforsaken on the cross, but the Son who gives himself up."[9]

God the Son dies. But it is a death the Father feels as his very own. The Father's grief is no less lacerating than the rods and whips opening up the back of the Son. Yet physical stress and pain are far from the worst of it. Godforsakenness means everything it portends. It is God who forsakes. It is God who is forsaken.

> The Son suffers dying, the Father suffers the death of the Son. The grief of the Father here is just as important as the death of the Son. The Fatherlessness of the Son is matched by the Sonlessness of the Father, and if God has constituted himself as the Father of Jesus Christ, then he also suffers the death of his Fatherhood in the death of the Son. Unless this were so, the doctrine of the Trinity would still have a monotheistic background.[10]

N. W. Clerk is a footnote to twentieth-century Christian writing, because it was under this pseudonym that C. S. Lewis first published his small work *A Grief Observed*. In coming to grips with the death of Helen Joy Davidman, Lewis shows his theological mettle and comes to the brink of a trinitarian theology of the cross. After Joy died, Lewis found no easy consolations. He was tempted to believe the worst about God. At times, to retreat to a loving God was only

> a door slammed in your face, and a sound of bolting and double bolting on the inside. After that, silence. You may as well turn away. The longer you wait, the more emphatic the silence will become. There are no lights in the windows. It might be an empty house. Was it ever inhabited? It seemed so once.[11]

Has anyone ever described Good Friday as "an empty house"? Could there possibly be a better description? Lewis admits trying some of these thoughts on a confidant, who reminded the grieving writer "that the

---

[9]Ibid., p. 243.
[10]Ibid.
[11]C. S. Lewis, *A Grief Observed* (San Francisco: Harper & Row, 1961), p. 18.

same thing seems to have happened to Christ: 'Why hast thou forsaken me?' "[12] Lewis is brave enough to state what many think but fear to say. The conclusion he dreads "is not 'So there's no God after all,' but 'So this is what God's really like. Deceive yourself no longer."[13] The truth of the Father who resurrects his Son in the power of the Spirit comes brightest of all to those who have asked Lewis's questions.

As grief-struck parents who have watched our eldest daughter's slow, halting and to this point incomplete recovery from traumatic brain injury due to an automobile accident, the academic exercise of the theology of the cross has wilted. A visceral, palpable, daily, watchful reality has taken its place. What feels like futility often overwhelms. Six months became twelve became eighteen as our ten-year-old fought her way from densely comatose to lightly comatose to nearly comatose to perhaps not at all. Speech returned, but did it really? Her first words, "Mom" and "No" are foundational, but it is hard to negotiate the world's complexities with a two-word vocabulary, especially considering her prodigious verbal talents before the crash. Our child's skull remains scarred and cratered, especially at the point of impact. The surgeon who replaced the "bone flap" about nine weeks after the incident said there were more pieces than he had remembered removing during that frightening but lifesaving emergency surgery just minutes off of the life-flight helicopter. Titanium plates and screws will forevermore show on her x-ray.

The daughter's near death felt very much like the father's real death. The father sometimes said, especially in the rude aftermath of that horrid collision, that he would gladly give his life if the child could be spared this horror. The father meant, and means, what he said. The closest the father can come to this may be the impersonal definite article, "the father" and "the daughter." Moltmann makes a similar point when he notes that out of all the times in the New Testament when Jesus addresses God, only as he is dying on the cross did he resort to the impersonal "my God, my God" formula. Otherwise it is always "Father."

God the Son died a real death. Like no mortal could, he died as an accursed man, bearing the world's sins (Gal 3:13). Horrific though our daughter's circumstance may be, it is scaled to human proportions. The

---

[12]Ibid.
[13]Ibid. p. 19.

trinitarian theology of the cross cuts to the center of God's very nature. As precarious as our daughter's condition remains and as brutalizing as was its onset, the frightening and at times paralyzing grief cannot match the Father's for his Son. Also unmatched in human terms is the blessed complicity Father and Son share in their common pathos. No, it is not complicity, not an evil scheme but something much finer: "This deep community of will between Jesus and his God and Father is now expressed precisely at the point of their deepest separation, in the god-forsaken and accursed death of Jesus on the cross."[14]

God the Holy Spirit is not a sympathetic bystander, not a dispenser of handy crying towels, still less a benign and powerless pressure valve. The Spirit is the activator who proceeds from the Son's death and the Father's grief commingled. The Spirit "justifies the godless, fills the forsaken with love and even brings the dead alive, since even the fact that they are dead cannot exclude them from this event of the cross; the death in God also includes them."[15] Plausibly, it is the Holy Spirit who speaks through those public library regulars who but for the Spirit would be silent.

Because the Holy Spirit brings to expression the Father's grief over the Son's death, the Holy Spirit is the voice of the defenseless and the exploited on the earth. The Spirit, who is in "Christ's death-cry on the Roman cross (Mark 15:34)," is also in the groaning creation "subjected to futility" (Rom 8:20) and yearning for redemption. Humankind, creation, triune God: "it is the one same Spirit who interpenetrates the depths of all creation and the depths of the Godhead."[16]

On the Internet site that helped friends and relatives keep track of our daughter's progress after the accident, this poem erupted from the father on the occasion of Pentecost, more than nine months after the accident. Here the Holy Spirit is invoked as the healing Spirit, as the enkindling Spirit, even as the burning Spirit.

> Her smoldering brain
> So battered, so emaciated
> So riven

---

[14]Moltmann, *Crucified God*, pp. 243-44. .
[15]Ibid., p. 244.
[16]Jürgen Moltmann, *The Spirit of Life: A Universal Affirmation*, trans. Margaret Kohl (Minneapolis: Fortress, 1992), p. 77.

Is ignitable
Is combustible
Is waiting
For You, Holy Spirit
You Who are
Where Father and Son
Meet in ecstasy
Can You not also
Wake our sleeping babe

The Holy Spirit is not the disaster-response specialist of the Trinity. Or if he is, the Spirit's arrival brings ecstatic joy as much as consolation and lifesaving relief. In what Moltmann names "the eucharistic concept of the Trinity," it is the Holy Spirit's special gift to navigate and narrate the passage of the lost back to God. Here "the homecoming of those who have been found begins, and that homecoming is also the beginning of God's love in its bliss."[17]

In this sketch of Moltmann's trinitarian theology of the cross we may conclude that he has done nothing less than configure a new theology, a new way of looking at God. God is no longer an abstract substance who must conform to this or that program of philosophy. God is not even the ethical horizon for human hope and accomplishment. After the history of the crucified God, all is changed. We no longer bring our fondest hopes and noblest aspirations to a powerful deity who will fill us with all good things. No, we look "retrospectively" at God through the lens of "the unity of the dialectical history of Father and Son and Spirit in the cross on Golgotha," even though this history is "full of tension."[18] In a similar vein Robert Jenson claims that "God's self-identification with the Crucified One frees us from having to find God by projection of our own perfections."[19] Jenson names this self-identification "Christianity's entire soteriological message."[20] The triune cross defeats all human schemes of self-salvation. In the company of the triune cross, no one can psychologize the gospel and distort it into mere emotional comfort. Ethical humanism, whatever its merits for social progress, is shown by

---

[17]Ibid., p. 299.
[18]Moltmann, *Crucified God*, p. 247.
[19]Robert W. Jenson, *The Triune Identity: God According to the Gospel* (Philadelphia: Fortress, 1982), p. 16.
[20]Ibid.

God's self-identification with the crucified Christ to be pretense masquerading as goodness.

Any lingering dichotomy between immanent Trinity and economic Trinity is overcome through our retrospective knowing of the trinitarian history of God.[21] Because Moltmann is a theologian of hope, our retrospective accounting must necessarily look forward also, for the Trinity is "an eschatological process" and not any "self-contained group in heaven."[22] Ted Peters sees the Trinity in similar terms, asserting that perichoresis means that God has a future to fulfill, that God's eternity "is inclusive—not exclusive—of natural and world history."[23] John Thompson adds that for Moltmann "the triune God is not complete until the end."[24]

While imprisoned by the Third Reich Dietrich Bonhoeffer summed up the basis for any theology of the cross:

> God allows himself to be pushed out of the world on to the cross. He is weak and powerless in the world, and that is precisely the way, the only way, in which he is with us and helps us. Matthew 8:17 makes it quite clear that Christ helps us, not by virtue of his omnipotence, but by virtue of his weakness and suffering.[25]

Moltmann here follows Bonhoeffer and adds the eschatological note of hope: "God allows himself to be forced out. God suffers, God allows himself to be crucified and is crucified, and in this consummates his unconditional love that is so full of hope."[26]

Does Moltmann take full cognizance of God's self-marginalization and yet at the same time underappreciate what the human Jesus suffered? This is Paul Fiddes's criticism. He sees Moltmann as so centering God's suffering within the immanent Trinity that Jesus Christ's human suffering—physical pain and being subjected to a sham trial, among other sufferings—is puny by comparison. Fiddes

---

[21]Moltmann, *Crucified God*, p. 245.

[22]Ibid., p. 249.

[23]Ted Peters, *God as Trinity: Relationality and Temporality in Divine Life* (Louisville: Westminster/John Knox Press, 1993), p. 175.

[24]John Thompson, *Modern Trinitarian Perspectives* (New York: Oxford University Press, 1994), p. 51.

[25]Dietrich Bonhoeffer, *Letters and Papers from Prison*, ed. Eberhard Bethge, trans. R. H. Fuller (New York: Macmillan, 1972), pp. 360-61, quoted in Jüngel, *God as the Mystery of the World*, p. 60.

[26]Moltmann, *Crucified God*, p. 248.

writes that "the cross is understood only in terms of suffering in the immanent Trinity, and so what is missing in this interpretation is the human response of Jesus."[27] This conclusion leads Fiddes to some corollary claims, that God "is the source of his own suffering,"[28] and even, in a disquieting phrase, that "God seems less the supreme victim than the supreme self-executioner."[29] Supporting Fiddes, John Thompson faults Moltmann for never really defining exactly what he means by suffering.[30]

In an op-ed piece in *The New York Times* the Nobel laureate Isaac Bashevis Singer once asked, "What is God to do—discuss his book with every reader?"[31] The Jewish writer Singer was not essaying a theology of the cross but his own personal religious statement. He believes that "all problems concerning God can be reduced to a single one: Why the suffering?" Moltmann may not agree with Singer's answer, that "without suffering there is no art." Yet the criticisms of Paul Fiddes not withstanding, Moltmann's trinitarian theology of the cross, while not an aesthetic approach to suffering like Singer's, may be the most truthful Christian answer to the problem of human suffering and even of cosmic and other forms of evil.

In Elie Wiesel's harrowing narration of the Holocaust, *Night*, the depth of his own suffering is mirrored and intensified by that of his father. The interplay between father and son situates *Night* as a kind of Jewish contribution to a trinitarian theology of the cross. At the initial selection, not long after the days-long cattle-car ride from the Jewish ghetto of Sighet, Transylvania, to Auschwitz, father and son were separated from mother and daughters. Eliezer was his father's only son. As their sojourn unfolds from one concentration camp to another, as periods of relative calm and repose give way to increasing forced labor, conscripted marches, deprivation and brutalization, Elie finds himself "riveted to my father's agony."[32] In this world a stronger son is sometimes not above killing his own father for bread.[33] Furthermore, when

---

[27]Fiddes, *Creative Suffering*, p. 138.

[28]Ibid., p. 136.

[29]Ibid., p. 137.

[30]Thompson, *Modern Trinitarian Perspectives*, p. 63.

[31]Isaac Bashevis Singer, "What Is God to Do—Discuss His Book with Every Reader?" *New York Times*, (May 18, 1979), sec. A, p. 29.

[32]Elie Wiesel, *Night*, trans. Marion Wiesel (New York: Hill & Wang, 2006), p. 109.

[33]Ibid., p. 101.

life ebbed from the elders, "sons abandoned the remains of their fathers without a tear."[34]

The last word that Elie's father spoke was the name of his son. Although this seems to reverse the Christian order of things—the father dies, the son survives—the grief of the son, Elie, trapped and forced as he was to endure the father's decline to death, is a fit human representation if not altogether a recapitulation of the grief of God the Father as God the Son died on Golgotha.

Wiesel experienced great difficulty in publishing *Night*. Finally, it was the kind intervention of the French Roman Catholic novelist François Mauriac that made the difference. In the forward to Wiesel's testimony, Mauriac remembers meeting the young author:

> And I, who believe that God is love, what answer was there to give my young interlocutor whose dark eyes still held the reflection of the angelic sadness that had appeared one day on the face of a hanged child? What did I say to him? Did I speak to him of that other Jew, this crucified brother who perhaps resembled him and whose cross conquered the world? Did I explain to him that what had been a stumbling block for his faith had become a cornerstone for mine? And that the connection between the cross and human suffering remains, in my view, the key to the unfathomable mystery in which the faith of his childhood was lost?[35]

Can Mauriac's confidence that the cross is God's best answer to human suffering turn aside Wiesel's many objections doubting God's goodness? In the wrenching few days after the accident that has so injured our daughter it was difficult simply to look at her. Grace had to intervene just to allow the simplest gaze. Her head was crushed and swollen. Dark circles beneath her lovely blue eyes became pools of despair. In the pediatric intensive care unit, my altogether beautiful daughter suddenly "had no form or majesty that we should look at [her], nothing in [her] appearance that we should desire [her]" (Is 53:2). Of course her parents know she is not the Suffering Servant Christians find in the incarnate One, but her severe wound spoke beyond itself and reminded us of the crucified One.

The wounds of the crucified One inflicted only one body, but an entire civilization of compassion sprung from their singularity. Simi-

---

[34]Ibid., p. 92.
[35]François Mauriac, forward to ibid., p. xxi.

larly, one daughter's crushed skull pulled dozens and really hundreds into the drama. Few if any could remain apathetic bystanders. The story was either compelling or repulsive, and often both at the same moment.

Although Jesus Christ suffered abandonment by his Father, and upon him alone was heaped the world's curses and sins, his direst abandonment was at the same time the Spirit's fusing of Father's grief to Son's death. Jesus Christ died alone, yet not alone.

The last song on the greatest album from the world's greatest rock 'n' roll band closes with ascending strings and a crashing chord. "A Day in the Life" from the Beatles' *Sgt. Pepper's Lonely Hearts Club Band* climbs to "the orchestral seizure" and ends with a "long, dying piano chord" that lingers long after switching off the stereo.[36] The song is over. The song remains.

The gospel telling of the crucifixion might lead one to think that nothing happens in its wake. Death is death. "It is finished" cries Jesus (Jn 19:30); "Father, into your hands I commend my spirit" (Lk 23:46). The temple curtain tears from top to bottom and the earth shakes amid splitting rocks (Mt 27:51).

But the Christian faith is not only a crucifixion faith. Patriarch Philareth of Moscow views the triune cross as love and power redemptively applied: "The Father is crucifying love, the Son is crucified love, and the Holy Spirit is the unvanquishable power of the cross."[37] This great love is proven and validated when the Father raises the Son through the Holy Spirit. The resurrection of Jesus Christ must also be seen not as the remarkable virtuosity of a single performer, God the Son, nor as an ensemble cast of three great actors, but as triunely wrought, accomplished, corroborated and sealed. For Moltmann one unifying theme of resurrection is glory: "God the Father glorifies Christ the Son through his resurrection, while the Son glorifies the Father through his obedience and his self-surrender. The event of their mutual glorification is the work of the Holy Spirit."[38]

THE TRINITARIAN LOGIC

Elie Wiesel's sufferings reverberated throughout his lifetime. His being awarded the Nobel Peace Prize in December of 1986, more than four

---

[36]*Rolling Stone: The 500 Greatest Albums of All Time*, ed. Joe Levy (New York: Wenner, 2005), p. 9.

[37]Patriarch Philareth of Moscow, quoted in Moltmann, *Trinity and the Kingdom*, p. 83.

[38]Moltmann, *Trinity and the Kingdom*, p. 124.

decades removed from the terrors of *Night*, was only a temporary pause on a lifelong trajectory. What has been called the banality and the futility of evil has marked the twentieth century as few if any others. In the midst of that century, in the midst of a civilized world thrown to barbarism, Wiesel doubtless witnessed suffering that was unredeemed, unforgiven, unaccounted for, unobserved. Who speaks for these anonymous sufferers? Dorothee Sölle reminds us that "those who suffer in vain and without respect depend on those who suffer in accord with justice. If there were no one who said, 'I die, but I shall live,' no one who said, 'I and the Father are one,' then there would be no hope for those who suffer mute and devoid of hoping."[39]

In the terms of Sölle's convictions, Jesus Christ may have died forsaken by God, but not without hope. Jesus died not with curses on his lips but with a sense of finality and accomplishment. It was a real death but not a futile death, not a death turned in upon itself, not a dead-end death. Even as the meaning of Jesus' death leaped beyond his own subjective experience of it, what we might even call his strictly human experience of it, so also his resurrection. To finish Sölle's thought: "There is a history of resurrections, which has vicarious significance. A person's resurrection is no personal privilege for himself alone—even if he is called Jesus of Nazareth."[40] Sölle's saying this does not dilute the force of the resurrection. Resurrection power is rather extended and heightened when its history and transferability are underscored.

Eberhard Jüngel helps to make the transition from a trinitarian theology of the cross to the resurrection of Jesus Christ. In the cross, for Jüngel, "*God defines himself* when he identifies himself with the dead Jesus. At the same time he defines the man Jesus as the Son of God, as an old New Testament formulation puts it (Rom. 1:4). The kerygma of the Resurrected One proclaims the Crucified One as the self-definition of God."[41]

Without this acknowledgement, that God defines himself in the crucified Christ, no theology of the resurrection is possible. Indeed no res-

---

[39]Dorothee Sölle, *Suffering*, trans. E. R. Kalin (London: Darton, Longman & Todd, 1975), p. 150, quoted in Fiddes, *Creative Suffering*, p. 147.
[40]Ibid.
[41]Jüngel, *God as the Mystery of the World*, pp. 363-64.

urrection is possible. The crucifixion says *something* about God's inner being. It says that "God *as God* has declared himself identical with the crucified Jesus."[42] The resurrection of Jesus Christ is not just an episode within God's triune life. In the resurrection God's action and God's being coinhere and interpenetrate. This coinherence marks the resurrection as the axis upon which the entire world revolves. It must then be the case, as Jüngel writes:

> The statement "he lives," justifiably asserted about one dead man, turns the relationship of death and life around. Resurrection means the overcoming of death. But death will cease to be only when it no longer consumes the life which excludes it, but when life has absorbed death into itself. The victory over death, which is the object of faith's hope on the basis of God's self-identification with the dead Jesus which took place in the death of Jesus, is the transformation of death through its reception into that life which is called eternal life.[43]

The influence that the dialectical philosophy of Georg W. F. Hegel (1770-1831) has exerted on the renewal of trinitarian theology has been often noted. For Jüngel, Hegel's philosophical theology addresses and even contradicts the modern human devolution into atheism. Hegel's philosophy allows for what Jüngel calls "the Christian truth of the death of God."[44] Here Christian theology meets atheism on its own terms, which is the attempt to negate if not destroy the theological. But if the death of God can be expressed in a *christological* way, through a trinitarian theology of the cross, then atheism can never pose as a usurping and presumptuous religion.[45]

Claude Welch's overlooked midcentury work, *In This Name*, reports that for Hegel "the Christian doctrine of the Trinity expresses the true thought that God is not the abstract unity, the barren identity without difference conceived by rationalism or by Judaism, but a richer concrete entity composed of inner movement and process."[46] Hegel informed Jüngel's theology of the cross. He quotes Hegel's aphorism: "God sacri-

---

[42]Eberhard Jüngel, *God's Being Is in Becoming*, trans. John Webster (Grand Rapids: Eerdmans, 2001), p. 102.

[43]Jüngel, *God as the Mystery of the World*, p. 364.

[44]Ibid., pp. 63-100.

[45]Ibid., p. 97.

[46]Claude Welch, *In This Name: The Doctrine of the Trinity in Contemporary Theology* (New York: Scribner's, 1952), p. 10.

fices himself, gives himself up to destruction. God himself is dead; the highest despair of complete forsakenness by God."[47]

Every sophomore philosophy student learns of the Hegelian dialectic of thesis-antithesis-synthesis. Hegel understands all thought to move through "a kind of double negation," the first being from thesis to antithesis and the second from antithesis to synthesis.[48] The double negation is not one pop star's continual reinvention of him- or herself to solidify the fan base and explore inner creativity. It is much more elemental than that. Hegel pointed to the "simple truth of negative self-relation" and called it "the innermost course of all activity, of living and spiritual self-movement, the dialectical soul, which all truth has in it and through which it alone is truth."[49]

Stanley Grenz says that after Hegel, all theologians "would need to think not only of the God of history but, more importantly, of the history of God."[50] To excavate the history of God is one of the chief impulses of today's trinitarian theology. Not only the traditionally conceived history of salvation but the entire history of the world—past, present, future—is where the triune God is to be found. That no fissure can be discovered between the immanent Trinity and the economic Trinity only means that the history of the world happens within and among God the Father, God the Son and God the Spirit.

If on Hegel's terms God is himself this process of unfolding dialectic, then God must be described, in the words of Hans Küng, "not in abstract propositions, but in a living process, focusing not on an abstract, dead divine essence, but on the concrete, living act that God himself is."[51] Jüngel's description of the resurrection of Jesus Christ as life absorbing death into itself has a Hegelian flavor to it.

Hegel's philosophy is a grand sweeping vision, whose summation is often given as "what is rational is actual and what is actual is rational," and not a logical tit-for-tat.[52] Hence any exact identification

---

[47]Georg W. F. Hegel, quoted in Jüngel, *God as the Mystery of the World*, p. 74.

[48]Grenz, *Rediscovering the Triune God*, p. 25.

[49]Georg Wilhelm Friedrich Hegel, *The Science of Logic*, trans. W. H. Johnston and L. G. Struthers (London: George Allen & Unwin, 1929), 2:477, quoted in ibid.

[50]Grenz, *Rediscovering the Triune God*, p. 32.

[51]Hans Küng, *The Incarnation of God: An Introduction to Hegel's Thought as Prolegomena to a Future Christology*, trans. J. R. Stephenson (New York: Crossroad, 1987), p. 362, quoted in ibid., p. 27.

[52]Georg Wilhelm Friedrich Hegel, *Philosophy of Right*, trans. T. M. Knox (London: Oxford Uni-

of, for example, the crucifixion with the "first negation" from thesis to antithesis and the resurrection with the "second negation" from antithesis to synthesis dilutes his rich complexity. But the foundational point of Hegel's finding of inner-trinitarian movement within the divine life remains. Love, which Hegel took as equivalent to spirit, is central for God. Like spirit, love "embraces differentiation and unity (or reconciliation) simultaneously."[53] Hegel's often abstruse philosophy can be, according to Grenz, fitted to the traditional language of trinitarian theology, namely, that "God apart from the world is an inherently complete dynamic of love in which the Son is separated from the Father only to be reunited in the Spirit."[54] The reunion of Father and Son in the Spirit will never supplant more traditional Easter affirmations of the resurrection, but in some minds it may bear the power of explanation.

The Lutheran theologian Robert Jenson has emerged as perhaps the brightest American star in the trinitarian firmament. Throughout Jenson's writing career, approaching four decades, he has often turned to trinitarian themes.[55] His two major contributions are *The Triune Identity* (1982), leading to his being named "the first American theologian to write a systematic construction of the Trinity," and the first of his two volumes of *Systematic Theology, The Triune God* (1997).[56]

God According to the Gospel is Jenson's subtitle for *The Triune Identity*. This speaks volumes. It identifies Jenson as a narrative theologian, someone who cares about *both* the history of God and the God of history, to cite Grenz's earlier couplet. Grenz asserts that for Jenson "theology arises out of the divine self-disclosure that displays a narrative, radically temporal, and eschatological character."[57] When Jenson avers

---

versity Press, 1967), p. 10, quoted in Grenz, *Rediscovering the Triune God*, p. 26.

[53]Grenz, *Rediscovering the Triune God*, p. 28.

[54]Ibid.

[55]For example, see Robert W. Jenson, "The Triune God," in *Christian Dogmatics*, ed. Carl E. Braaten and Robert W. Jenson (Philadelphia: Fortress Press, 1984), 1:79-191; *Essays in Theology of Culture* (Grand Rapids: Eerdmans, 1995), pp. 84-94, 190-201; "The Point of Trinitarian Theology," in *Trinitarian Theology Today*, ed. Christoph Schwöbel (Edinburgh: T & T Clark, 1995), pp. 31-43; as listed in Grenz, *Rediscovering the Triune God*, p. 249 n. 178.

[56]Carl E. Braaten, "God and the Gospel: Pluralism and Apostasy in American Theology," *Lutheran Theological Journal* 25, no. 1 (1991): 47, quoted in Grenz, *Rediscovering the Triune God*, p. 107.

[57]Grenz, *Rediscovering the Triune God*, p. 108.

that "Jesus is risen into the future that God has for his creatures" the eschatological cast of his theology is revealed.[58]

Here we will briefly explore what Jenson calls the trinitarian logic, with special attention to the resurrection of Jesus Christ. In the Old Testament God makes himself known in many ways, but primarily in the calling, forming, purging, chastening and ultimately freeing of his people, the Israelites. The exodus is the summary of the Hebrew Scriptures, and the summit also. Jesus Christ understands himself as carrying forth, perfecting really, the prophetic work he has inherited. He is understood as an enemy of Rome and as a blasphemer of the God of the Jews.

Who or what can vindicate this slain prophet, Jesus Christ? It can only be the resurrection. An unraised Jesus can no longer be the Christ. A place of honor, maybe, among Jewish prophets awaits the unresurrected Jesus, but not the status of God the Son. Phrasing all of this with his peculiar lucidity, Jenson writes that "only the resurrection of the dead will verify Yahweh's self-introduction as God, and when that event occurs the trinitarian logic promptly becomes explicit experience."[59]

To speak of the trinitarian logic would seem to hold the Trinity hostage to the strictures of philosophy, yet nothing is further from Jenson's mind. This trinitarian logic is of simple and consummate beauty, and Romans 8:11 is its clearest expression, this verse being for Jenson the "conceptual and argumentative heart" of "the most remarkable trinitarian passage in the New Testament, one amounting to an entire theological system."[60]

> If the Spirit of him who raised Jesus from the dead dwells in you, he who raised Christ from the dead will give life to your mortal bodies also through his Spirit that dwells in you. (Rom 8:11)

Jenson lines out the proper emphasis, lest there be no mistaking the majestic scope of this verse: "the *Spirit* is 'of him *who* raised *Jesus*.' "[61] This grammar is simply too glorious to hide under a bushel. *Whose Spirit raised Jesus!* The Holy Spirit is for hymn-writer Brian Wren

---

[58]Robert W. Jenson, *Systematic Theology*, vol. 1: *The Triune God* (New York: Oxford University Press, 1997), p. 198.

[59]Jenson, *Triune Identity*, p. 39.

[60]Ibid., p. 44.

[61]Ibid.

"their mutual friend," who in the resurrection of Jesus Christ transforms the Father's grief into glory.[62] The room with a view that is Romans 8:11 opens up to nothing short of the full panoply of Christian
salvation, one "which sweeps justification and the work of Christ and
prayer and eschatology and ethics and predestination into one coherent
understanding."[63]

Trinitarian logic is not syllogistic logic. The inexorability of "if A,
then B" cannot bind the divine will. The resurrection follows the crucifixion not because it *has* to but because God *wills* it. The Father's raising
of the Son in the Spirit's power is an event in the history of God that
in its wake defines and shapes God's historical dealings with all of the
world. Resurrection means there are no real boundaries between sacred
history and secular history, or that such boundaries as there may be are
erected because of human sin and not divine willing.

Resurrection seen in a trinitarian light may also mean that traditional formulas need to be revised or at least allow for perspectives that
are valid if underrepresented. The trinitarian logic allows, as implied
in some of Jesus' utterances, that the Son of God raised himself from
the dead. Christ being raised "from the dead by the glory of the Father" (Rom 6:4) may be most typical of New Testament theology, but as
Thomas Oden explains, "it is not inconsistent, according to the triune
premise, also to affirm that Jesus rose by his own power. For the Son,
being God, had power to raise himself. Christ explicitly stated of himself that he had authority to lay down his life and 'authority to take it up
again' (John 10:18)."[64] Oden believes that if the resurrection is seen as
the vindication of Jesus' divine power, then it may be viewed as the Son's
own act, although clearly enabled by the Holy Spirit. If the Father acts
to confirm and validate the Son's life, work and death, then proclamation of being "raised by the Father in the Spirit's power" may be more
fitting. Either way, nothing has been comprised. John Chrysostom well
expressed that "Whatever the Father does the Son also does."[65]

Those trained in syllogistic logic will approach the trinitarian logic
with questions poised. If God the Son really dies on the cross, if his

---

[62]Brian Wren, *What Language Shall I Borrow?* (New York: Crossroad, 1990), p. 215.
[63]Jenson, *Triune Identity*, p. 44.
[64]Thomas C. Oden, *The Word of Life*, Systematic Theology: Volume Two (San Francisco: Harper-
    SanFrancisco, 1989), p. 467.
[65]John Chrysostom, quoted in ibid.

death is the Trinity's greatest possible internal crisis, at least two questions arise. Jenson names them: "But then was God a binity between Good Friday and Easter? Or is the Incarnation subject to temporary suspension?"[66] The trinitarian logic does not blink when it replies. The only plausible and defensible answer is that "Jesus' abandonment and death do not interrupt the relation to the Father by which he is the Son but, rather, belong to that relation. But that is to say that these blatantly temporal events belong to his very deity."[67]

The word *event* is liberally sprinkled among the trinitarian theologies of Moltmann, Jüngel and Jenson. If an event is "inner-trinitarian," that event may not be subject to public scrutiny and review, but the agreed upon identity of immanent Trinity and economic Trinity means that what is "inner" is manifested in what is "outer." To modify *events* by "blatantly temporal" as Jenson does, serves to locate God's trinitarian history in human history, which is exactly Jenson's intent.

The confluence of theology and spirituality, the necessary linkage of creed and worship is never far from view in today's trinitarian theology. Jenson's descriptive phrase "three-arrowed time," is demonstrated in that most ecumenical of the Christian creeds, the Nicene.[68] In this creed there is a "daily trinitarian liturgical naming of the gospel's God."[69] One of time's arrows launches forward, from which vantage point one can still see the anticipated future as well as the accomplished past. Our knowing of Jesus Christ encompasses and enfolds "all three temporal directions," and it is for Jenson "just by this circumstance our God differs from the culture-God of Western civilization."[70] Jenson believes that today's religiously diverse climate demands that Christians distinguish the Christian God from this culture God.[71]

As our daughter has surged, trickled really, back to consciousness, the whole event has been semiotic, or pertaining to signs. By now hundreds and really thousands of signs have accumulated in, under,

---

[66]Jenson, *Triune God*, p. 49.

[67]Ibid.

[68]Jenson, *Triune Identity*, p. 85. See *Triune God*, p. 91, where Jenson explains that the Nicene creed is really a combination of the creeds issued by the first ecumenical council, at Nicaea in 325 and the second at Constantinople in 381. This creed has come "to dominate liturgical use" and "has since been an ecumenical rule of all talk in the Christian church."

[69]Ibid., p. 85.

[70]Ibid., pp. 91-92.

[71]Ibid., pp. ix-xii.

over and around our daughter—medical, physical, emotional, psychological and a host of other identifiers—but to read them all truthfully belongs to God and God alone. Not long after the accident, while the child was still in the densest of comas, her aunt risked calling out to her, "Rebecca, move your leg!" And lo and behold our daughter did move her leg ever so slightly. Many months into the drama, into the hermeneutical tangle of trying to figure our child out, that smallest of signs, an errant, stray eyelash, sent her from a pediatric nursing home back to the hospital. With no way to tell us of her discomfort except by elevated heart rate and heavy breathing, the eyelash, which probably abraded her cornea, defeated the smartest diagnostic strategies of the best medical practitioners.

What are the *signs* of the resurrection of Jesus Christ? Robert Jenson finds three such signs in the theologian Peter Brunner. These are (1) "Jesus in the identity of his person" is the resurrected Christ; (2) Jesus is "neither the ghost of a dead man nor a dead man returned"; (3) Jesus Christ "lives in the glory of God."[72] What is meant by the identity of the person of Jesus Christ? It is that in one human there is a perfect identity of the crucified Jesus and the resurrected Jesus. This identity is "nothing other than the oneness of God" and can be realized only through the doctrine of the Trinity. Jenson writes that "the Spirit who raises the Son is the Spirit of the Father, and had already rested on this Son. The unity of the crucified son with the risen Son is posited in the essential unity between this Father and this Spirit."[73] This is the trinitarian logic.

If the resurrected Christ is neither a ghost nor a returned man, who then is he? As the risen Son intercedes before God the Father, Jenson believes that it is the life Jesus lived "from Mary's womb to Golgotha" that "identifies him to the Father by the Spirit in the triune life."[74] After all, "it is the Crucifixion as the completion of the life lived in Palestine that settles what sort of God establishes his deity at the Resurrection."[75] Alive in the glory of God, Brunner's third sign of the resurrection, means for Jenson that "Christ is risen into the Kingdom, and Christ is risen into God. . . . He is located in the triune life."[76]

---

[72]Ibid., p. 198.
[73]Ibid., p. 200.
[74]Ibid.
[75]Ibid.
[76]Ibid., p. 201.

4

Toward a
Trinitarian Spirituality

In the year of his death the Anglican bishop of Calcutta Reginald Heber wrote a hymn that will endure forever. His 1826 composition "Holy, Holy, Holy, Lord God Almighty" may owe some of its nuanced cadences to his three years on the Indian subcontinent. "Early in the morning our song shall rise to thee" may be an accurate telling of how Indian Christians gathered for morning prayers and worship.

Heber's great hymn is one of the trinitarian classics of the church's hymnody. The twice-repeated "God in three persons, blessed Trinity" is the theological anchor for the entire work, notwithstanding the criticism of some that "God in three persons" sounds tritheistic. Because the triune God created time, he is the Lord of all of its expressions: "which wert and art and evermore shalt be." In describing God as "perfect in power, in love, and purity," Heber seems to be aware of the traditional trinitarian appropriations. According to this ancient wisdom, God the Father best expresses power, wisdom is the province of the Son, and love is the Holy Spirit's special gift.[1]

Recently, a one-word alteration has asserted itself. Instead of singing

---

[1]Roderick T. Leupp, *Knowing the Name of God* (Downers Grove, Ill.: InterVarsity Press, 1996), p. 149.

"our song shall rise to Thee," some are substituting "my song shall rise to Thee." Is this a difference worth noting?

Certainly, different interpreters will attach various weights to the relative importance of "our song" or "my song." Some may view this shift as a dangerous privatization of the Christian faith. Heber's second stanza is drenched with the company of the saints and with cherubim and seraphim. The hosts of heaven are not to be understood as each celestial being in isolation from the rest, but all together in unison. To sing "my song" to the triune God may make as much sense as preaching to a vacant sanctuary, which was Martin Luther's criticism of the obligatory Mass to be said by every priest each day in an empty chapel.

To raise "our song" early in the morning to God is a much better fit with the trinitarian intent of Heber's hymn. To sing among the faithful is to mirror the triune God's own spiritual practice, that being choruses of love resounding among Father, Son and Holy Spirit. "Our song" underscores again that this is no solitary God, but a God who arrives as promise and remains as gift.

The boundaries of any definition of Christian spirituality can only be the triune God himself. Every description of spirituality must inhabit the space created by God alone. Every intuition of what spirituality might be able to accomplish in the world can be realized only by God's acting through humanity. This God who acts is the triune God. The experience of this God, which is all that spirituality really means, must be on the terms that God has himself set forth. To say, with John Zizioulas, that "spirituality is an ecclesial and not an individual experience" is only to say that the God who is the source and end of spirituality is not a God unto himself, but a God who is a communion of love.[2]

The call of Christian spirituality asserts itself throughout the "organic continuum" of the order of salvation: "conscience, conviction of sin, repentance, [justification], reconciliation, regeneration, sanctification, glorification," to borrow Albert Outler's description of John Wesley's theology of salvation which, adapted to various historical and cultural contexts, can be judged as standard for all Christian theology.[3]

---

[2]John D. Zizioulas, "The Early Christian Community," in *Christian Spirituality: Origins to the Twelfth Century*, ed. Bernard McGinn and John Meyendorff in collaboration with Jean Leclercq (New York: Crossroad, 1992), p. 30.

[3]Albert C. Outler, *John Wesley's Sermons: An Introduction* (Nashville: Abingdon, 1984), p. 88.

Along this train of spiritual stations it is sanctification that is the clearest window into what spirituality intends, the life of God in the soul of the human.

It is God the Holy Spirit who sanctifies. "The Spirit summons us to a transforming friendship with God that leads to sharing in the triune life" is Clark Pinnock's summary statement.[4] Although to sanctify may be the Spirit's special gift and impartation, as the Holy Spirit sanctifies, he brings the believer into conformity with Jesus Christ. Every act and intuition toward knowing the triune God is at the same time an entry into all that God promises and delivers. To know one is to know all; to know all is to know one. If there is trinitarian "specialization" such that sanctification is assigned to the Spirit and justification to God the Son, the specialization is meant to promote and not to thwart triune life.

The Spirit's vivifying infusion into the world and humankind is grounded in Christian antiquity, such that "it is axiomatic for the writers of the New Testament and for the theologians of the early church that it is impossible to know God without holiness."[5] The fourth-century Eastern father Athanasius appealed to the Spirit's sanctifying work as one proof of his divinity against Arian detractors. Athanasius elegantly stated his logically compelling case. Sanctification was widely held to be a crucial component of the economy of salvation. Only those "who have clean hands and pure hearts" (Ps 24:4) will be able to ascend the hill of the Lord and stand in his holy place. If only the truly divine can save, and if the Holy Spirit's sanctifying work is honestly salvific, then not only the Spirit's work but also his person must be divine.

The apostle Peter opens his first letter by saying that the Spirit sanctifies. The Russian saint Seraphim of Sarov would later declare that "the true aim of the Christian life is the acquisition of the Holy Spirit," yet everyone knows that the Spirit cannot give himself without at the same time giving the Father and the Son.[6] Peter understands the triune implications of true sanctification, writing that the Spirit sanctifies into obedience to Jesus Christ and immersion in his blood, which is all ac-

---

[4]Clark H. Pinnock, *Flame of Love: A Theology of the Holy Spirit* (Downers Grove, Ill.: InterVarsity Press, 1996), p. 150.

[5]Gary D. Badcock, *Light of Truth and Fire of Love: A Theology of the Holy Spirit* (Grand Rapids: Eerdmans, 1997), p. 144.

[6]Seraphim of Sarov, quoted in Pinnock, *Flame of Love*, p. 162.

cording to the call and destiny of God the Father (1 Pet 1:2). Thus is the course of personal and cosmic salvation captured in a sentence.

The doctrine of the Trinity is the meeting point between Christian theology and spirituality. All intimations of God as triune are in the same moment directions for living a life in that very same God. Because Christian spirituality is simply God's life forming human decisions and passions, to investigate God's triune life is also to promise that this investigation is not merely intellectual, not merely spiritual, but both simultaneously. Theology and spirituality are not identical apprehensions of God as triune, but neither can be fulfilled apart from the other.

Prayer is the gate between theology and spirituality. More fittingly put, prayer is the permeable membrane where theology and spirituality meet and in fact interpenetrate. If theology is *thinking about God* and spirituality is *living in and toward God*, the obvious link is God, and God is Trinity. The structure of trinitarian prayer as being *to* the Father *through* the Son and *in* the Holy Spirit is not a lifeless protocol meant to destroy spontaneity and inhibit the free movement of the Spirit. Still less is this structure training wheels on an otherwise wobbly and misdirected prayer engine. To pray triunely in this way is foundational and not formulaic. The apostle Paul's summary encouragement to "pray without ceasing" (1 Thess 5:17) is simply an invitation to share in what has eternally happened from Father to Son to Spirit.

For those who experience everything about the Trinity as more a bewildering thicket than an inviting and negotiable landscape, to pray triunely is the best recourse and the only sure beginning. Praying after the historic pattern is not baby steps, not learning to crawl, not Christian obscurantism. It is Christian intuition fully realized, as Robert Jenson expresses:

> Believers know how to pray to the Father, daring to call him "Father" because they pray with Jesus his Son, and so enter into the future these two have for them, that is, praying in the Spirit. Those who know how to do this, and who realize that just in the space defined by these coordinates they have to do with God, do understand the Trinity.[7]

The triune God is not three divine personalities competing for superiority. The Trinity is not a theory of multiple personalities within

---

[7]Robert W. Jenson, *The Triune Identity* (Philadelphia: Fortress, 1982), pp. 47-48.

the one God. Ancient Christian consensus asserts that there are no degrees of divinity within God. Because God is one in essence if three in expression, any spirituality that is triunely drawn must follow this pattern. Christian spirituality is a heart toward the one God, yet this turning can be expressed and carried out in many ways. Trinitarian spirituality is both deep and wide. Its depth is the one God, and its breadth is the flexibility of the interplay of Father, Son and Holy Spirit. Simon Chan is correct to claim that "for a spirituality to be holistic it must be trinitarian."[8]

Chan suggests that a trinitarian spirituality is characterized by three realities. The first note is that of form and stability coupled with a sacramental vision of the created world. The triune God is ordered ecstasy. He is ecstatic speech that continually transcends itself, the sheer joy of being God. Yet all speech, even divine speech, follows certain patterns of intelligibility, cadence and meaning. The interplay among Father, Son and Holy Spirit is speech whose intent is to bring humans to the knowledge of God.

The second note of trinitarian spirituality for Chan is that it seeks to know God personally through knowing Jesus Christ, in whom the Father's eternal Word came into flesh. God the Spirit's working through the power of signs and wonders, and in the daily round of the ordinary, is Chan's third identifier of trinitarian spirituality.[9]

If we begin at the theological end of the continuum rather than that of spirituality, Chan believes that we will still converge on the center of the triune God. Any trinitarian theology, Chan believes, forms spirituality in three decisive ways. First, because the triune God is a relational God, to know this God must be a relational knowledge of "personal union with God."[10] Chan believes that this personal urgency is reinforced by Augustine's psychological understanding of the Trinity, where Christ and the Spirit are known as Word and Love descending from the Father. This personal immersion into the divine has been the traditional province of mystical and contemplative Christianity, and more recently that of Pentecostal and charismatic expression.

---

[8]Simon Chan, *Spiritual Theology: A Systematic Study of the Christian Life* (Downers Grove, Ill.: InterVarsity Press, 1998), p. 49.
[9]Ibid.
[10]Ibid., p. 52.

Chan understands that any mysticism, even a trinitarian one, can become amorphous and undifferentiated. It is possible to be carried away by the Spirit who "blows where it chooses" (Jn 3:8). The second way, therefore, in which trinitarian theology shapes the spiritual life is that such a life is "essentially relational without ceasing to be particular."[11] The counterbalancing social analogy of the Trinity fills out and completes the psychological analogy. Life is personal because it is social, and social because it is personal. Since the personal and the social converge in the family, trinitarian spirituality is a family spirituality grounded in the triune God as the primordial family.

Trinitarian theology teaches in the third instance that life and work, or theology and ethics, cannot be separated. Chan correctly notes that for Roman Catholics and Eastern Orthodox the church's mission is to join in the trinitarian mission, "in which the Father sent the Son and Spirit into the world."[12] The tendency of some Protestant theology to separate the works of the Son from those of the Spirit is hence overcome. To see the respective works of Son and Spirit as complementary is to believe that "the goal of the spiritual life is the indwelling of the holy Trinity through receiving the Son and the Spirit as they are sent into the world—visibly, in the incarnation and Pentecost, sacramentally, in baptism and confirmation, and experientially in new birth and baptism in the Spirit."[13]

ENRICHED BY THE HOLY SPIRIT

Jürgen Moltmann enhances our understanding of the Holy Spirit, and hence of trinitarian spirituality, by proposing a dozen ways of experiencing the Holy Spirit. This dozen is arranged in four groups of three each, which is Moltmann's arrival at what he calls a "triadic complementarity."[14] The old and the new, the biblical and the philosophical, even the psychological, the traditional and the innovative all coalesce in Moltmann's discussion, wherein he sets forth four broad metaphorical classes: the personal, the formative, the movement and the mystical.

---

[11]Ibid., p. 53.
[12]Ibid.
[13]John L. Gresham Jr., "Three Trinitarian Spiritualities," *Journal of Spiritual Formation* 15, no. 1 (1994): 29, quoted in ibid.
[14]Jürgen Moltmann, *The Spirit of Life: A Universal Affirmation*, trans. Margaret Kohl (Minneapolis: Fortress, 1992), p. 269.

The personal metaphors are the Holy Spirit as lord, as mother, as judge. These metaphors, Moltmann plainly states, belong to the Spirit's economy in the world, to the Spirit's effects on human subjects, and say nothing about the immanent Trinity, how the Holy Spirit knows the Son and the Father and is known by them.[15] In other words, the linkage between Holy Spirit and mother does not claim that somehow the Holy Spirit is to be considered as feminine. The mothering acts of the Holy Spirit are not at the same time the constitution of the Spirit as feminine. As lord and mother, the Holy Spirit promotes freedom, the Spirit's lordship and new life as the mothering quality symbolized by the Spirit in whom believers are "born anew." Freedom and life best thrive in a climate of justice, for "it is only in justice that life can endure."[16] These three—lord, mother, judge—belong together. Moltmann believes that "every counter-check will at once discover how one-sided the viewpoint becomes if any of these facets is left out."[17]

The Holy Spirit as energy, space and gestalt is the second triad. These are the formative metaphors. If the personal metaphors describe how agents act in the world, the formative symbols "describe forces which impose a profound impress."[18] While energy denotes power, and power is frequently impersonal, it is not Moltmann's intent to depersonalize the Holy Spirit. The ancient Hebrew concept of *ruach* stands behind the Spirit as power. This power can be observed in nature, but is given primally to humans. Moltmann says that "we sense in ourselves the personal dynamic given to us, and then perceive it in everything else that lives."[19] Expressed in infinite variety, this energy is yet for Moltmann "a *single* vital power." The church can itself be a model for this single pulsing power, if only the church will relate "itself to the diversity and the unity of everything living in the cosmos, and does not separate itself, withdraw into itself, and make itself poorer than it is."[20]

The Spirit's formative metaphors are not diffuse or wayward, but together are more embracing and expansive than the personal metaphors.

---

[15]Ibid., p. 274.
[16]Ibid., p. 272.
[17]Ibid.
[18]Ibid., p. 274.
[19]Ibid.
[20]Ibid.

Formatively, the Spirit appropriates, or rather can be found within, inner genetics, ecology and cultural history.[21]

Together, these dynamics comprise the gestalt of the Holy Spirit, which Moltmann illustrates with a phrase from the writer Goethe, gestalt as "minted form which takes shape as it lives."[22] This notion of form and configuration can also be rendered in more evangelical terms, as the Christian's hope for "the body of our humiliation" to be "conformed to the body of [Christ's] glory" (Phil 3:21). Dietrich Bonhoeffer knew this as "Christ's taking form in us."[23]

If the personal metaphors are about agents who act, the Holy Spirit as lord, mother and judge, and if from the formative metaphors we gain and appreciate the cosmic and the historical power of the Holy Spirit, the movement metaphors of tempest, fire and love "express the feeling of being seized and possessed by something overwhelmingly powerful, and the beginning of a new movement in ourselves."[24] Like the formative metaphors, tempest is rooted in the *ruach* of Yahweh, where in Moltmann's expression "the divine is the living compared with the dead, and what is moving compared with the things that are petrified and rigid."[25] In God's showing of himself to Elijah on Mount Horeb (1 Kings 19:11-18) the movement metaphors are on full display. Not in the great wind, not in the earthquake, not in the fire, but in "the voice of a hovering silence" is Yahweh to be known.[26]

The movement metaphors are thus more explicitly theological than are the formative metaphors, for they tell of the heart of divinity. The fire of the Holy Spirit represents for Moltmann the wrath of God, but this wrath is "not the antithesis of his love. It is nothing other than his love itself, repulsed and wounded." The divine anger may judge the creation but yet holds the universe even in this judgment. To withdraw and to forsake is not within the divine character: "only the withdrawal of God from his creation would be deadly. But his anger contains within itself his persevering and enduring love, and in his judgment is his grace."[27]

---

[21]Ibid., p. 277.

[22]Ibid.

[23]Dietrich Bonhoeffer, *Ethics*, trans. N. H. Smith (London: SCM, 1955), cited in Moltmann, *Spirit of Life*, p. 278.

[24]Moltmann, *Spirit of Life*, p. 278.

[25]Ibid., p. 279.

[26]Ibid., p. 280, borrowing Martin Buber's evocation of Yahweh in the "hovering silence."

[27]Ibid.

The Day of Pentecost is where the movement metaphors cohere as one. Taken together, the Holy Spirit as tempest, fire and love illustrates two strengths of Moltmann's theology of the Holy Spirit. For one, the centrality of Pentecost means that the Spirit's full descent upon the church and the world came after the resurrection of Jesus Christ. This means, in the words of Gary Badcock, that "it is through the trinitarian history of the Christ-event that the Spirit has *become* the Spirit of the risen Christ."[28] The Holy Spirit, to make the second point, is hence recognized "as a personal agent within the Trinity" and not as some impersonal point of contact between Father and Son who is not their equal.[29]

There are many mystical hints in virtually all of the nine descriptions of the Holy Spirit we have considered up until now. It is in Moltmann's fourth cluster of metaphors that these mystical strands come together around his final triad of light, water and fertility. Here the divine and the human come so close together "that it is hardly possible to distinguish the two" in his estimation.[30] In surveying the considerable biblical evidence of "God is light," Moltmann centers on the famous psalm "in your light we see light" (Ps 36:9) to show that "in our experience God is both the object of our knowing and its source."[31]

To a greater degree than with the other clusters of metaphors, Moltmann understands that to limit God's light only to the Holy Spirit is to deny that light suffuses the entire Trinity. The principle that where one divine person is involved all are present allows a wider reading of James 1:17, where God is "the Father of lights." Still farther along the trinitarian path, because naming more than one Person, is 2 Corinthians 4:6, the great text where the Creator God who once proclaimed "let light shine out of darkness" has also "shone in our hearts to give the light of the knowledge of the glory of God in the face of Jesus Christ."

To step outside of the metaphoric, Spirit as light means for Moltmann that "reality is characterized by a divine rationality."[32] Bequeathed to humans, the Spirit of God within us allows for intelligible perception. This perception may be most naturally found in the eyes, yet for Moltmann "it

---

[28]Badcock, *Light of Truth and Fire of Love*, p. 201.
[29]Ibid.
[30]Moltmann, *Spirit of Life*, p. 281.
[31]Ibid., p. 282.
[32]Ibid.

also means the streams of energy which we cannot see but sense, and which flood through us, transposing our life into vibrations and resonances."[33]

Through these manifold and ultimately complementary metaphors of knowing the Holy Spirit, a trinitarian spirituality can be discerned. It is a spirituality that strikes a balance between the passive, waiting for the Holy Spirit to energize and infuse God's passionate love, and the active out-flowing of this love into the world. This spirituality is neither heedlessly contemporary nor obdurately traditional. It is fresh yet ancient and hopeful in a responsible way. To close and punctuate his discussion Moltmann appends the liturgical hymn "Veni, Creator Spiritus" (Come, O Creator Spirit, Come) from the German Rabanus Maurus (780-856). Here are two key stanzas:

> Our senses with thy light inflame,
> Our hearts to heavenly love reclaim;
> Our bodies' poor infirmity
> With strength perpetual fortify.
>
> May we by thee the Father learn,
> And know the Son, and thee discern,
> Who art of both; and thus adore
> In perfect faith for evermore.[34]

FROM THE ONE TO THE THREE-IN-ONE

If it is true that there can be no single, all-encompassing theology of the Bible or even spirituality of the Bible, trinitarian spirituality likewise expresses itself variously.[35] God's unity or oneness is more easily interpreted by some trinitarian spiritualities; God's diversity or threeness by others. The Anglican spiritual writer Evelyn Underhill (1875-1941), owing to her fondness for unitive mysticism, more naturally gravitates toward the oneness end of the spectrum. As her life lengthened, as she pondered the imponderables of World War II, she became more aware of the corporate and institutional claims on her own Christian life, and her appreciation for the historical Christian witness to the Trinity deepened.

---

[33]Ibid.

[34]Rabanus Maurus, "Come, O Creator Spirit, Come," trans. Robert Bridges (1899).

[35]Urban T. Holmes III, *What Is Anglicanism?* (Harrisburg, Penn.: Morehouse, 1982), p. 71.

Underhill's two major works are *Mysticism* (1911) and *Worship* (1937), during whose quarter-century space Underhill came to own the Anglican covenant of her birth, keeping Anglican spirituality alive between the two world wars and evoking from T. S. Eliot the compliment that her writings address "the grievous need of the contemplative element in the modern world."[36] In *Mysticism* Underhill names Ephesians 4:6, "one God and Father of all, who is above all and through all and in all," as "the shortest and most perfect definition of [the infant church's] Triune God." Furthermore, this verse represents "all possible ways of conceiving this One Person in His living richness."[37] Salutary as is this recognition, Underhill has paid scant attention to the context of Ephesians 4:6, for it is the culmination of a trinitarian showing that Underhill seems to want to reduce to a unitarianism of God the Father. Perhaps Underhill's exegesis of Ephesians 4:6 finds the "one Spirit" of verse four and the "one Lord" of verse five somehow subsumed under the "one God and Father of all" with whom Paul concludes his thought.

Although Underhill may not be highly esteemed in some circles today, she continues to stand firm for all those who find unity more attractive than fractiousness.[38] Paul Marshall evaluates Underhill's contribution as showing that "Christian commitment provided a unifying factor in life, not a cause for dividing life into departments sacred and profane."[39] In *Worship* Underhill sees the primitive doxology, "Glory be to the Father, through the Son, in [the] Holy Spirit," as the only sure means of joining "the eternal and temporal worlds" together.[40]

In *Mysticism*, the doctrine of the Trinity is one, but not the only, means of understanding "the deep Abyss of the Godhead."[41] It is hard to escape the conclusion that Underhill makes the orthodox doctrine of the Trinity into the handmaid of mystical philosophy of the Neo-Platonic persuasion, which by definition is more at home with the Unconditioned One or the Undifferentiated One than the Three-in-One.

---

[36]T. S. Eliot, quoted in Dana Greene, *Evelyn Underhill: Artist of the Infinite Life* (New York: Crossroad, 1990), p. 2.

[37]Evelyn Underhill, *Mysticism: The Preeminent Study in the Nature and Development of Spiritual Consciousness* (1911; reprint, New York: Image Books, 1990), p. 113.

[38]Holmes, *What Is Anglicanism?* p. 67.

[39]Paul V. Marshall, "Anglican Spirituality," in *Protestant Spiritual Traditions*, ed. Frank C. Senn (Mahwah, N.J.: Paulist Press, 1986), p. 155.

[40]Underhill, *Worship* (New York: Harper & Brothers, 1937), p. 64.

[41]Underhill, *Mysticism*, p. 118.

The conventional mystical ladder of purgation-illumination-union may mean that the goal of mystical attainment need not be the Christian God but a pantheistic Other. Underhill herself suggests that the Trinity, or at least human attempts to understand it, may not be so much God's true and final essence as "a method of describing observed facts" of mystical experience. The Trinity is then reduced to an explanatory tool answering "the deepest instincts of humanity" to help one understand and implement "that diversity in unity" that is a prerequisite for the holy life.[42]

By the time *Worship* was published in 1937, Underhill was not less interested in unity, but now the shape of unity took on more explicit Christian content than it had in *Mysticism*. In the earlier work she had recognized that the natural tendency of all mysticism is toward pantheism, and that a stout adherence to the doctrine of the incarnation "is the only safeguard" against absorbing the historical, biblical Trinity into the ethereal Godhead beyond.[43] For Underhill the dialectic, and at times the very real personal struggle, between the christocentric, anchored in the incarnation, and the theocentric was no trivial pursuit. For the orthodox Christian, the Trinity means that "naked" monotheism, or the merely theocentric, is not God's fullest unveiling. If in Jesus Christ "all the fullness of God was pleased to dwell" (Col 1:19), then the simply theocentric does not adequately describe God.

Evelyn Underhill came to the brink of Unitarianism, but never quite dove in. But as Dana Greene analyzes it, she also never became fully christocentric either, and by extension truly Trinitarian.[44] In a 1922 letter to the Roman Catholic theologian Friedrich von Hügel, a great mentor for Underhill, she wrote that "I am still mainly theocentric; but the two attributes are no longer in opposition in my mind—they are two aspects of one thing."[45] In *Mysticism* Underhill allowed that the Trinity and the incarnation are the twin pillars of all Christian theology, and yet she never quite arrived there herself.[46]

---

[42]Ibid., p. 107.

[43]Ibid., p. 120.

[44]Greene, *Evelyn Underhill*, p. 102.

[45]Ibid., p. 83. See also Thomas S. Kepler, comp., *The Evelyn Underhill Reader* (New York: Abingdon, 1962), pp. 145-46.

[46]Underhill, *Mysticism*, p. 107.

It would be shortsighted and even cruel to write Underhill off because a fully realized trinitarian spirituality never truly grabbed her. She admires Julian of Norwich, "a simple and deeply human Englishwoman of middle age dwelling alone in her churchyard cell," and considers Julian "the poet of the Trinity."[47] Julian understood "this austere and subtle dogma" better than the learned theologians of Underhill's day.[48] Pondering a hazel nut in the palm of her hand, Julian exults that God made it, God loves it, God keeps it. Yet beyond the simple declaration that God is Maker, Keeper, Lover Julian is not inclined to peer.[49]

Underhill's ready identification with Lady Julian's simple nature trinitarianism agrees with her 1933 reservation regarding the regnant theologian of that day, Karl Barth, who for Underhill was "rather like a bottle of champagne . . . too intoxicating to be taken neat but excellent with a few dry biscuits!"[50] Along with Meister Eckhart, Underhill found Barth to be "too exclusively transcendent and abstract, carrying the revolt from naturalism too far."[51]

If someone was going to rein Karl Barth in, it was not likely to be Evelyn Underhill. She went part of the way with Barth, often favoring the language of the transcendent to name God the Father. She finds that "the richness and variousness of the simple Divine Nature" is best expressed as "God Transcendent, God Manifest, and God Immanent."[52] The collection of the church's ancient eucharistic prayers Underhill edited displays the Trinity as "God Transcendent, Incarnate, and Immanent."[53] More exotically, shifting the focus to how humankind may optimally receive the Real, the three divine traits of Transcendence, Desire, and Immanence collectively summarize "the whole gamut of symbolic expression."[54]

Although Underhill probably underutilized the specifically trinitarian name of God, she is familiar with many of the customary descriptions, for example, God as *above us, with us, within us*. The omission

---

[47]Ibid., p. 112.
[48]Ibid.
[49]Ibid.
[50]Evelyn Underhill, quoted in Greene, *Evelyn Underhill*, p. 109.
[51]Ibid.
[52]Underhill, *Worship*, p. 70.
[53]Evelyn Underhill, introduction to *Eucharistic Prayers from the Ancient Liturgies*, chosen and arranged by Evelyn Underhill (London: Longmans, Green, 1939), p. 10.
[54]Underhill, *Mysticism*, p. 133.

of the received language of Father, Son, Holy Spirit cannot throw one off the track of her trinitarian intent. Furthermore, these three divine "moments"

> are not exclusive but complementary apprehensions, giving objectives to intellect, feeling and will. They must all be taken into account in any attempt to estimate the full character of the spiritual life, and thus life can hardly achieve perfection unless all three be present in some measure.[55]

She finds humanity to be the "thing of threes," for example body, soul and spirit, as well as understanding, memory and will. Seeing the psychic profile as emotional, volitional and intellectual is of course a return to Augustine and his psychological analogy. Even human knowing, wherein a seeking subject and a found object are joined in the act of apprehension, suggests we are in the company of "a Trinitarian definition of Reality."[56]

Underhill's trinitarian impulse, while finally not beyond the pale of orthodoxy, is yet differently balanced and uniquely accented. According to her own words it is backward. Even in 1932, when she had outgrown the deepest trenches of her unitive mysticism, Underhill still confessed that "I came to Christ through God, whereas quite obviously lots of people came to God through Christ. But I can't show them how to do this—all I know is the reverse route."[57] She was chagrined and even embarrassed by her inability to find the more well-worn path to the Trinity, that leads more through revelation and less through ecstasy. "Left to myself," Underhill knew, she "would just go off on God alone."[58]

Yet Underhill was never one to split hairs when it came to doctrine and spirituality. Early and late, she had in view the practicality of knowing the triune God, especially the love of God. Dana Greene believes Underhill's best contribution is her rejuvenation of "the personal experience of the love of God that gives authenticity and authority to religion."[59] In *Mysticism* Underhill revisits and then revises the trinitarian symbolism of her countryman William Law in the direction of love. Law's Fire, Light, and Spirit Underhill finds too abstract, believing that Light,

---

[55]Evelyn Underhill, quoted in Marshall, "Anglican Spirituality," p. 156.
[56]Underhill, *Mysticism*, p. 111.
[57]Evelyn Underhill, quoted in Greene, *Evelyn Underhill*, p. 102.
[58]Ibid.
[59]Greene, *Evelyn Underhill*, p. 148.

Life, and Love are more in keeping with the persuasions and techniques of Christian mysticism. Love is "desirous and directive,"[60] a beautiful phrase that is all at once urgent, soothing, unsettling, and comforting. Theology, ethics, and spirituality happily congregate around the desirous and the directive. These words move one into the heart of God and out into the crush of humanity at the same time.

The short introduction Underhill contributed to her late compilation of eucharistic prayers (1939) is not a rigorous theological statement but suggests some directions her thought may have taken had her years lingered. Here she anticipates one of the cardinal concerns of today's trinitarian thought, to root out overblown individualism. To counterbalance the "excessive emphasis on the personal aspects of Holy Communion"[61] Underhill arranges the prayers of the liturgy into five groups that together mark the unfolding eucharistic mystery: the Preparation, the Offertory or Oblation, the Intercession, the Consecration, the Communion. Prayers of intercession remind the worshiper that "the Eucharist is not a private devotion."[62] Under the symbolic panoply of the liturgy "the whole mystery of redemption" and "the saving entrance of the Godhead into the human world" are made manifest, the conviction of which is perhaps chief among the goals of recent trinitarian theology.[63] To that extent Underhill is an economic trinitarian.

Taken as a whole, the prayer of consecration offers the clearest trinitarian focus of the entire collection of eucharistic prayers. Consecration is spoken in three parts: (1) adoration to God the Father, (2) a memorial to the Son's incarnation and saving work, technically called the *anamnesis* or remembrance of the Son's passion, (3) the *epiclesis* or invoking the Spirit's gift. "This great Trinitarian act of worship" culminates in the Lord's Prayer.[64]

The Communion completes the eucharistic mystery, and here, interestingly, Underhill notices slightly variant emphases between the Western liturgies, which drive toward redemption, and the Eastern liturgies, where the Holy Spirit's infusion prompts everyone to consider the claim of holiness. These "differences of devotional colour and emphasis" are

---

[60]Underhill, *Mysticism*, p. 115.
[61]Underhill, introduction to *Eucharistic Prayers*, p. 7.
[62]Ibid., p. 9.
[63]Ibid., p. 8.
[64]Ibid., p. 11.

not scaled to human liking or disposition, but are triunely propor-
tioned.[65] Within God, redemption and holiness are not in competition.

Underhill's comfortable and proper upper-middle-class English life was
deepened, if not totally dislocated, when in the early 1920s she started to
work with the poor.[66] If "the way of the Spirit" is the goal of the Christian
pilgrim, outward poverty must lead one to an inward poverty of spirit, it
being the sacrament of outward poverty. The Holy Spirit as "the Father of
the Poor" is the surest introduction to "the great simplicity of God."[67]

In the 1920s and 1930s Underhill cemented her own Anglican identity and drew her own loyal following by giving a series of retreats. The
freshest wisdom from these dozen or so retreats has been gleaned in
a collection appearing about a half-century after her death. *The Ways
of the Spirit* distills several triads, which upon investigation intuitively
recall the Trinity. Sometimes the triad names God: "Beauty, Wisdom,
and Power."[68] Borrowing from Ignatius of Loyola, founder of the Jesu-
its, Underhill presses this triad into definitional service. All of religion
is only a paraphrase of Ignatius's three-part movement: "I come from
God. I belong to God. I am destined for God."[69]

Theology and spirituality conjoin for Underhill in the vision of
God's loveliness that is at the same moment a call for humankind to
crave God's "eternal life, love, and light" in human souls. The triune
God is "holy, blessed, and glorious," and this translates to a Trinity of
"One Reality . . . redeeming love . . . mysterious, eternal Spirit."[70] The
contemplation of the Trinity is a spur to action, "to exercise the supreme human privilege: the encounter of our tiny spirits with the infinite Spirit."[71] Spirituality, worship and ethics are likewise entwined
by the One-in-Three God, who calls forth from his children: "Praise-
Reverence-Service."[72]

Underhill's long and active writing life spanned nearly forty years and
produced nearly as many books and many hundred more articles and

---

[65]Ibid., p. 12.
[66]Greene, *Evelyn Underhill*, p. 82.
[67]Kepler, *Evelyn Underhill Reader*, p. 193.
[68]Evelyn Underhill, *The Ways of the Spirit*, ed. Grace Adolphsen Brame (New York: Crossroad, 1994), p. 109.
[69]Ibid., pp. 103, 111, 115, 116-17.
[70]Ibid., p. 112.
[71]Ibid., p. 107.
[72]Ibid., p. 111.

book reviews. She deserves hearing today because where she worked and thought is where many people find themselves: not inclined to doctrinal niceties and grand declarations, but in search of a God who loves them and whom they can love. If at times, especially early in her career, Underhill forsook standard Christian verities for mystical rapture, she can be pardoned. She came home, if not to a Trinity of revelation, then to a Trinity of love that impelled worship and compelled service to the least among us.

CAN THE TRINITY BE FEMINIZED?

Elizabeth Johnson also has much to contribute to contemporary trinitarian theology and spirituality. It may be coincidental that the year of her birth, 1941, is also the year of Underhill's death. There is no real sense of passing along a mantle of feminist advocacy from elder to younger, because Johnson is a feminist in ways that Underhill never was and, given the times she inhabited, probably never could be. Underhill's death preceded the sort of feminism that would propose fundamental "reimagings" or "revisionings" of such Christian truths as God, creation, redemption, eschatology and many other components of the Christian faith.[73]

Of greater moment is their being joined by a fondness for Roman Catholicism, in Underhill's case a somewhat conflicted relationship that never quite allowed her to join the Roman way, for Johnson a calling as a member of the Congregation of Saint Joseph. They are also joined by a fondness for the analogical, with many representative trinitarian examples Underhill borrows from the history of Christian mysticism answering that call. Analogy is a fundamental ordering principle for both thinkers. Underhill's "Trinitarian definition of Reality" already alluded to is the climax of the process wherein "the very principle of analogy imposes" upon the human mind the ease and sensibility of this conclusion.[74] Since God, for Johnson, cannot be comprehended by finite minds, analogy must stand in the gap. Between

---

[73]*Freeing Theology: The Essentials of Theology in Feminist Perspective,* ed. Catherine Mowry LaCugna (San Francisco: HarperSanFrancisco, 1993). See especially LaCugna's essay on the Trinity, "God in Communion with Us." The essays in *Speaking the Christian God: The Holy Trinity and the Challenge of Feminism,* ed. Alvin F. Kimel Jr. (Grand Rapids: Eerdmans, 1992), are consistently challenging and illuminating.

[74]Underhill, *Mysticism,* p. 111.

human unknowingness and God's inscrutability "the only building
blocks near to hand are creaturely experiences, relationships, qualities,
names, and functions," concludes Johnson.[75] We have already seen how
Dorothy Sayers finds analogy to be the only reliable way to express what
is truthful.

Whereas Evelyn Underhill's spirituality starts from "the limitless Divine Abyss" who is the "true Country of the Soul" in spite of remaining
impersonal and indescribable,[76] Johnson's beginning is no less breath-
taking but somehow more accessible. The Spirit who is "God's livingness
subtly and powerfully abroad in the world" is where Johnson begins her
constructive trinitarian theology.[77] Additionally, in keeping with her
feminist convictions, the experiences of women are a privileged source
of theological knowing and reflecting. If women's experiences do not
always arise directly *from* Sophia, who is in a sense the incarnation of
wisdom, because this would be to set aside the freedom of the woman,
Sophia clarifies, extends and judges these experiences in her prophetic
light. Indeed this Spirit of Wisdom is nothing less than the lens through
which Johnson views *all* divinity.

Johnson's writing manages at the same time to be both poetic and ana-
lytical, evocative and somewhat convoluted, descriptive and opaque. She
chooses each word with care, knowing that across the vast expanse of the
trinitarian terrain, one little signifier makes a world of difference. Stanley
Grenz assesses Johnson's employing of Wisdom as centrally defining to
be masterful, and so it is.[78] Wisdom is yesterday, today and forever; wisdom can both shape and transcend history; wisdom is both singular and
plural; wisdom fills both tiny cracks and huge panoramas.

In *She Who Is*, which must rank as one of the greatest constructions
of feminist theology ever essayed, Johnson employs Sophia to form a
new Trinity of Spirit-Sophia, Jesus-Sophia, Mother-Sophia. In contrast
to traditional trinitarian theology, there are two reversals here. The
first, the recasting of all of the triune persons in the image of Sophia,
has already been noted. But what is the reason for the second, the rever-

---

[75]Elizabeth A. Johnson, *She Who Is: The Mystery of God in Feminist Theological Discourse* (New
    York: Crossroad, 1992), p. 113.
[76]Underhill, *Mysticism*, p. 110.
[77]Johnson, *She Who Is*, p. 122, quoted in Stanley J. Grenz, *Rediscovering the Triune God: The
    Trinity in Contemporary Theology* (Minneapolis: Fortress, 2004), p. 172.
[78]Grenz, *Rediscovering the Triune God*, p. 171.

sal of the traditional order of Father-Son-Spirit? Instead, Johnson proposes Spirit-Jesus-Mother.

Consistent with her valuing of human and specifically women's experience, Johnson reverses the received order of the Trinity because so doing demonstrates that the Trinity is founded on love and perpetuates love. Her new paradigm, furthermore, "allows a starting point more closely allied to the human experience of salvation, without which there would be no speech about the triune God at all."[79]

Is Johnson's prioritizing of human experience, especially that of women, to put the theological cart before the horse? Theologians such as Karl Barth and Paul Molnar would certainly think so. Any theological speech about the triune God is possible for Barth and his followers only as God allows it, only as God's speech is given in revelation. The speech of God is powerful and, by grace through faith, can save humanity. But no *merely* human experience, whether of beauty, of love or indeed of salvation, can ever hope to lead us to speaking of the triune God. God reserves the privilege of speech for himself. Johnson's demonstrated raising of human experience above all else validates Charles Marsh's criticism: "In the end, her primary commitment to experience compromises her ability to explicate the Trinity as a mystery that patterns human social and moral experience."[80] Molnar characterizes the whole tenor of Johnson's theology "as an imaginative way to achieve that goal [liberation of women] politically, socially, and religiously," whereas theology's true obligation is "an attempt to understand who God really is and what he has actually done and is doing in history."[81]

These criticisms not withstanding, how does Johnson see that the experience of love justifies her reversing the traditional order? Our initial contact with love is never through threats or hostility, but through warmth and acceptance. Love's warmth and approachability is for Johnson the third person of the Trinity, or Spirit-Sophia. Love must first be personal before it can be anything else. We must pass through love's entry into our lives "before we are moved to inquire after a definitive historical manifestation of this love," and this historical display is the

---

[79]Johnson, *She Who Is*, p. 122.

[80]Charles Marsh, "Two Models of Trinitarian Theology: A Way Beyond the Impasse?" *Perspectives in Religious Studies* 21 (1994): 63, quoted in Grenz, *Rediscovering the Triune God*, p. 179.

[81]Paul D. Molnar, *Divine Freedom and the Doctrine of the Immanent Trinity* (London: T & T Clark, 2005), p. 10.

second person, or Jesus-Sophia. Our progress from receiving the initiating act of love to locating this act historically quite naturally moves
us "toward the mystery of the primordial source of all," who is the first
person of Johnson's feminized Trinity, Mother-Sophia.[82]

This progression of Spirit-Sophia to Jesus-Sophia to Mother-Sophia
serves two purposes for Johnson. The primary one of grounding our
knowing of the Trinity in the human experience of love has been noted.
Second, this strategy also avoids the real or implied subordination of
the Holy Spirit enshrined in the traditional order, where the Holy Spirit
may be only a theological afterthought.

How does Johnson understand Spirit-Sophia, and how does a Spirit-
driven spirituality emerge from her theology? Of what moment is Spirit-
Sophia for Christian spirituality? Will our ending be that "we instinctively know your presence is not distant or theoretical, but close-by,
consonant with what we know of true communitarian life, and over-
flowing with relationship within and without?" in the words of William
Cleary, who authored a whole collection of prayers based on Johnson's
book, prayers that lack the conceptual heft of *She Who Is* but still impart
some of its splendor.[83]

Like Evelyn Underhill, Johnson appropriates selected figures from
the history of Christian spirituality, including Hildegard of Bingen
(1098-1179), a German mystic whose revelations have been called *sui gen-
eris*, who is also esteemed as "the first great woman theologian in Christian history."[84] In Johnson's paraphrase of the great German visionary:

> The Spirit . . . is the life of the life of all creatures; the way in which every-
> thing is penetrated with connectedness and relatedness; a burning fire
> who sparks, ignites, inflames, kindles hearts; a guide in the fog; a balm
> for wounds; a shining serenity; an overflowing fountain that spreads to
> all sides. She is life, movement, color, radiance, restorative stillness in
> the din. Her power makes all withered sticks and souls green again with
> the juice of life. She purifies, absolves, strengthens, heals, gathers the
> perplexed, seeks the lost. She pours the juice of contrition into hardened
> hearts. She plays music in the soul, being herself the melody of praise
> and joy. She awakens mighty hope, blowing everywhere the winds of re-

---

[82]Johnson, *She Who Is*, pp. 122-23. Cf. Grenz, *Rediscovering the Triune God*, p. 173.

[83]William Cleary, *Prayers to She Who Is* (New York: Crossroad, 1995), p. 89.

[84]Bernard McGinn, *The Presence of God: A History of Western Christian Mysticism*, vol. 2: *The Growth of Mysticism* (New York: Crossroad, 1994), pp. 334, 333.

newal in creation. And this is the mystery of God, in whom we live and move and have our being.[85]

Johnson seeks to lift Spirit-Sophia out of the neglect she has suffered through centuries of theological reflection. After sampling what eminent theologians have pronounced about the Holy Spirit, Johnson summarizes this sorry past in biting words: "faceless, shadowy, anonymous, half-known, homeless, watered down, the poor relation, Cinderella, marginalized by being modeled on women."[86]

If *She Who Is* presents one foundational premise, without which the entire project collapses, it is the compact but textured aphorism: "The symbol of God functions."[87] This symbol functions in more ways than can easily be lined out in a paragraph. Functionality for Johnson is no mechanized, routinized process. Functionality is more like an overarching gestalt than like the confounding directions a parent struggles with in assembling Christmas toys. Functionality does not cower, dodge or evade. Functionality functions, and Johnson's hope in *She Who Is* relies on new and more just and righteous functions to arise for women as the symbol of God is changed from one favoring patriarchy to one strictly hewing to biblical mandates for justice, mercy, love and inclusion.

If we apply Johnson's generative hypothesis of the symbol of God's functionality to Spirit-Sophia, what do we find? How does Spirit-Sophia *function*? "Where can I go from your spirit? Or where can I flee from your presence?" (Ps 139:7) is one of the most universally spoken psalms because it is so true, so in keeping with any human experience of the God of the Bible. This verse may have inspired Johnson's recognition "that in speaking of Spirit-Sophia's deeds we are pointing to the gracious, furious mystery of God engaged in a dialectic of presence and absence throughout the world, creating, indwelling, sustaining, resisting, recreating, challenging, guiding, liberating, completing."[88]

Any combination of these nine action words is surely sufficient to describe Spirit-Sophia's action, but Johnson discovers the Spirit's execution to be in three particular ways: vivifying, renewing/empowering and gracing. Johnson's general strategy is to toss the Spirit-Sophia net as

---

[85]Johnson, *She Who Is*, pp. 127-28.
[86]Ibid., p. 131.
[87]Ibid., p. 5.
[88]Ibid., p. 133.

far as she can loft it, and included in the catch are these three pregnant
metaphors. Johnson's methodology is not an act of indiscretion or care-
lessness, but of inclusion. Her net is as wide as all creation. The vivifying Spirit-Sophia pervades everything that is. "In the beginning," writes
Johnson, "she hovers like a great mother bird over her egg, to hatch the
living order of the world out of primordial chaos (Gen. 1:2)."[89] Spirit-
Sophia is a torrent, not a trickle, not a dammed-up river that turns a
downstream waterfall from a lion into a housecat, as sometimes happens to the Shoshone Falls of the Snake River in south-central Idaho.
The "Niagara of the West," deserving of this title during the river's un-
fettered spring runoff, is by summer's close a puny wisp. Natural effects
and farmers' irrigation see to that.

The spatial coordinates of Spirit-Sophia insure that Sophia never
dries up or fades away. Indwelling all, embracing the aching world "as a
great matrix (Acts 17:28)" flown throughout the universe—this is Spirit-
Sophia.[90] Because the dialectic of creation implies dissipation, destruction and decay, Spirit-Sophia is also the renewing and empowering
Spirit. Her presence is evergreen, not like the spewed chemicals that
falsely green a local funeral home's front lawn in winter. Spirit-Sophia
would never stoop to falsity. "She initiates novelty, instigates change,
transforms what is dead into new stretches of life."[91]

The ministry of Spirit-Sophia is worldwide and even cosmic. Johnson
buttresses her case by frequent reference to the biblical witness to the
Holy Spirit. The Spirit renews the face of the earth (Ps 104:30); the tra-
vailing Spirit awaits the wholeness of all creation (Rom 8:22); the Spirit
agitates for peace and justice (Is 61:1-2); she turns desolation row into a
fruitful field (Is 32:15-17); she is a midwife (Ps 22:9-10); she bears witness
to Jesus Christ (Jn 15:26-27); like a baker, the Spirit "keeps on kneading
the leaven of kindness and truth, justice and peace into the thick dough
of the world until the whole loaf rises (Matt. 13:33)."[92]

If there are two realms, the sacred and the secular, Spirit-Sophia
refuses to recognize any arbitrary bifurcation, because she ministers
to all. Especially to the ragged and the despised, she is God. Leonardo

---

[89]Ibid., p. 134.
[90]Ibid.
[91]Ibid., p. 135.
[92]Ibid., p. 137.

Boff's affirmation that "the Spirit sustains the feeble breath of life in the empire of death" is in keeping with the activity of Spirit-Sophia.[93] To call the Spirit's third area of activity, gracing, "more" religious than the first two is not to divide the Spirit against herself. Spirit-Sophia's holiness is not somehow more holy as gracing than as vivifying or renewing/empowering. *Gracing* is a simple signifier indicating the Spirit's movements among persons, communities, institutions and callings that have traditionally identified themselves as religious.

The Spirit's grace is no less potent and effectual for its universal spread. Johnson quotes Irenaeus that "there is but one and the same God who, from the beginning to the end by various dispensations, comes to the rescue of humankind,"[94] in support of her veiled hypothesis that Spirit-Sophia is productive outside the explicitly biblical religions of Judaism and Christianity. "No people are devoid of the inspiration of the Spirit."[95]

Yet, predominantly, Spirit-Sophia's grace is given in Christian ways. Through this grace the primitive Christian community emerged. The baptism of Jesus Christ, the witness to the power of his resurrection and Christian mission are all inconceivable without the Spirit's grace.[96] Cultivating, pruning, fertilizing—whatever it takes to bring the fruit of the Spirit (Gal 5:22-23) to perfection—this is what Spirit-Sophia does.

Cautioning, in the words of Marcia Falk, that "dead metaphors make strong idols," Johnson proposes a new metaphor to describe God: SHE WHO IS.[97] She believes that the Latin of Thomas Aquinas's phrase HE WHO IS will welcome "a feminist gloss."[98] "With this name," SHE WHO IS, Johnson concludes, "we bring to bear in a female metaphor all the power carried in the ontological symbol of absolute, relational liveliness that energizes the world."[99]

---

[93]Leonardo Boff, *Trinity and Society*, trans. Paul Burns (Maryknoll, N.Y.: Orbis, 1988), p. 217, quoted in ibid., p. 137.

[94]Irenaeus, quoted in Johnson, *She Who Is*, p. 139.

[95]Johnson, *She Who Is*, p. 139.

[96]Ibid., pp. 139-41.

[97]Marcia Falk, "Notes of Composing New Blessings," in *Weaving the Visions: New Patterns in Feminist Spirituality*, ed. Carol Christ and Judith Plaskow (San Francisco: Harper & Row, 1989), p. 132, quoted in ibid., p. 45.

[98]Johnson, *She Who Is*, p. 242.

[99]Ibid., p. 243.

It is "the mystery of God in feminist theological discourse," the subtitle of *She Who Is*, that Johnson wishes to explore. Her subtitle illumines the path ahead for both spirituality and theology. "Feminist theological discourse" retrieves aspects of "the mystery of God" obscured and at times obliterated by patriarchal theology. The act and art of discourse is to engage the needs of the world on their own terms. A live component of Johnson's spirituality is the gift of friendship, which overcomes and fuses and joins. "Friendship entails a reciprocity of relationship that exists independently of one's place in the social order, making it possible to cross boundaries of race, sex, class, and even nature."[100]

If spirituality can be sung, and it can be, then Brian Wren's hymn "Who Is She?" would be page one in Elizabeth Johnson's book of hymns:

> Who is She,
>   neither male nor female,
>   maker of all things,
>   only glimpsed or hinted,
>   source of life and gender?
> She is God,
>   mother, sister, lover;
>   in her love we wake,
>   move, grow, are daunted,
> triumph and surrender.
>
> Who is She,
>   mothering her people,
>   teaching them to walk,
>   lifting weary toddlers,
>   bending down to feed them?
> She is Love,
>   crying in a stable,
>   teaching from a boat,
>   friendly with the lepers,
> bound for crucifixion.
>
> Who is She,
>   sparkle in the rapids,

---

[100]Ibid., p. 145.

> coolness of the well,
>   living power of Jesus
>   flowing from the Scriptures?
> She is Life,
>   water, wind and laughter,
>   calm, yet never still,
>   swiftly moving Spirit,
> singing in the changes.[101]

What are we to make of Johnson's feminized approach to the Trinity? The ethical and the experiential elements of Johnson's trinitarian theology are pronounced and well spoken, and to that degree helpful and refreshing. The Holy Spirit as Spirit-Sophia is where the triune God really feels the world's pain. Johnson has a vivid and believable sense of exactly how the Holy Spirit truly operates in the world. Overall, however, Johnson's way of obtaining and processing theological truth, plus her view of God's triunity as a whole, is subject to at least two criticisms.

The more particular criticism arises from Johnson's "failure to distinguish the immanent and economic Trinity," in Paul Molnar's words, which must also mean a failure "to acknowledge the immanent Trinity as the norm for truth."[102] Johnson herself states that "the symbol of the Trinity is not a blueprint of the inner workings of the godhead, not an offering of esoteric information about God. In no sense is it a literal description of God's being *in se* [in itself]. . . . Our speech about God as three and persons is a human construction that means to say that God is *like* a Trinity, like a threefoldness of relation."[103] While everyone will applaud Johnson's humility in the face of the triune mystery, for Molnar her saying that God is *like* a Trinity is the rankest denial of who God really is, because the Christian God *is* the Trinity, in Molnar's description "the one who is one and three from all eternity."[104]

The more general criticism follows from Johnson's heedless placing of human and especially feminine experience over revelation. What

---

[101]Brian Wren, *Who Is She?* (Carol Stream, Ill.: Hope Publishing Company, 1986), quoted in ibid., p. 191.

[102]Molnar, *Divine Freedom*, p. 24.

[103]Johnson, *She Who Is*, p. 204, quoted by Molnar, *Divine Freedom*, p. 24.

[104]Molnar, *Divine Freedom*, p. 24.

William Abraham said of another feminist theologian must also be true of Johnson: "Commitment to the full humanity of women is a moral endeavour as much as it is a theological principle. Yet this moral principle is surely not something derived from experience, but something brought to experience."[105] For Abraham as for Molnar, feminist theology commits the category mistake of prioritizing the human over the divine.

---

[105]William J. Abraham, *Canon and Criterion in Christian Theology: From the Fathers to Feminism* (Oxford: Clarendon, 1998), p. 443, referencing Rosemary Radford Ruether.

5

The Triune
Life Is Our Life

"C rossing the bar" may be an ancient expression with poetic punch,
but in the case of the mighty Columbia River the reality matches the
metaphor. Only the skilled and the intrepid need apply for the tricky
labor of negotiating watercraft through the unforgiving sand bars that
guard the Columbia's mouth as it empties into the Pacific Ocean. Do
those who successfully negotiate the passage from fresh water to salty
sea know exactly *when* they are ocean dwellers? Is a cup sent water-
ward to sample the taste sweet or bitter?

Something dimly like this—the mingling of the pure and the pun-
gent—may be happening when the church is viewed in a trinitarian
light. Every understanding of the church desires to remain true to its
trinitarian roots and bearings. Every assembly longs for the mishmash
of people who come in the door to become a koinonia fellowship that
shines forth an ecclesial communion that strives to imitate the communion shared among Father, Son and Holy Spirit. Any ecclesiology that is
both relevant to human needs and anchored in the reality of God must
be triunely figured, constructed and realized. Just *how* a theology of the
Holy Trinity can bear fruit in the everyday workings of the church is a
test case for the relevance of trinitarian theology. It is not, obviously,

the truth of God that is on trial here, but how well this truth can be realized, *incarnated* even, in the life of the church. If a doctrine of the church runs after alien models, be they economic, cultural, psychological or corporate, then ecclesiology becomes futility.

Few of theology's main constituent parts other than ecclesiology lend themselves so readily to a trinitarian makeover, or at least scrutiny. There is a desire to fashion the many of the church, the cloud of witnesses (Heb 12:1) who are easily observed on Sunday morning, into a congregation recreated in the triune image. Ethicists ponder how to bring the *ought* of conscience, with its implied purity of motive, to the *is* of performance and doing the right thing. Christians can easily apply this logic to the ought of the triune God and the is of the church. The wisdom of Catherine LaCugna's simple statement "the nature of the church should manifest the nature of God" shines in its own light.[1] The "should" LaCugna expresses is not a regimented coercion but a gracious enablement. She further believes that "the Christian community is the image or icon of the invisible God when its communitarian life mirrors the inclusivity of divine love."[2]

When Jesus Christ prayed to unify his disciples, he situated their union in the love he and his Father shared in the Holy Spirit. John 17:21, "As you, Father, are in me and I am in you, may they also be in us," is clearly a foundational text for any ecclesiology that aspires to be trinitarian. On the terms of Jesus' prayer the church could never be just an arbitrary assembly of thrown-together humans. The church is always a divine endowment. More familiar, perhaps, to a Roman Catholic than to a Protestant sensibility, the church has been defined as a sacrament of Christ or a sacrament of the Holy Spirit.[3] Yet Catholic theologian William Hill finds an even richer vein to mine: *community*, a concept that when applied to the church is more representatively trinitarian than is sacrament.[4] When Cyprian, third-century bishop of Carthage, named the church as "a people united by the unity of the Father, Son, and Holy Spirit," he admitted that the church's unity can be secured

---

[1]Catherine Mowry LaCugna, *God for Us: The Trinity & Christian Life* (San Francisco: Harper-SanFrancisco, 1991), p. 403.
[2]Ibid.
[3]William J. Hill, *The Three-Personed God: The Trinity as a Mystery of Salvation* (Washington, D.C.: Catholic University of America Press), p. 289.
[4]Ibid.

only in God.[5] "As God is a unity in communion," writes John Thompson, "those called by him through Christ by the Holy Spirit will show this, however imperfectly, and be drawn to participate in the fellowship of God within himself as Father, Son, and Holy Spirit."[6]

To formulate the ideal is not the same as hitting the mark. The intuitive sense that the divine family in heaven should be able to replicate itself on earth in the church meets the hard reality of human sin. Miroslav Volf notes that in today's climate "the thesis that ecclesial communion should correspond to trinitarian communion enjoys the status of an almost self-evident proposition."[7] Volf sees that the interconnections between trinitarian communion and ecclesial communion lead to two platitudes: (1) there is a necessary and urgent oscillation between unity and multiplicity, each needing the other; (2) humans must rise to the heights of God's selfless love. He finds the first platitude "so vague that no one cares to dispute it," while the second is "so divine that no one can live it."[8]

Sixty years ago, in the aftermath of World War II and before the recent resurgence of trinitarian theology had taken flight, H. Richard Niebuhr published a wise article titled "The Doctrine of the Trinity and the Unity of the Church." Niebuhr brought the studied attentiveness of the Christian ethicist and social critic to this task, if not necessarily the detail of the constructive theologian. Niebuhr believes that the doctrine of the Trinity, which he called "this most formidable and interesting Christian doctrine," should be pressed into greater ecumenical service than he currently observed.[9] Trinitarian thinking is uniquely poised to address the whole gamut of existential and social concerns because it represents the church's more encompassing vantage point over against the strictly individual.[10] The doctrine of the Trinity, Nie-

---

[5]Cyprian, quoted in ibid. Also quoted in John Thompson, *Modern Trinitarian Perspectives* (New York: Oxford University Press, 1994), p. 80.

[6]Thompson, *Modern Trinitarian Perspectives*, p. 80.

[7]Miroslav Volf, *After Our Likeness: The Church as the Image of the Trinity* (Grand Rapids: Eerdmans, 1998), p. 191.

[8]Ibid.

[9]H. Richard Niebuhr, "The Doctrine of the Trinity and the Unity of the Church," in *Theology, History, and Culture: Major Unpublished Writings*, ed. William Stacy Johnson (New Haven, Conn.: Yale University Press, 1996), p. 62. Article originally published in *Theology Today* (1946): 371-84.

[10]Ibid., p. 50.

buhr argues, "has great importance for an ecumenical theology as a formulation of the whole Church's faith in God in distinction from the partial faiths and partial formulations of the Church and of individuals in the Church."[11]

The peculiar and lasting genius of Niebuhr's article is his identification and explication of three different stripes of Unitarianism. Niebuhr admits that Unitarianism traditionally specifies God the Father as alone in his essential divinity, an impulse that is "a perennial and unconquerable movement in Christianity."[12] Yet from nearly the earliest Christian times there has been a Unitarianism of the Son, that cared little for the philosophical speculations of Father Unitarianism but rather for personal salvation. For these Christians, who sometimes veered into heresy, as with the second-century figure Marcion, "Christ was the Lord who brought them redemption, hence though they might have in mind the presence of other deities and even of a high God beyond the natural world, their worship was concentrated on Jesus Christ, the Lord."[13] Hymns such as "Fairest Lord Jesus," the liberal appropriation of Jesus as a moral exemplar, and the evangelical embrace of pietism all demonstrate that Jesus Unitarianism is not an isolated impulse in Christian history, although Niebuhr admits that devotion to Jesus does not always preclude devotion to the Father and the Holy Spirit.[14]

The Spirit Unitarianism that Niebuhr explicates tends to absorb the Father and the Son into the third person of the Trinity, and this Unitarianism "may be the most prevalent of all," Niebuhr suggests.[15] Rather than focus on God the Father as "the Being beyond nature," or God the Son as "the Redeemer in history," Spirit Unitarianism seems to spring from self-reliance, or at least self-reflection. This third Unitarianism has its own certain appeal, as Niebuhr explains: "The reality with which men come into touch when they turn to reasoning itself, to awareness as subjective, to conscience and self-consciousness—this is the reality on which they are absolutely dependent and from which alone they can expect illumination, purification, perfection."[16] In the familiar equation

---

[11]Ibid., p. 51.
[12]Ibid., p. 53.
[13]Ibid.
[14]Ibid., pp. 53-54.
[15]Ibid., p. 55.
[16]Ibid.

of "Holy Spirit and human spirit," this third Unitarianism locates or even imprisons the work of the Holy Spirit within human boundaries. The wisest sort of Spirit Unitarianism has always realized its incompleteness. Because revelations and interior experiences may arise from anywhere, Niebuhr allows that "it has been necessary for spiritualism to employ criteria taken from the religion of the Son," on the principle of Romans 8:9, "Anyone who does not have the Spirit of Christ does not belong to him."[17]

The three Unitarianisms Niebuhr identifies are not just Christianity in triplicate, with no significant differences from one Unitarianism to another. For American Protestants, at least, Niebuhr's three Unitarianisms have been at times lived out in various theological traditions and denominational families. The Reformed tradition's esteem of God's sovereignty may correlate with a Father-Unitarianism. Pentecostals may thrive on a Spirit-Unitarianism. The evangelical emphasis on redemption may be most naturally represented by a Son-Unitarianism. Even recognizing these differences, it remains that these three Unitarian impulses "are logically and historically interdependent," as well as psychologically linked.[18] Niebuhr convincingly explains how none of the three Unitarianisms can really go it alone, that the layers of mutual reference among the three are real and enduring, that while each one of them may speak truth that the other two miss, none of them is complete, showing that after all "the three Unitarianisms are interdependent."[19]

Niebuhr's insightful article is more descriptive than prescriptive, more valuing of historical demonstration than of forward-looking theological proposals. He holds forth the hope that the doctrine of the Trinity may serve to unite the church. This central confession occupies a place no other Christian declaration possibly can. Niebuhr urges that "the Trinitarianism of the whole Church must undertake to state what is implicit in the faith and knowledge of all of its parts though it is not explicit in any one of them."[20] In Niebuhr's hands the doctrine of the Trinity becomes a welcoming irenic passage and not a polemical cudgel. Trinitarian theology should be a synthesizing theology, "an ecumenical

---

[17]Ibid., p. 61.
[18]Ibid., pp. 57, 58.
[19]Ibid., p. 62.
[20]Ibid.

doctrine providing not for the exclusion of heretics but for their inclusion in the body on which they are actually dependent."[21]

Niebuhr's ecumenical instincts have been in the consciousness of many trinitarian ecclesiologists. Of whatever confessional identity, all would embrace the move proposed by Leonardo Boff, where the regnant "church-as-society" becomes "church-as-communion."[22] This movement can only come to palpable fruition through God-as-Communion, the Trinity. Historically, the moment for a truly trinitarian ecclesiology is now. No one has seriously contested Colin Gunton's claim that ecclesiologies of the past have flunked the Trinity test. Thinking about the church "has never seriously and consistently been rooted in a conception of the being of God as triune."[23] Just as a small engineering error may lead to a huge mistake in constructing a suspension bridge, so also faulty philosophical and theological presuppositions have often undermined ecclesiology. The monistic or hierarchical thinking that has often dictated past ecclesiology has led to disastrous consequences that ranged from identifying the church with a political regime to inflexible and robotic structures that sacrificed compassion and mercy to efficiency.[24]

If past ecclesiology has often failed to catch the trinitarian vision, then what remedy can God's triunity offer? Gunton avers that "to base a theology of the church in the Trinity is of great practical moment."[25] Why and how? For Catherine LaCugna, consistent with her stress on the economic Trinity who creates the world and works toward its salvation, the church must be "run like God's household: a domain of inclusiveness, interdependence, and cooperation, structured according to the model of *perichoresis* among persons."[26]

The remaking of the church following a perichoretic pattern, which is the mutual indwelling of the divine persons each within the others, solves many ecclesiological problems. The relationship between the local church and the church universal is no longer problematic because

---

[21]Ibid.

[22]Leonardo Boff, *Holy Trinity, Perfect Community*, trans. Phillip Berryman (Maryknoll, N.Y.: Orbis, 2000), pp. 65-67.

[23]Colin E. Gunton, *The Promise of Trinitarian Theology* (Edinburgh: T & T Clark, 1991), p. 58.

[24]Ibid., p. 71.

[25]Ibid., p. 81.

[26]LaCugna, *God for Us*, p. 402.

there is no longer any competition between the local and the universal. The goal of Christian union, and how perichoresis advances this, is aptly put by the Conference of European Churches:

> The whole church of Christ is constituted not by adding together part church to part church, but is expressed by the communion of local churches in mutual interpenetration (perichoresis). Conciliar community of churches is thus an integral part of the concept of the trinity.[27]

To make the same point in a more theological way, Dumitru Popescu advises that "we need to see the organic unity of the church as the body of Christ as inherent in the diversity of local churches just as the persons of the trinity are inherent in the divine nature and the divine nature in the persons of the trinity."[28]

Popescu's two-word signifier "just as" reminds us that an analogy between the triune God and the church is being proposed. Standing behind and validating the analogy is not psychological or sociological or institutional or even philosophical truth. It is theological truth. The movement from trinitarian communion to ecclesial communion is possible only because God is perfect communion. The Greek Orthodox theologian John Zizioulas has worked out an entire ontology of communion in his book *Being as Communion*. To live in the church is to live as an ecclesial being, an order of being that "is bound to the very being of God."[29]

We must say more than that. Ecclesial being is not one order of being among many other options. Ecclesial being reshapes human existence and ecclesiastical life because God's being is fully realized communion, and through the Holy Spirit this gift is made available to humankind. Zizioulas believes that "the Holy Trinity is a primordial ontological concept and not a notion which is added to the divine substance or rather which follows it. . . . The substance of God, 'God,' has no ontological content, no true being, apart from communion."[30] Because God is perfect communion, every Christian is called to live likewise, an ecclesial life begun in baptism and sustained through the eucharistic worship of

---

[27]Conference of European Churches, quoted in Thompson, *Modern Trinitarian Perspectives*, p. 87.
[28]Dumitru Popescu, quoted in Thompson, *Modern Trinitarian Perspectives*, p. 89.
[29]John D. Zizioulas, *Being as Communion: Studies in Personhood and the Church* (Crestwood, N.Y.: Saint Vladimir's Seminary Press, 2002), p. 15.
[30]Ibid., p. 17.

the church. This ecclesial life may begin inward, but it moves outward in love. Ecclesial being is a truly catholic life that universalizes itself.[31] To live ecclesially is to be not an individual or even a "personality" but truly personal.[32] This must be the case if ecclesial life is grounded in God, whose very being is constituted in the relationships among Father, Son and Spirit. Zizioulas believes that no one can be imagined or realized only self-referentially. No, persons are made only through, with and in their relationships. "No man is an island" has met its theological match.

Ecclesial communion must always aspire to trinitarian communion. To phrase it thus is not quite right; it sounds like ecclesial communion is some sort of human striving or human capacity. But it is more like a gift of grace. The local church, a gathered community of those so graced with ecclesial life, always looks to God to perfect its koinonia. God remains uniquely communal because God is uniquely personal. Zizioulas asserts that only when being and communion coincide is personhood really present, and this coincidence is absolutely true only with the triune God. The conclusion to which Zizioulas's theological reasoning stretches is this: "The triune God offers in Himself the only possibility for such an identification of being with communion; He is the revelation of true personhood."[33]

When communion is seen in a trinitarian light, both unity and uniqueness are realized. Perichoresis, the expression of divine communion, brings along both threeness and oneness. Jürgen Moltmann knows that "*perichoresis* combines the threeness and the oneness without reducing the threeness to the oneness or the oneness to the threeness."[34]

Furthermore, perichoretic life among Father, Son and Holy Spirit "is a process of most perfect and intense empathy."[35] If unity and uniqueness are not in dire competition, and if trinitarian empathy can begin to work itself into the fabric of every Christian congregation, then trinitarian communion can begin to replicate itself in ecclesial communion. If

---

[31]Ibid., p. 58.

[32]Ibid., p. 105.

[33]Ibid., p. 107.

[34]Jürgen Moltmann, *History and the Triune God: Contributions to Trinitarian Theology*, trans. John Bowden (New York: Crossroad, 1992), p. 86.

[35]Jürgen Moltmann, *The Trinity and the Kingdom*, trans. Margaret Kohl (San Francisco: Harper & Row, 1981), p. 175.

institutional and personal patterns are frozen in predictable structures of subordination and superordination, a perichoretic ecclesiology breaks this logjam. The church that is fluently perichoretic is the church with "overlapping patterns of relationships,"[36] which Colin Gunton finds more representative of the churchly relationships Paul describes in 1 Corinthians 12—14, where "the notion of a permanent order of leadership is completely absent."[37]

To follow the template of perichoresis will energize and perfect church life, whether on the corner or across the world. No finer pattern may be found for conforming the life of the church to the life of God. The creative interplay between unity and multiplicity signified by perichoresis means that spiritual gifts and charisms and ministries are given to *all* Christians, a universal bestowing standing for multiplicity. In that these gifts are given exactly to benefit all Christians we see unity. Miroslav Volf, who makes this point about the interplay between multiplicity and unity, finds the correspondence between the divine persons and the local church here: "Like the divine persons, they [congregants] all stand in a relation of mutual giving and receiving."[38]

Yet no one is mistaking a meeting among three members of the clergy, or even the laity, as heaven finding its way to earth. Trinitarian perichoresis is a perennial bloom always in full maturity, which the imitative human perichoresis struggles even to conceptualize. Volf reminds us that "because of the creaturely nature of human beings, ecclesial communion is always a communion of the will,"[39] and the divine will congregates, effectuates and solidifies in ways the human will, torn and sin prone, never can. To say, as Colin Gunton does, that "the being of the church should echo the dynamic of the relations between the three persons who together constitute the deity" is to ground ecclesiology in the only sustainable place, the perichoretic life of the triune God.[40] To acknowledge both this foundation and that the church's reach toward a perichoretic life will always exceed its grasp is not to be negative or defeatist, but only truthful.

---

[36]Gunton, *Promise of Trinitarian Theology*, p. 80.
[37]Ibid., p. 81.
[38]Volf, *After Our Likeness*, p. 219.
[39]Ibid., p. 207.
[40]Gunton, *Promise of Trinitarian Theology*, p. 81.

The relationship between trinitarian communion and ecclesial communion ought not to be construed platonically, with the former the eternally perfected and the latter a second-rate copy. To think thus sells short the vivifying power of the Holy Spirit to breathe the communion of the Trinity upon otherwise earthen vessels.

Although Martin Buber is not a trinitarian, his philosophy of dialogue is not unlike perichoresis, with its stress on real meeting and "experiencing the other side of the relationship." Furthermore, Buber's God is "the Eternal Thou" in whom all lines of relationship converge. The mature Buber looked back many years to when he was eleven, reflecting on his daily meetings with a "broad dapple-grey horse," Buber's darling. Recalling that with Buber's I-Thou evocation the human and the nonhuman world can meet around the "Thou," he remembers "the still very fresh memory of my hand" that decades before had stroked his darling horse's neck and mane. "What I experienced in touch with the animal was the Other," Buber remembers, "the immense otherness of the Other, which, however, did not remain strange like the otherness of the ox and the ram, but rather let me draw near and touch it." Buber's horse was "really the Other itself; and yet it let me approach, confided itself in me, placed itself elementally in the relation of *Thou* and *Thou* with me."[41]

Buber's hand on the horse's neck was ecstatic; it lifted him outside of himself. But when one day Buber took note of the pleasure he received from the stroking ritual, he suddenly became conscious of his hand, and Buber's I-Thou knowing of his horse ceased, never to return.

The point of this equine parable is certainly not to compare God to a horse and still less that no pleasure should be taken when in the company of God. And yet the Otherness Buber received from the horse reminds us that the triune God always comes to us on his own terms, and that the meeting place of trinitarian communion and ecclesial communion is a meeting point of grace.

A TRINITARIAN FOCUS ON WORSHIP, PRAYER, SACRAMENTS

The deep structures and pervasive rhythms of trinitarian theology mean that no realm of Christian theology or spirituality falls outside

---

[41]Martin Buber, *Between Man and Man*, trans. Ronald Gregor Smith (New York: Macmillan, 1965), p. 23.

of trinitarian oversight and governance. From revelation to eschatology, from ecclesiology to the doctrine of creation, from pneumatology to christology, the Trinity is there. It is not so much a force to be reckoned with, although it may be that, as the formative reality behind and beyond which one cannot go.

It has been wisely said that the church has three main callings: to worship God, to nurture believers, to evangelize the world. Earlier in the book we touched on Christian spirituality as shaped by the Trinity, one component of which is to nurture believers, and now we examine the worship of God, including a trinitarian accounting of the Eucharist and baptism, the two sacraments agreed to by very nearly all Christians. Throughout our discussion we will be guided by Robert Jenson's assertion that unique among all Christian doctrines, the Trinity "is that doctrine which finally interprets all Christianity's claims about its verbal proclamation and sacraments."[42]

Whatever else divine worship may include, the proclamation of the gospel and the practice of the sacraments are crucial. To the extent that worship is defined and enacted in a trinitarian way, it is true worship. James B. Torrance defines trinitarian worship as "the gift of grace to participate through the Spirit in the incarnate Son's communion with the Father," a gift in marked contrast to human efforts to please God, which Torrance calls a Unitarian perspective on worship.[43] Sadly, many Christians mistake Unitarian worship for the real thing, because to worship thus can be immensely satisfying psychologically. Unitarian worship, for Torrance, "has no doctrine of the mediator or sole priesthood of Christ, is human-centered, has no proper doctrine of the Holy Spirit, is too often nonsacramental, and can engender weariness."[44] Unitarian worship fails every conceivable test that might be put to it: theological, sacramental, existential, ethical, communitarian. In fact, Unitarian worship can soon devolve to narcissism. But when worshipers receive the gift of trinitarian worship, "the Spirit lifts us out of any narcissistic preoccupation with ourselves to find our true humanity and dignity in Jesus Christ, in a life

---

[42]Robert W. Jenson, *Visible Words: The Interpretation and Practice of Christian Sacraments* (Philadelphia: Fortress, 1978), p. 32.

[43]James B. Torrance, *Worship, Community & the Triune God of Grace* (Downers Grove, Ill.: Inter-Varsity Press, 1996), p. 59. Cf. pp. 15, 30, 36, 107.

[44]Ibid., p. 20.

centered in others, in communion with Jesus Christ and one another, in a loving concern for the humanity of all."[45]

The adjective *Pelagian* may not often be affixed to *worship*, but cut off from the sustaining grace that "actually includes the provision of the very response demanded" by grace, Christian worship falls away into human-centered religious ritual.[46] This is the self-salvation scheme of Pelagianism translated into the terms of worship. Alan Torrance argues thus, keeping covenant with his father James B. Torrance and his uncle T. F. Torrance: "Worship is not some valiant subjective response," the younger Torrance asserts, because "Christian worship shares in a human-Godward movement that belongs to God and which takes place within the divine life."[47] Torrance sees the "form and content" of Christian worship as being "from above," so that "the Father is the author of worship, the Son the worshipper and the Spirit the agent of worship (where the worship may be identified with the presence of the Spirit)."[48]

A Protestant minister of a theologically conservative church was preparing to lead the Sunday morning pastoral prayer. Prior to prayer, he remarked: "I haven't had family altar recently," meaning a time when congregants may come to the front to kneel and pray during the pastoral prayer. While a casual remark should not be overinterpreted, what the pastor said rings a Pelagian and not trinitarian worship note. As a representative of all of the congregants the pastor should seldom, if ever, use the singular personal pronoun, because the pastor does not stand before God alone but as one of the priesthood of believers. The gathered speech of "ours" and "us" must take precedence over the self-regarding speech of "I" and "mine." Alan Torrance is correct: divine worship is so designated because it begins within the triune God, and only then moves to include humans. It is good when congregants gather to pray around the altar, but this particular means of invitation negated the truly trinitarian place of all Christian worship. Instead, it sounded more like a checklist from the pastoral study that needed to be satisfied.

The language of prayer is the language of worship. Christian prayer is today, even when carefully wrought and reverently voiced, more often

---

[45]Ibid., p. 107.
[46]Alan B. Torrance, *Persons in Communion: Trinitarian Description and Human Participation* (Edinburgh: T & T Clark, 1996), p. 314.
[47]Ibid.
[48]Ibid.

than not binitarian, prayer to the Father and through the Son, shelving the Spirit.[49] But of course the Holy Spirit is actually present in all prayer, even if not explicitly acknowledged, because Jesus Christ cannot be named Lord except in the Holy Spirit (1 Cor 12:3).[50]

To pray triunely is the perfect union of Christian theology and spirituality. Prayer that finds its true trinitarian footing is at the same time a deep theological exercise and the truest Christian doctrine. Christian prayer begins in boldness and ends in our being God's children. Jenson astutely explores trinitarian prayer:

> Christians dare address God, however others may do it, only because Jesus permits us to join *his* prayer, appropriating his unique filial term of address and relying on his fellowship in the prayer. We pray *to* "our Father." We pray *with* the one who, by uniquely addressing God as "my Father," makes himself the Son, and us as his adoptive siblings children, of his Father. Just so, we enter into the living personal community between them, that is, we pray *to* the Father, *with* the Son, *in* the Spirit.[51]

The exercise of a particular calling of prayer—the intercessory—becomes for Paul Fiddes and his pastoral understanding of the Trinity "an experience of connectedness and mutuality, because it is praying 'in God' who lives in relationships."[52] The Holy Spirit guides our prayer life to places and persons we could never reach on our own, and prayer as "supremely social" is in that regard an imitation of and a following after the social or the perichoretic God. "We enter into the life of prayer already going on within the communion of God's being," Fiddes believes; "we pray to the Father, through the Son and in the Spirit. This is why the everlasting God 'has time for us.'"[53]

This God who makes time for us is the one about whom humans theologize, and the act of theology is, in Jenson's nifty phrase, a "thinking what to say to be saying the gospel."[54] Forgiveness, reconciliation,

---

[49]Archimandrite Ephrem, "The Trinity in Contemporary Eucharistic Language," in *The Forgotten Trinity*, ed. Alasdair I. C. Heron (London: Council of Churches for Britain and Ireland, 1991), p. 50.

[50]Ibid., p. 52.

[51]Robert W. Jenson, *Systematic Theology*, vol. 1: *The Triune God* (New York: Oxford University Press, 1997), p. 37.

[52]Paul Fiddes, *Participating in God: A Pastoral Doctrine of the Trinity* (Louisville: Westminster John Knox Press, 2000), p. 123.

[53]Ibid.

[54]Jenson, *Systematic Theology*, p. 32.

holiness are all parts of what the gospel says. As the gospel proclaims and encourages communion, which is essential to gospel integrity and wholeness, three interrelated aspects of communion can be identified. All three are instinctively trinitarian, and all three invite human participation: (1) that between the Son and the Father *in* the Holy Spirit, (2) between Christ as the head of the body and the church, realized in the Spirit's utterance and the Eucharist, and (3) between the members of the body through life in the Spirit, as for example in Christian marriage (Eph 5:25-33).[55]

This desired communion is especially sustained and refined through the Eucharist, which "is the ongoing sacramental sign of communion."[56] Some communion liturgies begin with what has been called one of the clearest New Testament expressions of God's triunity, Paul's benediction to the Corinthians: "The grace of the Lord Jesus Christ, the love of God, and the communion of the Holy Spirit be with all of you" (2 Cor 13:13).[57] Launching the Eucharist from the triune premise serves, for Catherine LaCugna, to remind us "that God is not generically or abstractly God, but is the loving God who comes to us in Jesus Christ by the power of the Holy Spirit."[58] The Orthodox monk Archimandrite Ephrem is encouraged at renewed and ongoing efforts to understand "the mystery of the Eucharist as the revelation to us today of the mystery and presence of the Most Holy Trinity."[59]

Trinitarian mystery fills a stage as wide as all creation. Eucharistic mystery is therefore found not only within the rapt solitary worshiper, and not even as just the binding spirit knitting observant Christians into the eucharistic community. This mystery works in those ways, but at its widest reach is an entire ontology of the cosmos. The Eucharist articulates the primal triune reality. The relational ontology we have already noted in John Zizioulas, where "the basis of ontology is the person," is that which brings the worshiper into the company of the triune God.[60]

Zizioulas's eucharistic theology is splendidly layered, and its riches can only be hinted at here. In contradiction of much Protestant indi-

---

[55]Torrance, *Worship, Community & the Triune God of Grace*, p. 38.
[56]LaCugna, *God for Us*, p. 405.
[57]Ibid.
[58]Ibid.
[59]Ephrem, "Trinity in Contemporary Eucharistic Language," p. 61.
[60]Zizioulas, *Being as Communion*, p. 55.

vidualism, where one's selfhood is defined without regard for church affiliation, whether through one's upbringing, education, occupation or travel, to cite obvious examples, for Zizioulas one's selfhood cannot be *Christianly* defined outside of an ecclesial existence. And the truest expression of this ecclesial being is the Eucharist, which for Zizioulas is the pinnacle of the church's worship. He writes that "it was in the eucharist that the Church would contemplate her eschatological nature, would taste the very life of the Holy Trinity; in other words she would realize man's true being as image of God's own being."[61]

The church's eschatological quality, brought to sharpest focus in the Eucharist, allows the church to look two ways at once: back to the life, death and resurrection of Jesus Christ, and ahead to time as sacredly weighted and reckoned, time as "eucharized." This means that "the eucharist is thus the affirmation par excellence of history, the sanctification of time, by manifesting the Church as historical reality, as an *institution*."[62] Yet if the Eucharist sacralizes time, this means that the church is not only an institution. Rather than being conformed to the patterns of national and secular history, through the Eucharist the church is freed "from the causality of natural and historical events, from limitations which are the result of the individualism implied in our natural biological existence."[63] The church is constituted, is in effect created, by the celebration of the Eucharist. When the church eucharistically gathers, what unfolds is nothing less than "an event of free communion, prefiguring the divine life and the Kingdom to come," thereby overcoming the dichotomy between church as event and church as institution.[64]

Not every Christian tradition will embrace Zizioulas's ontology of the Eucharist. Yet all will acknowledge that the proper celebration of holy Communion brings the church into the company of the holy Trinity. The climax of any service of communion is the prayer of consecration, in liturgical churches often known as the Great Thanksgiving, which is addressed to both God and the congregation. In analyzing this prayer Robert Jenson finds its structure to be trinitarian.[65] The basic pattern

---

[61]Ibid., p. 21.
[62]Ibid., p. 22.
[63]Ibid.
[64]Ibid.
[65]Jenson, *Visible Words*, p. 94.

is doxology, or praise to God the Father, a recounting of the sacred history of Jesus Christ's redemptive act and the inviting or invoking of the Holy Spirit. The petition to "Send, O God, your Spirit" reminds us that "God the Spirit is God as the transforming power of the eschaton, now to be goal and judgment of what now is."[66] The Holy Spirit offers the world the hope already won by Jesus Christ through his cross and resurrection, and holds the accomplishments of the present age up to the scrutiny of this high standard.

The desired melding of trinitarian communion and ecclesial communion is seen as efficaciously in baptism as in the Eucharist. Baptism is the sacrament of initiation, through which the neophyte joins the ecclesial community. Jenson believes that "in the mission of the gospel, the decisive event is baptism."[67] Miroslav Volf exudes great hope that baptism is no formal ritual but is in fact the correspondence between trinitarian and ecclesial communion. When Christians are baptized they come to share in "concrete, anticipatory experiences" of "the one communion of the triune God and God's glorified people," made real by the Spirit's intervention.[68] Volf finds that Scriptures such as 1 Corinthians 12:4-6, 2 Corinthians 13:13 and Ephesians 4:4-6 reveal a parallel between the church's growing sense of its trinitarian shape and its understanding of God's triunity. He concludes that "if Christian initiation [baptism] is a trinitarian event, then the church must speak of the Trinity as its determining reality."[69]

What we have briefly taken up here—worship, prayer, Eucharist, baptism—are four compass points that taken together define the Christian devotional and spiritual life. They are not so much discrete indicators, prodding one to walk there but shun here, as they mark out the playing field where the communion shared by Father, Son and Spirit, trinitarian communion, can be realized and enacted as ecclesial communion.

Andrei Rublev's early fifteenth-century icon, "The Old Testament Trinity," is rightly hailed as one of the greatest icons of Eastern Orthodoxy. In Rublev's hands, the three visitors to Abraham and Sarah by the oaks of Mamre (Genesis 18) represent the persons of the Trinity. The

---

[66]Ibid., p. 95.
[67]Jenson, *Triune God*, p. 35.
[68]Volf, *After Our Likeness*, p. 195.
[69]Ibid.

three persons are ranged around a table, roughly equidistant from each other. We are made to understand that the figure on the left represents God the Father, probably because the gazes of the other two move in that direction, thus solidifying the general Orthodox point of the Father as "first among equals" and the principle of origination in the Godhead. The Son and the Holy Spirit are poised as to give the overall sense of perichoresis, the mutual regard of each for all and all for each.

The viewer is invited into the icon, ecstatically to join the divine life. This is salvation. Geoffrey Wainwright elaborates: "Salvation is to be drawn, in a way appropriate to creatures, into the very life of God, to be given by the graciousness of God a share in the communion of the divine persons."[70] Salvation is not a once-only simplicity but a continual immersion. This immersion is initiated and sustained sacramentally, and sacraments nourish the person's (*not* the individual's) progress into the life of God. Wainwright concludes:

> The sacramental sign of the beginning of that process is baptism in the name of the Father, the Son, and the Holy Spirit. In the Eucharist, the Holy Spirit touches us and the bread and wine so that we may receive the body and blood of Christ and so be included in the Son's self-gift to the Father. To the one God we cry, "Holy, holy, holy."[71]

---

[70]Geoffrey Wainwright, "Trinitarian Worship," in *Speaking the Christian God: The Holy Trinity and the Challenge of Feminism*, ed. Alvin F. Kimel Jr. (Grand Rapids: Eerdmans, 1992), p. 221.
[71]Ibid.

6

A Trinitarian Light on Christian Ethics

Charles Wesley reached to the final book of the Hebrew Scriptures to find a suitable signifier for the messianic age. Wesley's classic Christmas evocation "Hark! the Herald Angels Sing" mines Malachi 4:2 for its lovely metaphor of a rising sun and healing wings. No mere sun of fire but a sun of righteousness would rise, with deliverance in its wings. Wesley's appropriated metaphor is both universal and particular: the sun shines everywhere, on the just and the unjust, and yet in Christian terms this sun beams most brightly as the Holy Spirit shines and focuses and even harnesses its rays. This sun of righteousness is at the same time the only begotten Son of God, Jesus Christ, whose advent ushers in a new age of hope and peace.

In this chapter we will examine Christian ethics in a trinitarian light. Christian ethics is not the handmaid to some presumed theological superior, and yet Christian ethics is traditionally a theological discipline. Paul Tillich affirms that "theological ethics is an element of systematic theology, present in each of its parts."[1] Tillich knows that every theological statement, whatever it may be, necessarily has an ethical

---

[1]Paul Tillich, *Morality and Beyond* (New York: Harper & Row, 1963), p. 13.

element, even if often unspoken. Additionally, Christian ethics never turns its back on trends in the natural or social sciences, and listens when philosophical ethics speaks, but fundamentally Christian ethics is a theological task.

We observed earlier that trinitarian theology is not so much a particular theological conclusion that can be sealed off from other parts of the theological whole, but is rather the very best way of approaching and examining theology's vast terrain in an synoptic manner. That insight will serve us well in this chapter. More than exacting and definitive stopping points our thoughts may more closely resemble tentative and hopeful probes. We will wonder if the recent revival of trinitarian doctrine has bypassed ethical reflection. If not, then what refinement, gains and confirmations can Christian ethics take away from its conversation with trinitarian theology? For all of its argued and certain practicality, if trinitarian theology fails to leaven and complete Christian ethics, of what value is it? To slide the shoe on the other foot, could a close ethical examination conducted in its own house by trinitarian theology subtly shift certain theological protocols and priorities? Christian ethics and trinitarian theology may be a marriage made in heaven, but this marriage can only be consummated on earth.

I agree with Frans Jozef van Beeck's assertion that "doctrines arise in worship and witness, and must never be allowed to belie their pedigree; their key function is and remains to ensure worship and to enable witness."[2] Worship plus witness is one approximation to Christian ethics. Immanuel Kant was famously rapt by the starry skies above and the moral law within, but can any divine Lawgiver really compel worship? The ethics of the greatest happiness of the greatest number, otherwise known as the teleological principle of utilitarianism, may for some people create the perfect society. But is the ethic of utilitarianism an ethic of witness, to say nothing of an ethic of suffering and redemption? In neither Kant's duty ethics of the categorical imperative, often called the deontological approach to ethics, nor utilitarianism do we find worship and witness so seamlessly joined.

Christian ethics, as its very name implies, must take with great seriousness the ethics of Jesus Christ. Accordingly, it has been more cus-

---

[2]Frans Jozef van Beeck, "Trinitarian Theology as Participation," in *The Trinity*, ed. Stephen Davis, Daniel Kendall and Gerald O'Collins (New York: Oxford University Press, 1999), p. 313.

tomary to describe ethics as "christocentric" than as trinitarian. Paul Ramsey's mid-century work *Basic Christian Ethics* envisions Christian ethics as rooted in Jesus Christ, and therefore as being more than just theocentric, but Ramsey did not push on to a trinitarian conclusion:

> Christian ethics stands therefore in decisive relation to Jesus Christ for the strenuous measure taken of human obligation. As a consequence, Christocentric ethics contrasts both with humanism's cutting the pattern to fit man and also with any religious or mystical ethics which may indeed be theocentric and pious enough but in a general or cosmic sense not historically related to this particular man, Christ Jesus.[3]

There is no competition in naming Christian ethics where "christocentric" must necessarily yield to "trinitarian." It is in fact difficult to define "christocentric" without constant reference to the Trinity. Paul Lehmann is correct to claim that "the doctrine of the Trinity is the most comprehensive statement of the christological dogma."[4] While Paul Tillich's thoughts on the Trinity are not conventional, because always controlled by his philosophical priorities, he yet agrees with Lehmann, stating that "the Christian doctrine of the Trinity is a corroboration of the christological dogma."[5] Christology would be woefully unfinished without the doctrine of the Trinity, having no real way to speak believably about the divinity of Jesus Christ. In that same sense every christocentric ethics has the seeds of a trinitarian ethics within. Gregory Jones believes that while "the moral life should receive its decisive specification in the person and work of Jesus Christ," to live morally is a more complicated matter than merely following Jesus Christ, which can be reduced to an ethical humanism.[6] Any christocentric ethics must be cultivated in the direction of a trinitarian ethics, for a trinitarian ethics adds dimensions, possibilities and complexities unknown to an exclusively christocentric ethics.

To say this is not to usurp the role Jesus Christ has historically carried for Christian ethics. As Ramsey knows, the particularity of the man

---

[3]Paul Ramsey, *Basic Christian Ethics* (New York: Charles Scribner's Sons, 1950), p. 23, partially quoted in James M. Gustafson, *Ethics from a Theocentric Perspective, Volume Two: Ethics and Theology* (Chicago: University of Chicago Press, 1984), p. 87.

[4]Paul Lehmann, *Ethics in a Christian Context* (New York: Harper & Row, 1963), p. 105.

[5]Paul Tillich, *Systematic Theology* (Chicago: University of Chicago Press, 1967), 1:250.

[6]L. Gregory Jones, *Transformed Judgment: Toward a Trinitarian Account of the Moral Life* (Notre Dame, Ind.: University of Notre Dame Press, 1990), p. 74.

Jesus Christ ought always to be kept in view, although this particularity always opens up to the expansive trinitarian view. Joe DiMaggio's stellar baseball statistics are an impressive record standing alone, but astoundingly so in light of winning ten American League pennants and nine World Series crowns in a career lasting only thirteen years, with three additional years given to World War II duty. To think of DiMaggio is to think of the New York Yankees; to think of the Bronx Bombers in the years 1936-1951 is to think of DiMaggio. The man and the team are inseparable.

The ethics of Jesus Christ may be trivialized if his moral sense is reduced to an especially vigorous execution of team-playing, because the perfectly realized community of the three-in-one God strictly speaking has no human analogies. Yet human metaphors may crack open a little light on divine mysteries. Jesus Christ never claimed to be a self-made Savior. "I can do nothing on my own," declared Jesus, "because I seek to do not my own will but the will of him who sent me" (Jn 5:30). Jesus Christ was no empty robe wandering around the Galilean countryside, picking up moral cues on the cheap. His Jewish heritage may have grounded his moral vision, but this vision was truly effectuated as a calling from his Father enabled by the Holy Spirit.

Is the way to develop a christocentric ethics into a fully trinitarian one simply to add the Holy Spirit? The significance of the Holy Spirit for Jesus' own moral awareness and accomplishment cannot be ignored. Edward Long's careful compendium of Christian ethics, *A Survey of Christian Ethics*, has dozens of references to Jesus Christ but only one to the Holy Spirit. Athanasius, in the explanation of Paul Lehmann, eloquently explained the relationship between God the Father and his Son, but left to others, notably Ambrose and Augustine, to flesh out the Holy Spirit's significance for the Trinity. However, the history of subsequent Christian theology sadly suggests that the theology of the Holy Spirit "is largely an unfinished assignment."[7] Lehmann's own project is what he calls a koinonia ethics, which must answer this question: "What am I, as a believer in Jesus Christ and as a member of his church, to do?" This ethic "can only be faithful to its messianic occasion and character upon a trinitarian foundation."[8] Furthermore, in contrast to a general

---

[7]Lehmann, *Ethics in a Christian Context*, p. 106.
[8]Ibid., pp. 45, 111.

or philosophical ethics, Lehmann insists that "Christian ethics . . . is oriented toward revelation and not toward morality."[9] A christocentric and a trinitarian ethics are therefore in the hands of Lehmann a seamless whole.

AN IMPLICITLY TRINITARIAN ETHICS

Many pertinent questions might be asked of any Christian ethics in order to gauge the overall shape, force and direction of the ethical proposals. How are the biblical materials handled? What is the relationship between Christian ethics and philosophical ethics? What is the balance between ethical thinking and action, between theory and practice? What are the direct and implied ties between the ethical formulations and more particularly theological ideas, especially christology and ecclesiology? These several questions, to suggest only the most obvious, promote the sort of dialogue between Christian ethics and broader theological inquiry that will be mutually enriching. Since trinitarian theology makes itself felt everywhere the theologian works, the conversation between Christian ethics and theology will illumine how and why a Christian ethics can be a trinitarian ethics.

Joseph Sittler's small book of three lectures, *The Structure of Christian Ethics*, appeared fifty years ago. This "creative little book,"[10] from a preacher-theologian who was "a poet at heart,"[11] is probably mistitled, if by "structure" one expects to find "a fully developed scheme of logically interrelated categories and subcategories."[12] Sittler's presentation answers either directly or indirectly the several questions posed in the previous paragraph. He does so in a way that might be called "implicitly trinitarian." His work is trinitarian more in the way of the seed growing secretly (Mk 4:26-29) than the shouting stones (Lk 19:40) that cannot abide the Pharisaic shutting of the disciples' mouths.

God is, in Sittler's understanding, supremely a relational God. Human life and the life of God are for Sittler "so organically related that nothing but misunderstanding can arise by treating them separately from each

---

[9]Ibid., p. 45.

[10]James M. Gustafson, *Ethics from a Theocentric Perspective*, vol. 1: *Theology and Ethics* (Chicago: University of Chicago Press, 1981), p. 49.

[11]Franklin Sherman, introduction to *The Structure of Christian Ethics* by Joseph Sittler (Louisville: Westminster John Knox, 1998), p. xii

[12]Ibid., p. ix.

other," in Edward Long's explanatory phrase.[13] Hence a better title for Sittler's work might have been *Christian Ethics Organically*. He takes "a radically theocentric and radically christocentric approach to Christian ethics, yet one that was open also to input from a wide range of secular thought."[14] His tastes in secular thought often run toward the literary, among his favorite authors being Boccaccio, Cervantes, Montaigne, Blake, Hardy, Jane Austin, Hawthorne, Melville, Eliot, Cummings, Shaw and Tennessee Williams.[15] The lone female on Sittler's reading table, Jane Austin, is for Sittler "an instance of the fundamentally ethical nature of the craft of the artist."[16] While the artist may not proclaim the gospel directly, it is to the artist that everyone looks for the truth about "the human dilemma."

Sittler's ethics is so far removed from legalism, stating the case for relational ethics "as colorfully and as radically" as anyone, that people have wondered if he is a situation ethicist.[17] An episode Sittler lifts from the novel *The Cruel Sea* would for some paint Sittler as a situationist. He ponders the choice facing the commander of a destroyer that is protecting a fleet of commercial vessels. In an instant the commander must decide whether or not to destroy a submarine that has recently wreaked havoc, that has already sunk many of the merchant ships and forfeited hundreds of lives. The commander's dilemma? If he takes out the submarine he will at the same moment kill hundreds of men hanging on to life preservers, victims of the submarine's previous attacks. Sittler explains that "there was but an instant to make his choice, and the commander made it knowing that no choice available could be anything but death-dealing."[18] "One must do what one must do—and say one's prayers" is Sittler's description of the commander's postdecision mindset, and this "is an eloquent condensation of the ethical situation."[19]

But does this fondness for using literary episodes to make ethical points that Sittler's shares with Joseph Fletcher, author of *Situation Eth-*

---

[13]Edward LeRoy Long Jr., *A Survey of Christian Ethics* (New York: Oxford University Press, 1967), p. 143.

[14]Sherman, "Introduction," p. x.

[15]Sittler, *Structure of Christian Ethics*, p. 17.

[16]Ibid., pp. 20-21.

[17]Long, *Survey of Christian Ethics*, p. 126.

[18]Sittler, *Structure of Christian Ethics*, p. 83. Long mentions this story in *Survey of Christian Ethics*, pp. 296-97.

[19]Sittler, *Structure of Christian Ethics*, p. 83.

ics, make Sittler a situationist? Franklin Sherman does not think so. Unlike Fletcher, Sittler refuses to reduce everything to love as the chief deciding factor. This was Fletcher's strategy. For Sittler, love can never become its own absolute, and is "never commanded for its own sake." That is because there can be only one absolute, God, who gives to love such strength as it has. Sittler believes that "the strength of love is in the love of God and the love of the neighbor in God."[20]

True to his Lutheran heritage and its valuation of faith, in distinction to Fletcher, Sittler posits a profound interplay between faith and love, which in the New Testament are never "alternative or opposing terms." Sittler closes his second lecture with this deep analysis of how faith and love intertwine: "Faith is the name for the new God-relationship whereby the will of God, who himself establishes the relationship, is made actual. And that will is love. Faith active in love is alone faith; and love is the function of faith horizontally just as prayer is the function of faith vertically."[21]

Edward Long correctly assesses that "the language of faith is relational, not imperative"[22] for Sittler. If the "organic" more than the "structured" is the best description of Sittler's overall thrust, it is because of his attention to "engendering," as in the engendering deed, and the concomitant engendered response. Hence the language of faith, in Long's description, "is constantly engendered, continuously elicited," for it "presupposes an intimate relationship between two persons."[23]

The "two persons" referenced by Long are the human and the divine. Sittler himself uses organic language in describing how the human stands perpetually before the divine, awaiting a holy impress.

> The organic content of Jesus' address to men was not composed of highly personal epigrams consensed *[sic]* from the most elegant moral idealism ever envisioned by man in his quest for the good. This content was constituted, rather, by a lived-out and heroically obedient God-relationship in the fire of which all things are what they are by virtue of the Creator, all decisions are crucial in virtue of their witness to his primacy and glory, all events interpreted in terms of their transparency, recalcitrancy, or service to God's Kingly rule.[24]

---

[20]Ibid., p. 44.
[21]Ibid., p. 64.
[22]Long, *Survey of Christian Ethics*, p. 127.
[23]Ibid.
[24]Sittler, *Structure of Christian Ethics*, p. 12.

While Sittler is not here deriding the "elegant moral idealism" of philosophical ethics, any ethics that arises from an engendering God and returns to God through an engendered response is a Christian and not a philosophical ethics, for only the Christian God *engenders*. Here is how James Gustafson describes Sittler's foundational idea:

> The Christian life is conformity to, re-enactment of, the shape of the en-gendering deed. But the shape that is re-enacted is the shape of the *deed* that engenders our re-enactment, and thus *engenders* our deed. We are conformed to that by which we are formed. We act or do in accordance with that which enacts or enables us. In this sense, Christian ethics is Christological.[25]

If Sittler's trinitarian profile is more implied than expressed, what can be done to bring out the trinitarian provenance of his Christian ethics? We must connect the dots among Father, Son and Spirit in ways Sittler would approve. The Holy Spirit needs particular atten-tion here. He is underrepresented. Yet not absent. On the penultimate page of his book Sittler advises that "the Christian is to accept what God gives as Holy Spirit the Sanctifier."[26] The Christian awaits the Holy Spirit's giving not as a mute piece of wax but as a pliant recep-tacle. This is a holy passivity that is in line with the New Testament ethos. Sittler avers that "the passive verb dominates the New Testa-ment story! I love because I am loved; I know because I am known; I am of the Church, the body of Christ, because this body became my body; I can and must forgive because I have been forgiven; I can speak because I have been spoken to."[27]

Two things must be noted here. For one, Sittler's stress on the passiv-ity of waiting before God is as far removed from apathy as the East from the West. One Lutheran theologian, Sittler, was remembering another, Kierkegaard, when the American Lutheran said, "The continuity of the love wherewith we are loved and the love which we are commanded to exercise, passes through the passion of faith."[28] Here Long's summa-tion of Sittler as "talking about a state or condition of life, not about a

---

[25]James M. Gustafson, *Christ and the Moral Life* (Chicago: University of Chicago Press, 1979), pp. 174-75.
[26]Sittler, *Structure of Christian Ethics*, p. 87.
[27]Ibid., p. 11.
[28]Ibid., p. 62.

group of opinions or even a mere decision of the will" is appropriate.[29] Christian ethics is not a piecemeal grab bag of moral choices that can be plugged into arising moral situations. It is the deep orientation of the soul toward the God who engenders.

The engendering God is the second reality we must note. Engenderment, if the term be allowed, describes the God who engenders, who creates the engendering deed, in whose presence humans are called toward the engendered response. In one theological word, the engendering deed is the incarnation. This is nothing less than the gospel of God, as Sittler knows:

> The story says that God has acted for man's healing, that this action became concrete in an Incarnation, that in consequence human life has available a new relation to God, a new light for seeing, a new fact and center for thinking, a new ground for forgiving and loving, a new context for acting in this world.[30]

The clear christological contour of Sittler's ethics should not throw us off the trinitarian track. A well articulated christology can be one of the building blocks of the doctrine of the Trinity. The career of Jesus Christ, demonstrating as it does "the total self-giving of God,"[31] is a career offered up to God the Father through the reality of the Holy Spirit. Sittler's avowedly christological ethics is at the same time a fully trinitarian ethics. It is not as if the Holy Spirit is a missing ingredient, needing to be added to the batch to complete the recipe. No, surely the Holy Spirit is already present whenever Jesus Christ is found. The Spirit may be the hidden ingredient, but he is never the missing ingredient.

Of the many words that seem to be the equal of "engenders," none quite rises to its unique summit. "God's deed does not simply call," Sittler believes, "or present a pattern in front of, or evoke, or demonstrate. It *engenders*; that is, it brings into existence lives bred by its originative character."[32] Sittler's last two words may harken back to a distant theological time and place, when appeals to the immanent Trinity were somehow more urgent and expected and therefore compelling than they are today. At that time, how the triune God expressed his "origi-

---

[29]Long, *Survey of Christian Ethics*, p. 144.
[30]Sittler, *Structure of Christian Ethics*, pp. 17-18.
[31]Ibid., p. 29.
[32]Ibid., p. 25.

native character" was inescapably necessary to begin to know God's complexity. Within the immanent Trinity, God the Father was the principle of origination of the Godhead, God the Son being eternally generated as the Word of the Father, with the Holy Spirit proceeding, being breathed or in the technical term *spirated*, from the Father and through the Son, to use the ecumenical phrase of consensus favored by Eastern Orthodoxy and becoming increasingly accepted throughout the entire Christian world.

What might "originative character" mean for Christian ethics? Is this to say that any Christian ethics aiming to be fully trinitarian *must* begin with the immanent Trinity? This is unlikely, yet acknowledging the importance of the immanent Trinity serves to illustrate the point made earlier by Paul Molnar, that is, that trinitarian reflection, whether it be theological or ethical, begins with the economy of salvation, which then can take one to the immanent Trinity and back again to the economy. Sittler has a very firm grip indeed on what happens in the economy of salvation: "What God gives is the theme of the Bible. This going out from Himself in creative and redemptive action toward men is, within the Bible itself, the basic meaning of the *Word of God*."[33] Sittler does not here interpret the "Word of God" in an incarnational or trinitarian way, but such a meaning is consistent with his enduring arguments in *The Structure of Christian Ethics*.

However inelegant or elegant a restaurant may be, its menu says a great deal about its priorities: culinary, clientele, market niche, reputation and so forth. Whatever a restaurant intends to be, the menu is of first consequence. It expresses the desires of the restaurant's owners or originators. A theological analogy may be apt. In the same way that every menu item participates in the overall menu coherence, from appetizer to entrée to dessert to drinks, every theological doctrine participates in the theological coherence of Christian belief, which necessarily is marked out and fulfilled in God's triunity. No theological doctrine may willingly absent itself from its obligation to represent and be found in God's triunity.

To shift the analogy to Joseph Sittler's work, how does his unifying idea of the engendering God serve to congregate the rest of his ethical proposals? More to the point, how is God's being triune reflected

---

[33]Ibid.

and demonstrated in how God engenders? Sittler's view of biblical reality coincides with God's triunity. In the Bible there are no dangling modifiers or freely roaming separate realities. Biblical reality is God's reality. Every ethics perforce addresses and accounts for humanity and nature. However a philosophical ethics may choose to ground these two, Sittler sees that "in the Bible [they are] but aspects of a single actuality, God himself."[34]

As already remarked, the biblical God is supremely relational, not in parallel form with the created order, as is true of so much of process theology, but organically sovereign over creation, such that human existence "is a subsistence."[35] When Sittler allows that the "radical vocabulary of relatedness characterizes every primary term of the Bible," he is not asserting any sort of human equality with God.[36] He is saying, however, that the human enterprise is to be inescapably relational. God's creation of Eve is not so much about what Eve can do to secure the future of the human race as to prove "that a solitary person is no person," the whole point of human life being "for organic relation to God . . . [and] also for organic relation to other persons."[37] To find oneself among those so described as "the called" or "the household of faith" is at the same time to delight in membership in the church as the body of Christ. It is also to realize there can be no final distinction between personal and social ethics.[38]

It is how the biblical God relates to the world and its inhabitants, organically so, that connects God's engendering with God's triunity. No abstract principles, no general rules, not even a structured legality marks Sittler's God. How God is in the world is totally consonant with God in Christ. This is the content of Christian ethics.[39] The kenotic or "emptying-out" christology of Philippians 2:6-11 is how Jesus Christ relates to his Father, and here we are called to imitate Jesus. Remembering that the engendering God expects an engendered response, the kenotic christology with its "enactment-reenactment" structure is "go thou and do likewise." In the light of Philippians 2 we can see that "the ripples

---

[34]Ibid., p. 4.
[35]Ibid., p. 5.
[36]Ibid.
[37]Ibid.
[38]Ibid., pp. 65-66.
[39]Ibid., p. 72.

of life's concrete decisions are continuous with the huge tidal wave of God's will in Christ."[40]

The engendering God is at the same time the God of mutual indwelling, the God of perichoresis. The God of ethical motion is the same as the God of theological motion. In both cases the motion is ultimately other oriented. The coming and going of perichoresis amounts to, with all due respect, divine effacement, for God's oneness is only deepened when Father, Son and Spirit enter into one another. By his engendering love, God compels human obedience to what he has already done, obedience to God first and then to the neighbor. The end of the ethical life therefore becomes not justice, for justice answers only to human aspirations. At such time that justice submits itself to "the creative and restorative will of God" justice enters the realm of righteousness. But righteousness is a life beyond ordinary justice, for the righteous life is "sprung from, determined by, and accountable to the life of God. It is a thoroughly theonomous term."[41]

THE ETHICS OF RESPONSIBILITY

Although not as renowned as his brother Reinhold Niebuhr, H. Richard Niebuhr is by any stretch one of the outstanding Christian thinkers of the twentieth century. His richly textured work is by turns theological, historical and ethical, always with a view toward cultural engagement and critique. The brief attention we will now devote to several of his works attests to Niebuhr's ongoing interest in the doctrine of the Trinity. In *Christ and Culture*, a monumental twentieth-century work on Christian ethics, his sporadic inclusion of the Trinity is a veiled testimony to the Trinity's impact on Christian moral formulation. Analytically, Niebuhr employs the Trinity especially in the "Christ Against Culture" paradigm, using a trinitarian lens to interpret Tertullian's ethical thought, as well as in the "Christ of Culture," chiding liberalism for its underdeveloped ethics that identifies Jesus Christ "with the immanent divine spirit that works in man."[42] A full-blown trinitarianism would stand to convince liberalism "that it is not possible honestly to confess that Jesus is the Christ of culture unless one can confess much more than this," namely, his appointment by God the Father and how

---

[40]Ibid., p. 38.
[41]Ibid., p. 78.
[42]H. Richard Niebuhr, *Christ and Culture* (New York: Harper Torchbooks, 1956), pp. 81, 114.

the Holy Spirit judges and winnows other spirits who animate and preserve a culture.[43] For the liberal who sees in Jesus Christ the conservator of culture, the Son's relation to his Father "is ultimately no speculative question . . . but [the] fundamental problem."[44] The doctrine of the Trinity is the answer to the question of how Jesus Christ relates to God his Father. This relationship is wrought through the Holy Spirit.

The Meaning of Revelation, which predates *Christ and Culture* by a decade, offers scant yet significant reference to the Trinity. In this work Niebuhr sees revelation as relational, as unfolding historically and in its unfolding judging humankind, realms, thrones and dominions, but decidedly not relativistic, meaning a cynical sameness where every divine pretense is equal to every other. For Niebuhr, God the Father "met us not as the one beyond the many but as the one who acts in and through all things, not as the unconditioned but as the conditioner."[45] God the Father transvalues or reverses values, not as Friedrich Nietzsche would have it but according to God's transcendent yet immanent purposes: "For him our last things are first and our first things last."[46]

Philosophically and culturally rooted wisdom offers glimpses of the divine unity, but the doctrine of the Trinity is for Niebuhr the best expression of this unity. Niebuhr is not nearly the trinitarian zealot that Karl Barth is, and as an articulation of the unity of God, Niebuhr suggests that "the doctrine of the Trinity is no satisfactory or final formulation" of this unity.[47] Yet the theology of the Trinity is even so the clearest glimpse into God's nature we are likely to get. This doctrine, writes Niebuhr,

> is more satisfactory than all the ancient and the modern pantheons wherein we ascend beyond the many gods or values to someone who is limited by them. The unity of the God who appears as Father, Son and Holy Spirit is not the unity which we conceive as the common source and spirit of beauty, truth and goodness, especially not as we conceive truth, beauty and goodness in our own image. And so the oneness which the God of Jesus Christ demands in us is not the integration of our purposes and values but our integrity, singleness of mind and purity of heart.[48]

---

[43]Ibid., p. 115.
[44]Ibid., pp. 114-15.
[45]H. Richard Niebuhr, *The Meaning of Revelation* (New York: Macmillan, 1941), p. 183.
[46]Ibid., p. 184.
[47]Ibid.
[48]Ibid., pp. 184-85.

In contrast to pantheons both ancient and modern, into which humans may ascend by strenuous effort, the triune God simply appears, his appearance being its own announcement and validation. The Greek triad of the Good, the True and the Beautiful is not the measure of value, because this triad is inevitably corrupted when expressed through human deeds. Even the sincere consolidating of human virtue is shy of trinitarian value because "singleness of mind and purity of heart" are not so much human attainment as divine bestowment.

Humanistic ethics concocts truth, beauty and goodness in the human image, and may even reach to "the integration of our purposes and values." Seen from a strictly human vantage, nobility and high purpose may attend upon this morality. But the ethics granted by, or really *demanded* by, the gift of revelation is the ethics of the single mind and the pure heart. Niebuhr calls us to imitate within ourselves the unity shared among Father, Son and Holy Spirit. This unity is at the same moment both *demand* and *gift*.

Niebuhr's desire to give to the theological world his definitive statement on Christian ethics was thwarted by his 1962 death, but *The Responsible Self* (1963) strides significantly in that direction. This book is not avowedly and intentionally trinitarian, but Niebuhr's awareness of a trinitarian impress on Christian ethics is never far from view. James Gustafson's introductory comments root Niebuhr's theology biblically and hence trinitarianly also. Explaining what is foundational for Niebuhr, Gustafson writes that

> it is in Scripture that we find the trinitarian pattern which is indispensable for understanding the ultimate authority for man's moral existence. God is disclosed as the Creator—the one in whom power is manifest, but goodness is uncertain. He is disclosed in the Son, as God with us—the one in whom goodness is present, but power is dubious. He is disclosed in the Holy Spirit—the one whose presence is manifest, but whose ultimate nature is shrouded in mystery.[49]

This summative statement is more theological than ethical, which is at it should be, because as Gustafson notes, "Christian ethics starts with Christian beliefs."[50] This statement is not reversible, in the same

---

[49]James Gustafson, introduction to *The Responsible Self* by H. Richard Niebuhr (New York: Harper & Row, 1963), pp. 24-25.
[50]Ibid., p. 14.

way that "God is love" (1 Jn 4:8, 16) cannot become "love is God." Theology ponders the nature and activity of God; ethics plumbs the depths of the human response to who God is, what God expects and how God enables our turning toward him expectantly.[51]

The set of lectures that appear in modified form in *The Responsible Self,* and bear *An Essay in Christian Moral Philosophy* as the subtitle, are psychologically informed, philosophically astute and theologically cogent. The definition of trinitarian theology need not be compromised or arbitrarily stretched to find in Niebuhr both a settled profundity and a springboard for further reflection. A half-century ago, emergent psychological trends summarized as "interactional" by Niebuhr were coming to influence perspectives on politics, economics, education and religion.[52]

Niebuhr's great gift may be to simplify complex ideas, to synthesize masses of data and interpretation into believable paradigms, which may then be critiqued, refined or validated, as the case may require. The linchpin of Niebuhr's argument is clearly the idea of responsibility, which across the ages and cultures has never had one fixed meaning. How could it?

As Niebuhr strives to rein in the abundance of meanings attached to responsibility, to make this idea "useful for the understanding of our self-action," he employs four rich words or phrases to clarify this crucial concept.[53] Responsibility happens within the matrix of *response, interpretation, accountability* and *social solidarity.*[54] Any action lifted up for moral scrutiny will necessarily engage all four elements of Niebuhr's definition. The Beatitudes of Matthew chapter five are not meant to be followed piecemeal or occasionally, but *all* nine "blessed ares" must be striven after at all times. So also are the four marks of responsibility to be taken as a whole, although one or two of the four marks may be more decisively applied to any given complex of actions than are the others.

If "what shall I do?" is the primal moral question, Niebuhr knows that two answers have been proposed historically. Teleological or utilitarian ethics fixes on "what is my goal, ideal, or telos?" Here the "my goal" is

---

[51]Ibid., p. 40.
[52]Niebuhr, *Responsible Self,* p. 57.
[53]Ibid., p. 61.
[54]Ibid., pp. 61-65.

not necessarily self-serving egotistically, because utilitarian ethics is after all "the greatest happiness for the greatest number," but in reality a teleological ethic often devolves into egotism. For the deontologist the corresponding danger is legalism. Strict adherence to the deontologist's guiding question, "what is the law and what is the first law of my life?" may eclipse other moral lights such as reason, emotion, tradition and happiness. In contrast to both utilitarianism and deontologism, the way of responsibility asks the disarming question, "What is going on?"

Marvin Gaye's great collection of songs released by the Motown label in 1971, *What's Going On*, may not have been done in homage to Niebuhr's identifying phrase for the ethics of responsibility. But when Gaye described the goal of his songs as causing listeners "to take a look at what was happening in the world," this was a tacit endorsement of the ethics of responsibility.[55] "What is going on?" blends rather seamlessly with another 1960s phrase: "What is happening?"

From his post at Yale Divinity School Niebuhr was not trying to dictate the rhythms of pop culture, but his phrase presciently pointed to the decade ahead, the 1960s. If each of these three ethical approaches can be summarized using only one word, then teleology is all about the *good*, deontology the *right*, and the ethics of responsibility the *fitting*.[56]

AN UNLIKELY TRINITY? ATTICUS FINCH, TOM ROBINSON AND BOO RADLEY

One can discern the ethics of the fitting in Harper Lee's only novel, *To Kill a Mockingbird*, which appeared in 1960, toward the end of Niebuhr's life. The moral center of this Southern novel is the attorney Atticus Finch, whom Lee modeled after her own father, a small-town attorney and newspaper man.[57] The match between A. C. Lee and Atticus Finch was not perfect, however. Lee's biographer notes that "Mr. Lee himself only gradually rose to the moral standards of Atticus."[58] A. C. Lee was of such a mind as was not uncommon to his time and place, to accept

---

[55] Marvin Gaye, quoted in *Rolling Stone: The 500 Greatest Albums of All Time*, ed. Joe Levy (New York: Wenner, 2005), p. 21.

[56] Niebuhr, *Responsible Self*, p. 60.

[57] Charles J. Shields presents evidence that the novelist drew on knowing her father to flesh out the character of Atticus Finch (*Mockingbird: A Portrait of Harper Lee* [New York: Henry Holt, 2006], pp. 44-45, 120-21, 185, 215, 229).

[58] Ibid., p. 121.

a sharp division between personal salvation and social justice, even to the point of acquiescing in the face of racial segregation.[59] Harper Lee's family had worshiped for generations in the mainline Methodist church of Monroeville, Alabama, where to one degree or other the antislavery—and by extension the antisegregation—teachings of Methodist founder John Wesley had been summarily ignored.

In the novel Atticus defends the African American Tom Robinson against the charge of raping the white girl Mayella Ewell. We do not know as much as we would like about how Atticus Finch was morally formed, but seemingly his vision of social justice was a generation or two advanced beyond that of his creator's father. As an attorney the strictures of the deontological way of law and obligation no doubt lodged in his mind. The communitarian good promised by the teleological approach was also necessarily a moral motivator.

Yet the ethical layers exposed and engaged and contemplated in Lee's masterwork, which for some readers is second only to the Bible as morally consequential, are best accounted for by the ethics of responsibility. Better than either deontology or teleology, the four components of responsibility—response, interpretation, accountability, social solidarity—integrate and illuminate *Mockingbird*. This is especially true considering that *Mockingbird*'s narrator is Atticus's girl, Scout, who is learning her moral bearings at a tender age.

Niebuhr's academic definition of responsibility, that it is "the idea of an agent's action as response to an action upon him in accordance with his interpretation of the latter action and with his expectation of response to his response; and all of this is in a continuing community of agents," can be applied to any of the major characters in Lee's novel.[60] This may sound like the domino theory of morality, where every action effects every other action, and in turn receives its effect, but it is not. It is closer to the symbiotic theory, wherein every action hangs together in a relational web with every other.

It is in Atticus Finch that Niebuhr's vision of responsibility most fully springs to life. He is not omniscient—it just seems so—bolstered by his daily reading of at least four newspapers. Atticus's knowledge is cagey,

---

[59]Ibid., pp. 121-22, documents A. C. Lee's conservatism regarding questions of race and social justice.

[60]Niebuhr, *Responsible Self*, p. 65.

measured and appropriate. He could apply it circumstantially at just the right moment. At length, Scout gathers that her father "knew a lot more about something than we thought he knew."[61] He surprises Scout and her older brother, Jem, by dropping a rabid dog with one shot, revalidating his best-in-county marksmanship with one squeeze of the trigger. As the novel closes, Atticus stands watch over Jem, drifting in and out of consciousness, gathering his strength after a vicious attack from Mayella's vengeful father, Bob Ewell, who was humiliated by Atticus at Tom Robinson's trial and who exacts revenge on Scout and Jem, too cowardly to confront Atticus on manly terms. Atticus "turned out the light and went into Jem's room. He would be there all night, and he would be there when Jem waked up in the morning."[62] Not unlike God the Father, Atticus never sleeps, certainly not while the well-being of his son hangs in the balance.

Niebuhr's four defining criteria of responsibility are incarnated in Atticus Finch. Unexpectedly widowed, Atticus eschews the easy remarriage option to close in solidarity with his children, realizing that his African American cook and housekeeper Calpurnia would do right by his children. After all, Calpurnia speaks two languages, the Negro vernacular of her people who live proudly and tidily in a little settlement beyond the town's garbage dump, and the finessed cadences expected in a professional home like Atticus's.[63] The "bilingual" raising of Scout and Jem is safe in Calpurnia's expert hands.

Atticus's largest challenge, of course, was one he had never sought, a court-appointed date to defend Tom Robinson, the judicial protocol of handing such a case to a rookie lawyer having been set aside. In this defense Atticus weaves Niebuhr's four strands of response, interpretation, accountability and social solidarity into a powerfully redemptive cord. Jem and Scout's presence among Tom Robinson's people in the courtroom balcony, unknown to Atticus but tacitly endorsed by him, represents the attorney's solidarity with those who need the defense of the law. After the crushing verdict against Tom, which Atticus pledges to appeal, Jem draws the line between the children of light and the children of darkness: "can't any Christian judges an' lawyers make up for heathen juries."[64]

---

[61]Harper Lee, *To Kill a Mockingbird,* 40th anniv. ed. (New York: Harper Collins, 1999), p. 279.
[62]Ibid., p. 323.
[63]Ibid., p. 143.
[64]Ibid., p. 247.

Harper Lee surely had in mind the character of Tom Robinson as exemplifying the harmless mockingbird that for its plangent yet hopeful song should never be harmed. Yet the elusive Boo Radley, who stuck a kitchen knife in Bob Ewell's ribs to save Scout and Jem as they returned home from a school pageant on a balmy Halloween night, is also the mockingbird. The frightfully reclusive Boo, whose given name is Arthur, comes out of his home only when he wants to; a quarter-century may lapse between manifestations.[65]

Atticus Finch, Tom Robinson and Boo Radley are so far from being a holy *Mockingbird* trinity that it may take a lot of literary imagination for them to rise even to the level of a triad. Certainly Atticus, Tom and Boo are three. But are they one? Not in any specifically trinitarian sense of unity around a common single story line, as is true with the economy of salvation and God the Father, God the Son and God the Spirit. We have noted that both Tom and Boo are the mockingbird in the flow of the novel, but they are strangers to one another, and the two presences who could most likely unite them, Jem and Scout, are deeply enamored of Boo, if not always for the right reasons, and deeply troubled, especially Jem, by the injustice suffered by Tom. But Jem and Scout have no reason to bring Tom and Boo together, and in Lee's novel Tom and Boo are less like two sides of the same narrative coin than two separate routes to the summit of Lee's moral vision.

It is not irreverent or even impertinent to say that for some readers Atticus Finch will bring to mind God the Father, Tom Robinson God the Son, and Boo Radley may eerily recall the Holy Spirit. In the small universe that is Maycomb, Alabama, Atticus is the closest representative to God the Father, being "related by blood or marriage to nearly every family in the town."[66] Atticus runs his family the way God runs the universe: loving but not arbitrarily dominating, showing power at crucial moments, empathic but not feeble. The maimed Tom, whose left-arm muscles were shredded in an early cotton gin accident, leaving his left arm fully a foot shorter than the right, is sacrificed on the altar of race prejudice, and hence emblematic of the Son of God. Like a lamb led to the slaughter, Tom is hit with seventeen bullets as he nearly escaped from a prison work farm after

---

[65]Ibid., pp. 219, 260.
[66]Ibid., p. 5.

losing his case. Boo's shy eccentricity was taken by the Maycomb townsfolk as belonging to "a malevolent phantom," all evidence to the contrary, as Boo left weird but wonderful gifts for Jem and Scout and ultimately gave them their very lives.[67] Boo's identification with the Holy Spirit is the hardest one to maintain with integrity, because of his manifold oddness, but Boo works behind the scenes to bring something beautiful out of the ugly, which trait is near the center of the Holy Spirit's identity.

To Kill a Mockingbird cannot be imagined as a novel without Atticus, Tom and Boo. Their respective characters may not interpenetrate as do Father, Son and Holy Spirit perichoretically, but with the removal of any of them the novel collapses. But having said that, three—or twenty-three—literary characters are not capable of carrying forth any story line in the same way the Father, Son and Holy Spirit create, sustain, indwell and finally consummate the narrative of salvation. The reason is simple: whereas all literary characters only *inhabit* the story and can be changed by the whim of their creator, Father, Son and Holy Spirit truly and really *are* the story. Without the three-in-one God there cannot be a Christian story. Atticus, Tom and Boo are, within and among themselves, the moral complexity of *Mockingbird*, but as illustrations of ethical problems and potentials they are as far from being creators and definers of those problems and potentials as—aside from God's graced overtures—humanity is from divinity.

But as illustrators of universal moral complexity, Lee's characters are always interesting, frequently perspicacious and sometimes even prophetic. All of them, even Boo Radley in his voluntary hiddenness, live forth "the fundamentally social character of selfhood," as Niebuhr phrases it.[68] Boo was a son to his father Nathan and a hero in Scout and Jem's time of need. Harper Lee chose not to take the reader inside the mind of Boo Radley to see how his moral juices flowed, but one can surmise that the ethics of responsibility was uppermost in this misunderstood and possibly brilliant presence. Boo answered not to the call of some onerous moral law or joined hands with some nebulous and fleeting greatest good calculation, but acted swiftly and decisively because in his own way he knew and loved both Scout and Jem. When

---

[67]Ibid., pp. 9, 321.
[68]Niebuhr, *Responsible Self*, p. 71.

Niebuhr describes the New Testament ethic in the words below we can easily see Atticus Finch, his two children, Calpurnia, Tom Robinson and Boo Radley:

> The God to whom Jesus points is not the commander who gives laws but the doer of small and of mighty deeds, the creator of sparrows and clother of lilies, the ultimate giver of blindness and of sight, the ruler whose rule is hidden in the manifold activities of plural agencies but is yet in a way visible to those who know how to interpret the signs of the times.[69]

Scout understands that the ethics of responsibility is the ethics of neighborliness. The circle of responsibility needs reciprocal participation to keep growing to perfection. Sounding much too wise for her pre-teen years, Scout reflects that

> neighbors bring food with death and flowers with sickness and little things in between. Boo was our neighbor. He gave us two soap dolls, a broken watch and chain, a pair of good-luck pennies, and our lives. But neighbors give in return. We never put back into the tree what we took out of it: we had given him nothing, and it made me sad.[70]

But maybe Scout and Jem had given to Boo Radley more than they knew. The fear Boo occasionally stirred in Atticus's children was never the fear of the grotesque but the respect for the mystery at the heart of Being. "Hey, Boo" were Scout's coaxing words to ease Arthur Radley from his corner hideaway in Jem's room to the full cognizance of responsibility.[71] Boo Radley examined his conscience and exercised his moral prerogative to kill Bob Ewell and deliver Jem and Scout. "Conscience is a function of my existence as a social being," Niebuhr believes, "always aware of the approvals and disapprovals of my action by my fellow men."[72]

When Atticus concludes that in the scuffle between man and boy, Jem must have killed Bob Ewell, Sheriff Heck Tate sets him straight. The "official" version of events is that Ewell fell on his own grubby knife, although Tate knows that Boo killed Ewell. It would be a sin to put Arthur Radley on trial for Ewell's death, on account of Boo's tortured shy-

---

[69]Ibid., p. 67.
[70]Lee, *Mockingbird*, p. 321.
[71]Ibid., p. 311.
[72]Niebuhr, *Responsible Self*, p. 75.

ness. "It's a sin and I'm not about to have it on my head," declares the sheriff. "If it was any other man it'd be different. But not this man, Mr. Finch."[73] The sheriff's legal reasoning is not meant to cheapen or dissipate the law, be it moral or criminal. But Heck Tate's stance shows the inadequacy of a strictly legalistic approach to morality, which is not flexible or durable enough to encompass all the contextual variables the sheriff has gathered, sifted and weighed during his forty-three years of living nowhere else but Maycomb County.

It has by now become common wisdom, approaching cliché status, that the communitarian dynamics within the Trinity, carried out among Father, Son and Holy Spirit, are a necessary blueprint for human affairs, be these political, familial, sociological or interpersonal. The logic is inexorably easy—that what is true of God is incumbent upon humanity—and rings true enough. Niebuhr's ethics of responsibility, the ethics of the fitting or *cathekontic* ethics, holds the greatest promise for channeling the ethical purposes and energies of the triune God to the human situation.[74] By this we do not mean that God breaks a moral sweat or is always trying to outdo himself, but simply that the perfections of the divine life might become human and societal perfections also.

Teleological ethics eventually seizes upon this question: What is the Form of the Good that is the form of the whole? For the triune God this question is meaningless, since God is himself the Form of the Good. The deontological ethicist finally wants to know: What is the universal form of the law? This may be closer to the triune reality; however, the fact that God as triune not only exhausts the universal but also completes every particular means that the "one size fits all" tendency of deontology is inadequate. Through the ethics of the fitting, so Niebuhr believes, "we find ourselves led to the notion of universal responsibility."[75] The ethics of responsibility is less about hewing to universal law or finding and realizing a universal ideal than it is "a life of responsibility in universal community."[76] An ethics of universal responsibility is possible only on trinitarian terms, where it is understood that God is the span and measure of community and not the reverse.

---

[73]Lee, *Mockingbird*, p. 318.
[74]Niebuhr, *Responsible Self*, p. 87.
[75]Ibid.
[76]Ibid., p. 89.

The ethics of idealistic teleology and regimented deontology can both be interpreted and viewed theologically. Each coheres most naturally with a mere monotheism that never becomes trinitarian. "Remember God's plan for your life" is where the teleologist lives, whereas the deontologist seeks to "obey God's law in all your obediences to finite rules." For Niebuhr, though, the ethics of responsibility declares: "God is acting in all actions upon you. So respond to all actions upon you as to respond to his action."[77] Niebuhr does not identify the God of responsibility ethics explicitly with the triune God. But in fact it could be no other God.

Theological truth is for Niebuhr always culturally and philosophically expressed, but never controlled by these enterprises. It is the God of biblical faith with whom the Christian ethicist must always deal. Niebuhr is himself a Christian who is an ethicist, not an ethicist who happens to be a Christian. This difference is decisive. Niebuhr's take on responsibility is always theocentric and christocentric, and hence biblical. The God whose Spirit calls forth from us responsible thought and action is the God of the Bible, and this God is the Trinity.

Is the Triune God the Divine Commander?

The acting God of the Bible is for some theological ethicists not so much the pondering God or the musing God or even the deliberating God. He is rather the divine Commander. Can the ethics of the divine command be reconciled with a trinitarian ethics, or perhaps even be the chief exemplification of such an ethics? Will God the Father, if divine command ethics be seen trinitarianly, take to himself all the privileges of the command, slighting Son and Spirit? Intuitively, a divine command ethics appears to work best when the one God is at the controls, not the three-in-one God. A "chain of command" as conventionally understood, as hierarchically conceived, cannot be applied to the Trinity, because the presumption is that the command emanates from only one source and is then "seconded" or corroborated all along the line. But to attach this chain of command to the Trinity obviously makes of the Son and the Holy Spirit lesser divinities, and trinitarian orthodoxy has consistently said that there can be no degrees of divinity within God.

Christian ethicist Richard Mouw sees God's triunity as lending it-

---

[77]Ibid., p. 126.

self to a divine command interpretation. His essay on the triune Commander begins with the unproven but probably true simplicity: "Christians play favorites with the members of the Trinity."[78] A child who has traversed the family discipline protocol from one parent to the second parent to the grandparents knows all about trying to play favorites with authority figures. Since in one sense all Christians are perpetually children in the face of God, similar tactics with God are not uncommon.

One should not sink all of Mouw's project on account of one errant word, but his description of the divine persons as "members" calls to mind a different range of meanings than does *persons*. A club, from which one might voluntarily withdraw or to which one might not be judged worthy of initial entrance, has "members" but not "persons." The Trinity is *not* an "invitation only" club but the heart of all reality. *Members* is thus an ill-advised descriptor, and yet, sadly, is probably an accurate reflection of the "every God for every human need" ethic and spirituality that, if it does not like what is behind door number one, asks to see what is behind door number two and door number three before making a final decision.

In fairness to Mouw, though, he is not really promoting a sort of "have it your way" approach to the Trinity. Only God knows the full complexity of every ethical quandary or conundrum. It is the Christian hope that in glory "we will see face to face" but until that day "we see in a mirror, dimly" (1 Cor 13:12). As we struggle toward moral clarity it is only natural that some people will be more persuasively drawn toward God the Son as a moral beacon, whereas others find their moral challenges met by the Spirit or the Father. Mouw's two questions, therefore, may be the beginning of moral calm and purpose rather than a concession to human obtuseness: "When you think about *obeying* God which member of the Trinity do you view yourself as relating to primarily? Which of the divine persons calls you to, or directly mediates, the strategies for your response of, obedience to the divine will?"[79]

Rather like the fruit of the Spirit (Gal 5:22-23), which is conceptually and linguistically singular but functionally plural, there being nine

---

[78]Richard Mouw, "The Triune Commander," in *The God Who Commands: A Study in Divine Command Ethics* (Notre Dame, Ind.: University of Notre Dame Press, 1990), p. 150.
[79]Ibid., p. 151.

demonstrations of this singular fruit, so also is there only one divine will but three ways of knowing it: the way of the Father, the way of the Son, the way of the Spirit. Any respectable mountain will have many proven ways to the summit. For the sake of illustration let us suppose that one mountain had three identified and oft-climbed means of ascent: the north face, the south face and the centennial glacier. No climber can be said to know all the moods and the possibilities of the mountain until gaining mastery over all three routes. Although no climber can simultaneously be on all three routes, the routes are complementary and not mutually exclusive. None of the three routes is a technically harder ascent than the other two. Each route offers unique ascending views. On a clear day the south face lines up with stunning peaks in the near and far distance. From the north face one can see nestled villages populating the valley below, and the centennial glacier soars over a mighty waterway tumbling toward the sea.

Richard Mouw does not illumine the connection between the triune God and the divine command through extended metaphors, but he does find connections between what are commonly regarded parts of the ethical whole and each of the three divine persons. He believes that the Father's divine directive is about principles. Interacting with H. Richard Niebuhr's essay "The Doctrine of the Trinity and the Unity of the Church" that we considered in the previous chapter, Mouw believes that the ethics of God the Father "features creational generalities" which evince, especially among Roman Catholic and Calvinian philosophers, "a strong interest in *law*."[80] Without the leavening provided by, respectively, the ethics of God the Son and God the Spirit it may be a short step from the Father's love of the law to a full-throated deontological perspective.

When Christian ethics avails itself of the entire riches of the triune God, there is a much better chance of avoiding any impasse between principles (the ethics of the Father) and narratives (the ethics of the Son). A strict appeal to a principles-only ethics may be unassailable logically but emotionally and even historically vacant. Alternatively, as Mouw analyzes, the ethics of the Son "focuses on redemptive-historical particulars."[81] Principles and narratives are not "natural enemies"

---

[80]Ibid., pp. 157, 155.
[81]Ibid., p. 157.

in the ethical forest and truly need each other to fulfill and complete any Christian ethics. To paraphrase Immanuel Kant, principles without narratives are empty; narratives without principles are blind.[82] If the ethics of God the Father is primarily creational, then this principle of creation is perfected only through the narrative of Jesus Christ. Principles are necessary but remain empty without the indicatives of the "redemptive-historical particulars" of Jesus Christ.

Mouw appears to doubt that any Christian could be fully trinitarian in ethical formulation and enactment. To be seized by this awareness is itself one mark of ethical maturity, for it will prevent one's chasing after this or that divine person to the neglect of the other two. The beauty of there being three identities, but not versions, of one moral wisdom is that one's conscience and moral parameters can be triply informed. The downside, of course, is that the taut balances of the Trinity may be displaced or improperly applied, as Mouw notes: "any one of the members of the Trinity can be emphasized in a manner that results in a harshness that must then be softened—often by an intratrinitarian shift of emphasis."[83]

This shift of emphasis, I must stress, is not to unfog the divine moral vision, as if to tell God how to be moral. But a Spirit-generated shift will allow God's full moral suasion to operate within us. It is the special gift of the Holy Spirit, Mouw believes, to promote and further moral clarity within every human being. To see clearly is to see discerningly; discernment is the contribution the Holy Spirit makes to an ethics that is functionally trinitarian. Mouw writes that

> discernment is crucial to the moral life, but it does not come automatically with the territory of any moral scheme. Laws and principles must be applied effectively. Moral examples cannot be properly imitated unless we know how and what to imitate. Character-formation requires the ability to place ourselves in those settings where the appropriate virtues can begin to "take" in our lives.[84]

In Papua New Guinea, so a medical missionary friend informs me,

---

[82]In bringing together the philosophical outlooks of rationalism and empiricism, Kant declared that "concepts without percepts are empty; percepts without concepts are blind." Kant had no use for the doctrine of the Trinity, either as a truth of revelation, which he categorically rejected, or as the anchor for a moral system.

[83]Mouw, "Triune Commander," p. 168.

[84]Ibid., p. 173.

prayer is routinely offered up to Papa God, Holi Spirit and Pikinini Jisas, as the divine persons are known in Melanesian Pidgin. This spirituality, when translated into ethics, is not so much a "cover all my bases" dodge as the acknowledgement that the full measure of human ethical experience can only be met by the full expanse of God: the Trinity. If moral consciousness consists chiefly of cognitive, volitional and affective elements, then each of Father, Son and Spirit will necessarily have something to say to each of these elements.[85] Like a soloist backed by a choir, each divine person may specialize in one of these three fundamental areas, although none of the three would contradict the other two.

John Calvin believed that the Trinity brings the cognitive to life in much the same way as the trinitarian economy of salvation unfolds. He saw that the Father, as the principle of fecundity, is the one who brings forth. God the Son arranges and orders this effusion of goodness and the Holy Spirit brings it to perfection.[86] One of the Holy Spirit's greatest works is the resolution and perfection of the human will, as the Spirit brings to mind how everything Jesus Christ performed was done in the power of the Spirit.

THE PRACTICE OF DISCERNMENT

Christian ethics that seeks and applies trinitarian expectations is not a simple oscillation between the austerities of God the Father and the accomplishments of God the Son, with the Holy Spirit called in for convenient mediations. No formula, simple or complex, can deplete the meaning of trinitarian ethics. James Gustafson muses on "moral life in theocentric perspective," and while the Trinity never rises to full articulation in his treatment, his centering question in "a theocentric construal of the world" is best answered if God is seen as triune: "What is God enabling and requiring us to be and to do?"[87] It is not as if *being* is parceled out to God the Father with *doing* the province of the Son. No, all of God must be involved throughout the entire gamut of the moral life. Gustafson's choice of verbal forms—*requiring* and *enabling*—points to the dynamism of God's triunity rather than to the relatively more narrow strictures of an unrelieved monotheism.

---

[85]Ibid., p. 172.
[86]Ibid.
[87]Gustafson, *Theology and Ethics*, p. 327.

The Holy Spirit works, in Mouw's understanding, toward "the enrichment and expansion of our moral subjectivity," which is to say that the Spirit grants discernment.[88] Even more than Mouw, Gustafson develops an ethics of discernment, finding in Romans 12:1-2, with its call "to present your bodies as a living sacrifice," the biblical warrant for and call to discernment.[89] As Gustafson amends and expands these two verses as follows, the One who inhabits these words and shines their specificities upon us is the Holy Spirit.

> Individually and collectively offer yourselves, your minds and hearts, your capacities and powers in piety, in devoted and faithful service to God. Do not be conformed to the immediate and apparent possibilities or requirements of either your desires or the circumstances in which you live and act. But be enlarged in your vision and affections, so that you might better discern what the divine governance enables and requires you to be and to do, what are your appropriate relations to God, indeed, what are the appropriate relations of all things to God. Then you might discern the will of God.[90]

The phrase of greatest moral and theological consequence is obviously "the divine governance," which inasmuch as it can be known, is known through the discipline of discernment. Divine governance is not an arbitrary and imposed morality that rules by divine fiat. God's oversight of the human and the natural worlds always takes into account developments where the divine and the human intersect, for example in the overlapping worlds of nature, culture, politics, history, society and the self, and the overwhelming reality of these developments "rules out a timeless and changeless moral order."[91] Gustafson is not here advocating the sort of moral free fall often associated with the decade of the 1960s. He stands not for the abolition of traditional principles and standards of conduct and misconduct, what is fitting and what is not, but rather for the occasional extension, revision and even radical alteration of these principles.[92] Human and historical progress is such that new situations and accomplishments may bring new ethical challenges.

---

[88]Mouw, "Triune Commander," p. 172.
[89]See James M. Gustafson, "Moral Discernment in the Christian Life," in *Theology and Christian Ethics* (Philadelphia: Pilgrim Press, 1974), pp. 99-119.
[90]Gustafson, *Theology and Ethics*, pp. 327-28.
[91]Ibid., p. 339.
[92]Ibid.

Gustafson believes that "the realities in which we experience the divine governance in nature and culture, for example, develop, and with them there must be development in ethics itself."[93]

Gustafson presents the ethics of discernment more thoroughly than does Richard Mouw, although Mouw links discernment with the Holy Spirit more decisively than does Gustafson. Even so, it is only through God the Spirit that Gustafson's exacting descriptions will come to life. In Gustafson's case the Holy Spirit is conceptually present even if descriptively and verbally absent. When it has reached its end, prior to inspiring action, the long glance of discernment is for Gustafson "an informed intuition; it is not the conclusion of a formally logical argument, a strict deduction from a single moral principle, or an absolutely certain result from the exercises of human 'reason' alone."[94]

The Holy Spirit is not "the God of the gaps," who fills in missing bits of cognition, not the rescuer of the lazy student who has not prepared for the examination. Human reason is not defeated by the Holy Spirit, not thwarted or embarrassed or shown up, but helps one to think more clearly and, when human reason seems at its frustrated end, there are always new persuasions and intimations offered by God the Spirit. To live by human reason that seeks only its own counsel and listens only to its own arguments is to live in the flesh, a life condemned by Paul in Romans 8. Throughout this capacious chapter, one of the greatest in the New Testament, the life of the Spirit can be equated with the life of discernment. Discerning life is contrary to fleshly life, and works toward the renewal of all things in Jesus Christ. There are markedly trinitarian phrases in this chapter, especially the witness of renewed life through the Spirit's vivifying work: "If the Spirit of him who raised Jesus from the dead dwells in you, he who raised Christ from the dead will give life to your mortal bodies also through his Spirit that dwells in you" (Rom 8:11).

There need not be, and in fact there is not, any hard and fast boundary between a trinitarian spirituality—the life of God in the human soul spilling over redemptively—and a trinitarian ethic, this same God-infused life engaged in the creating of community, the practice of virtue, the refinement of motive, the waiting upon the Lord. "In all theological

---

[93]Ibid.
[94]Ibid., p. 338.

ethics piety and morality are part of each other," Gustafson concludes. "All that is, including ourselves, is gift; it is given to us in reliance upon powers man does not create and on which all of life continues to rely. . . . The sustenance of piety is of fundamental importance for morality."[95]

For Kathryn Tanner, Christian experience, which includes everything Christians do in prayer, worship and work, necessarily "takes on its own trinitarian form: in the Spirit, who is given to us by the Son, we gain the Son, and through the Son, by the same power of the Spirit, we have a relationship with the Father."[96] The life Jesus Christ lived, knowing the Father and captivated by his will, centered on the Father through the Spirit's ministry, becomes through grace our own life. The trinitarian shape of Jesus' own life becomes our shape. The configuration of this life is service. Tanner names her own theology a task- and vocation-centered theology, whose fulfillment recreates in human life the trinitarian benefits of Jesus' life. This life looks like this:

> The Son is sent by the Father in the power of the Spirit to bring us into the gift-giving relations enjoyed among members of the Trinity; living our lives in Christ according to the mode of the Son, should involve, then, our service to that mission, spreading the gifts of the Father that are ours in Christ, empowered by the Son's own Spirit.[97]

---

[95]Gustafson, *Ethics and Theology*, p. 42.
[96]Kathryn Tanner, *Jesus, Humanity and the Trinity: A Brief Systematic Theology* (Minneapolis: Fortress, 2001), p. 62.
[97]Ibid., p. 68.

7

The Giver,
the Given and the Giving

The calendar said midsummer, and in the tropics midsummer meant the monsoon. It had been surprisingly dry, however, and front-page news photos showed half-empty reservoirs and voiced fears of impending crop failure without enough irrigation. But as I alighted from the metropolis's latest light-rail line and made my way along vaguely remembered streets, there was a welcoming moisture in the air. Humidity. Soon the metal back of my wristwatch would glisten with sweat and the stain on the leather band would deepen beyond removal.

Picking my way through one of the most congested places on the planet, past stalls crammed with cheap electronics, I felt a gentle touch on my lower arm just below the elbow. Too definite for an accidental brush from a passerby. Not prickly enough for a mosquito. The touch registered but I did not break my stride. Seven or eight more steps along the battered sidewalk came another touch. This time complete with a meek but determined solicitation. Prostitutes! What part of town had I stumbled into? And at the sun's peak in the early afternoon!

I raised my wedding ring into the prostitute's sight, elevated my voice just below prophetic rage and kept walking. Three weeks before on this summer teaching odyssey a woman and child asking for money had persisted in walking alongside of me for at least one hundred yards, making her case and insisting she was not lying (I was convinced she was lying, which is one reason I brushed her off). But the prostitute thankfully abandoned the hunt immediately.

My journey continued. I walked by one of the busiest U.S. embassies in the world, less than two miles from where I had rebuffed the prostitutes. Crossing the street I was again propositioned, this time not by a lady of the night but by a male fixer. It was only a golf shot's distance from the U.S. embassy where, presumably, along with the values of freedom, democracy and the rule of law, moral probity reigned. The fortified embassy anchors one end of a wide boulevard festooned with palm trees, much breezier and more tourist friendly than the place I had just vacated.

Three solicitations on a glorious summer day half a world from my home. Two verbal, one the merest touch. Three solicitations with the propagators' one lustful intent, to separate me from the virtue kept alive within me by the Holy Spirit. Were these three visitations from the world of sexual sin a kind of reverse or antitrinitarian assault on my Christian sensibilities? At that time the cumulative experience did not impress me in this way, and it does not now. While sin and moral evil can be highly organized, and may even conspire to imitate a triadic pattern, those three solicitations were a random matter of my being in the wrong places at the wrong times.

Many years before in the same tropical city, not in the heat of the day but at twilight, another three-in-one happening stirred theologically reflective juices within me. Arriving near a large shopping center, I parked the car in a crudely graveled parking lot and started to walk toward the mall. A girl of early teen years approached me. Her face was ordinary except for the sort of deformity one sees in this country from time to time, a condition not impervious to the surgery that is yet difficult for the poor to come by. This dusky young lady only wanted money.

By now, having lived in this country for seven years and being warned by veteran missionaries not to give to beggars, I hastened on, waving her away. Children only work for the syndicate, we were told. We gave to the poor, but in the tangible gift of a well-placed hamburger as street children scrambled outside of a fast-food eatery.

My shopping finished I walked back to the car. Had the girl forgotten my first refusal? I did not know, but here she was again. Again I refused.

Three or four minutes later I refused again, as she knocked on the car window as I was waiting for the traffic light to change so I could leave the area.

Three visits from one girl. Three requests for money and I refused them all. It was not until later that I thought that perhaps I had been visited first by God the Father, then by God the Son and last by God the Spirit, three visitations of one holy God. I did not feel especially guilty about my trio of rejections, but wondered by and by if I had done the right thing, if I should have quashed those missionary admonitions not to give to beggars and reached into my pocket. Indeed before those admonitions, as a new missionary, I had often given to beggars.

If life can imitate theology, and if our common experiences call for theological interpretation, my being met by one girl voicing three separate yet similar plaints struck me as being at the very least triadic, if not trinitarian. What theological name did this deserve? The whole episode would not leave me until I could dignify it theologically. Three random interruptions might be dismissed as coincidence, but my theological mind could not rest in this convenient solution.

My conclusion? My being stopped three times for one reason was a gritty visitation of Karl Barth's tri-iterative trinitarianism. Three speeches whose varying words did not yet forsake a common underlying grammar and purpose of God's will, even of God's command. Had my reluctance to part with a pittance been in direct violation of God's command of how I *ought* to respond at that particular time? God's speech is enduring and finally thwarts all efforts to muzzle it. My obtuseness, my failure to give, could never silence the Trinity. Yet not once, not twice, but three times I had turned a deaf ear.

Along with tri-iteration, could the girl's triply staked begging have been at the same time the perichoresis of the mutual self-giving and other-regarding of the Father, Son and Holy Spirit, any one of them indwelling the other two and receiving them into himself? This seemed an attractive possibility, for how often in the real world does perichoresis present itself? But the symbol of perichoresis would have been more powerfully available had the girl been working in a community of beggars (as possibly she was, unknown to me) or been old enough to have a child or two in tow as a prod to any stranger's generosity.

It is with tri-iteration that we therefore come to rest, the triply presented act of begging. If the triune God cannot show himself in the face of a beggar, then where else might he be found? Jesus himself knew that an act of mercy done unto the least was an act done unto him (Mt 25:40), and if unto him then unto the Father and the Spirit also.

Prostitutes and beggars were welcomed by Jesus Christ into the kingdom of God. After really meeting Jesus, those who would sell their bodies in one desperate act had the strength to go and sin no more; those who patrolled dirty streets looking for alms could buy without price. From one tropical city came two clusters of three events each. One traded in lust and was dissolute and debauched. But the triply humiliating act of begging was the Trinity unawares, the hidden Trinity reminding me that at any time, at any place, God's triunity can and will be known.

TRINITARIAN ACCENTS IN KARL BARTH'S ETHICS

Karl Barth likely never visited the tropics, and we hope he never suffered the indignity of solicitation. But doubtless Barth had abundant opportunities to put his theology into practice. At first consideration his theological ethics might be more accurately called christocentric than trinitarian. However this ethics be named, it surely allowed for his charity to manifest itself. In Barth there is of course no disagreement between Jesus Christ and the holy Trinity; his ethics must be a fully trinitarian ethics.

Edward Long describes Barth's ethics with three points: (1) while the ethical question is required of humanity, it cannot be humanly answered; (2) Jesus Christ is this answer; (3) Christ's answer authenticates and humanizes ethical existence in ways that alienated and distorted human attempts never could.[1] Thus Long asserts that for Barth Jesus Christ is "both the premise and the conclusion of the ethical enterprise."[2] Barth's theological ethics is widely described as that of the divine command, and yet for Barth to hear and obey is a joyous transport and not a debilitating surrender. Long classifies Barth as belonging to the "relational motif" of Christian ethics, relationality here

---

[1]Edward LeRoy Long Jr., *A Survey of Christian Ethics* (New York: Oxford University Press, 1967), p. 151.
[2]Ibid.

pointing, of course, first to the divine expectation and only then to ethical exertion and accomplishment in the human world. Barth's construal of the divine command as relational is "about its personal and spiritual nature, about its releasing powers, about the permissions it bestows rather than the actions it precludes, about its joyful features," in Long's summary explanation.[3]

Humans may struggle to hear God's command, and even in hearing turn away in cowardice and inertia, but there can be no second guessing the power and the force of God's utterance and requirement. "The divine decision," Barth knows, "in which the sovereign judgment of God is expressed on our decisions, is a very definite decision."[4] As Barth unpacks the logic of this definiteness, it is clear that his is a theological approach to ethics, stemming from his doctrine of God, and not a philosophical, psychological, historical, social, cultural or any other approach to ethics. James Gustafson offers this clarification of Barth's ethics:

> The point is that human beings are not to discern what is morally right and good by their assessment of the natural and social patterns of dependence and interdependence in life in the world, but are to hear and obey the command of God, to witness to God's gracious action in the world by conforming their actions to his actions, to testify in their lives and in the ordering of human activity to the prior gracious covenant of God with man.[5]

What is impossible for humankind, to survey the moral field and construct pathways for forward movement and standards for right and wrong, can only be realized by the triune God. To ignore this fundamental divine option and to careen recklessly into ethical territory that can only be marked and known by God is not merely foolish and irresponsible; it is also sin. If God's rightful place as the final ethical arbiter is usurped, if pretentious human analysis thwarts the divine prerogative, then it is sin. Gustafson explains that

> it is in this sense that ethics itself can become a grave sin, since the forms of ethics given in the philosophical and much of the Christian tradition

---

[3]Ibid., p. 153.
[4]Karl Barth, *CD* 2/2, ed. George W. Bromiley and T. F. Torrance (Edinburgh: T & T Clark, 1957), p. 663, quoted in Gustafson, *Ethics and Theology*, p. 29.
[5]Gustafson, *Ethics and Theology*, p. 29.

make the final point of reliance in moral life the reasonable judgments of persons, or make rules and principles (including those derived from biblical sources) the ultimate basis of decision.[6]

Barth's strenuous and even strident divine-command ethics turns philosophical ethics on its head, and even the sort of biblical ethics that strays from how Barth interprets the Bible. People manufacture ideas about good and evil, and assimilate these ideas from countless sources, but Barth claims that "at certain crucial points the Bible amazes us by its remarkable indifference to our conception of good and evil," instancing the exploits of Abraham, Jacob and Elijah that so-called enlightened minds find so repugnant.[7] If "The Strange New World Within the Bible"[8] is allowed to recreate one's morality, this new ethic abandons the former ways of imagined goodness for the bracing biblical goodness. Sounding at once biblical and trinitarian, Barth exclaims that "the reality which lies behind Abraham and Moses, behind Christ and his apostles, is the world of the Father, in which morality is dispensed with because it is taken for granted. And the blood of the New Testament which seeks inflow into our veins is the will of the Father which would be done on earth as it is in heaven."[9]

As is true for all of Barth's theology, in his theological ethics God's freedom is uppermost. Any presence to whom is accorded the stature and status of command is by definition the creator and configurer of everything about the command: its formulation, its appropriateness, its relation to corollary or competing commands, its judgment on the outcome and aftermath of the command. Everything, that is, except the enactment of the command, which must fall to the one of whom the command is required, the human. While the human response is more than an afterthought, it occupies a much more modest realm than normally accorded to the human will. For Barth, in the words of Robin Lovin, "Christian ethics is not about our deliberations but about God's determinative action."[10]

---

[6]Ibid., p. 31.

[7]Karl Barth, *The Word of God and the Word of Man*, trans. Douglas Horton (n.p.: Pilgrim Press, 1928), p. 38.

[8]Ibid., pp. 28-50; reprinted in *A Map of Twentieth Century Theology: Readings from Karl Barth to Radical Pluralism*, ed. Carl E. Braaten and Robert W. Jenson (Minneapolis: Fortress, 1995), pp. 21-31.

[9]Barth, *Word of God and Word of Man*, p. 40.

[10]Robin Lovin, forward to *The Holy Spirit and the Christian Life: The Theological Basis of Ethics* by Karl Barth, trans. R. Birch Hoyle (Louisville: Westminster/John Knox Press, 1993), p. x.

Imagine a cleanup hitter who ignored his coach's "take" sign on a 3-0 pitch and hit a home run to win the World Series. Under such a glorious outcome the batter would likely be forgiven, even lionized, but with a less propitious result the would-be slugger would be benched. The point is that the coach, as commander, knows moral terrain the batter does not, and the coach's signals are absolutely binding on the batter. A lifetime of baseball experience still does not entitle the batter to usurp the coach's command. Likewise, a lifetime of humanly generated moral living, or attempts thereat, may only be to deaden one's true ethical sensibilities.

What God believes about goodness is given only through revelation, and to the question Barth asks—"What is Christian life?"—there is a trinitarian answer, an answer that "cannot be ambiguous."[11] What motivates and enables all human turning toward God as the divine Commander, as with every divine intention for humanity, can only be grace, which Barth finds to be "ever and in all relations God's *deed* and *act*" and "never at all a quality of ours, inborn in us, such as would enable us to know of it in advance."[12] John Wesley's famous summation of grace, that grace is "free in all, and free for all," does not cheapen or degrade grace, but for Barth robs from grace the strange surprise he held so dear.[13]

The Christian life, as already hinted, is thoroughly trinitarian. It begins not with the human response (here Wesley agrees with Barth) but with God's gracious willing of the good for humanity. This good is no abstract, culturally measured and mediated goodness, but that of Jesus Christ, "the crucified and risen One." The moment of grace's onset and availability for humankind is God's chosen moment, but this moment becomes at the same time the human moment of readiness to hear God's grace, living in and for Christ, and hearing the Word of God.[14] When we talk of the subjective experience of receiving and applying revelation, we are in the company of the Holy Spirit, whom Barth describes as "the Paraclete who is not only speaking on our behalf but

---

[11]Barth, *Holy Spirit and Christian Life*, pp. 8, 6.
[12]Ibid., pp. 5-6.
[13]John Wesley, *John Wesley's Sermons: An Anthology*, ed. Albert C. Outler and Richard P. Heitzenrater (Nashville: Abingdon, 1991), p. 50.
[14]Barth, *Holy Spirit and Christian Life*, p. 6.

speaking to us so that we have to hear him, the speaking God."[15] To hear the speaking God is not a privilege handed to humans genetically, historically or culturally, but by God and God alone. In Barth's version of the philosophical puzzler—does a falling tree in an empty forest create any sound?—what legitimates the speech of God is not this or that human sifting or even hearing of God's speech, but the majesty of the speech itself. Human hearing adds nothing to divine utterance, and yet it is ultimately for human salvation that God deigns to speak at all. The Word of God can be heard, but its hearing is only possible on the terms of God's assignment, namely, the Holy Spirit, whose office for Barth is "to be continually opening our ears to enable us to receive the Creator's word."[16] God's tree still falls, God's speech still resonates, even in an empty forest or a forest populated with unhearing ears. To be a "hearer of the Word" comes not by human intuition but through divine intervention.

It would be a superlative teacher who could draw one deep breath and then in one great moment issue three classroom directives at one and the same time. Any number of pedagogic commands could unfold sequentially but never simultaneously. This analogy is stretched a little beyond a truly trinitarian shape, because in Barth's view of the divine-command ethic not three discrete directives are given by God but his singular command spoken in three distinct yet inseparable ways. All ethics happens within "the history of the covenant of grace established by God with humankind" in Nigel Biggar's explanation.[17] The realms or spheres of creation, reconciliation and redemption make up this covenant, and each sphere is enfolded within and welcomes the other two, as is true of the perichoretic indwelling of Father, Son and Spirit.[18] To return to our classroom analogy, creation, reconciliation and redemption are mutually intertwined in ways scarcely imaginable for recess, computer lab and lunchtime.

"Always in the ethical event," Barth attests, "God commands and man acts in all three spheres at once."[19] How can it be that when God's

---

[15]Ibid.

[16]Ibid., p. 8.

[17]Nigel Biggar, *The Hastening That Waits: Karl Barth's Ethics* (Oxford: Clarendon, 1993), p. 29.

[18]Ibid., p. 29 n. 99.

[19]Barth, *CD* 3/4, ed. George W. Bromiley and T. F. Torrance (Edinburgh: T & T Clark, 1961), p. 33, quoted in Biggar, *Hastening That Waits*, p. 29.

command is heard, all of creation, reconciliation and redemption are engaged in the human response? Is this a mere instance of Charles Wesley's stalwart admonition, or something greater?

> To serve the present age, my calling to fulfill;
> O may it all my powers engage to do my Master's will![20]

Here Wesley stresses the entirety of the human response—*all my powers engage*—more than the interwoven span of salvation history—creation, reconciliation, redemption—that calls forth this paramount human response. Barth stresses more the reality of salvation history, whereas Wesley knows the grace-aided response that this reality entails. The *truth* of the gospel is always prior to any human response, as Barth understands, and yet this truth is somehow strangely incomplete without the human knowing of it, being grasped by the gospel. That God's free grace enables humanity's free will is a staple of Wesleyan theology.

Barth believes that every engagement with the divine command is at one and the same time both an obligation and a chance to respond to the Father's grace of creation, the Son's work of reconciliation and the Holy Spirit's redeeming healing. In the words of Biggar,

> in each and every ethical event the human being confronted with the divine command is always thereby defined simultaneously as the creature and therefore the covenant partner of God; as the pardoned sinner; and as the child of God led by the Holy Spirit to live during the present time of contradiction, conflict, and suffering by hope in the presence of God's future.[21]

Since Biggar points to the specificity of "every ethical event," we might well put to Barth at least one ethical issue, abortion, and investigate whether his views mesh with the coinherence of creation, reconciliation and redemption. Abortion is for Barth a sinful act, capable of being forgiven, to be chosen only under the direst of circumstances. If someone denies the inherent gravity of abortion, Barth suggests a wakeup call: "the only thing which can help is the power of a wholly new and radical feeling of awe at the mystery of all human life as this is commanded by God as its Creator, Giver and Lord."[22] Barth takes

---

[20]Charles Wesley, "A Charge to Keep I Have" (1762).
[21]Biggar, *Hastening That Waits*, p. 30.
[22]Barth, *CD* 3/4, p. 418.

it as given that human life exists from the moment of conception.[23] Within the mother's womb is a human being for whom Christ died. Beautifully expressed, Barth urges that "this child is a man for whose life the Son of God has died, for whose unavoidable part in the guilt of all humanity and future individual guilt He has already paid the price. The true light of the world shines already in the darkness of the mother's womb."[24]

May there be any exceptions to Barth's prohibition against abortion? Yes, there may be exceptions, because human life, even that of the unborn child, is *not* an absolute. Human life is protected by God's commandment of life, but for Barth "it can be so only within the limits of the will of Him who issues it. It cannot claim to be preserved in all circumstances, whether in relation to God or to other men."[25] Barth does not enumerate every circumstance in which abortion may be allowed, but does admit that exceptions to the prohibition will be rare, and abortion can be contemplated only after "all the arguments for preservation have been carefully considered and properly weighed."[26] *Any* abortion at all is cause for great sadness and reflection, and those who make such decisions will find themselves in "situations in which all those concerned must answer before God in great loneliness and secrecy, and make their decision accordingly."[27]

God would never command an abortion, because God is the giver of life and not the warden of death, and yet Barth believes that any abortion happens under the provisions or within the parameters of the divine command. In regulating and standardizing any approach to abortion, the civil law can be of great value, but it is not the final authority. Civil laws against abortion cannot become the criteria of ethics, because the divine command, in Barth's view, "must have the freedom to move within limits which may sometimes be narrower and sometimes broader than even the best civil law."[28] The freedom of God is its own ethical explanation and can be subject to no external authority.

---

[23]Ibid., p. 415. "For the unborn child is from the very first a child. It is still developing and has no independent life. But it is a man and not a thing, nor a mere part of the mother's body."
[24]Ibid., p. 416.
[25]Ibid., p. 420.
[26]Ibid., p. 421.
[27]Ibid.
[28]Ibid., p. 422.

While Barth did not choose to frame his reflections on abortion with explicit reference to the doctrine of the Trinity, the impress of this doctrine is more than faintly visible. His reference to God as Creator, Giver and Lord sounds a trinitarian note, as does his poignant meditation on how Jesus Christ has died for the unborn child. Finally, all of Barth's discussion of abortion unfolds under the canopy that has universal stretch, coverage and obligation: the divine command.

The divine command overseas and integrates creation, reconciliation and redemption in ways human instrumentality cannot. We believe Barth at the point of his saying that "the command of God is based on His grace," and yet for many observers this divine grace seems to nullify human responsibility rather than to extend its reach.[29] Has Barth pushed his *sola gratia* approach to Christian ethics too far?

It is exactly this appearance of the taking of all "the ethical marbles" to the divine Self that has occasioned the most criticism of Barth. While no Christian ethics can allow fallen humanity to be lord and master of its own ethical kingdom, there are degrees of allowing and encouraging human responsibility, most obviously at the point of human choice and even in the rational search for defensible and operable principles, standards and laws. But Barth sweeps all of that away, with the exception of human accountability toward God's singular and unmistakable command. If the sovereign Lord gives not only the command but the only way to hear and heed the command, then any independent ethical thinking is crushed and subverted at the outset. Many would agree with Biggar's objection that Barth's ethics "removes the deep and mysterious seriousness of human moral responsibility, and accordingly diminishes human dignity."[30]

FROM COMMAND TO COOPERATION

Younger trinitarian theologians and ethicists, none of whom is likely to be a Barth loyalist on the point of his divine-command theory of ethics, have instead exerted their energies in the direction of human freedom, corporate responsibility and global sensibilities. One of the best representatives of this impulse, which stresses the practical relevance of the Trinity, this best-attested Christian teaching, is David S. Cunningham, who outlines the infectious applicability of trinitarian theology in his

---

[29]Ibid., p. 418.
[30]Biggar, *Hastening That Waits*, p. 162.

book *These Three Are One*. Among recent full-length treatments, this work stands out as a thorough and sympathetic accounting. The whole tenor of his book is practical and not speculative, although Cunningham is certainly a fine scholar of the nuances of the doctrine of the Trinity. He would have to be to produce a work as knowing and richly considered as this one.

The Promise of Trinitarian Theology, the chosen subtitle, is his enterprise in a phrase. Cunningham is a stylish and resourceful writer who hydrates the Trinity with a water metaphor, the Source (the Father) being trinitarian beliefs as such, the Wellspring (the Son) being trinitarian virtues, and the Living Water (the Holy Spirit) showing us the way of trinitarian practices. Each of these three main parts is presented in three segments, for a total of nine, all nine of them arrayed in the alliterative splendor of *p:* the Source is about positioning, producing, paralleling; polyphony, participation, particularity comprise the Wellspring; Living Water must eventuate in the trinitarian ways of peacemaking, pluralizing, persuading. Some might dismiss this technique as theological cuteness, derailing the main event of trinitarian theology and ethics by a grab at literary polish. While Cunningham no doubt could have said the same thing in other words, shelving alliteration, overall it is not a distraction.

I will not attempt a systematic survey of Cunningham's insightful and profuse book. A brief tour will have to suffice. The big ideas of the book are relatively few in number and are reinforced constantly, nearly on every page. Just as every sovereign nation has a foreign policy that it then applies to particular situations, so also every coherent ethics first insures the solidity and viability of its pronouncements before parading them in public view or applying them to particular cases. Cunningham follows this pattern. When his attention turns to particular ethical issues, such as peacemaking or same-sex relationships, he always keeps in mind the trinitarian doctrines that brought him to these issues in the first place. It is for the sake of illustrating the wider point of the Trinity's ethical relevance that the case studies are undertaken at all.

When Cunningham asserts that "we should not think of divine and human agency as essentially contrastive," many of his underlying assumptions are laid bare.[31] The God so identified may be closer to the relationally available God of so much recent theology than to the "infinitely Other" God of Kierkegaard and Barth. Cunningham admits that at some points his God acts identically to the God of process theology, although he came to this conclusion via a different route.[32] Cunningham attests that the "double agency" that God, and especially the Holy Spirit, shares with us is evident in such Scriptures as:

> For you did not receive a spirit of slavery to fall back into fear, but you have received a spirit of adoption. When we cry "Abba! Father" it is that very Spirit bearing witness with our spirit that we are children of God. (Rom 8:15-16)

> Likewise the Spirit helps us in our weakness; for we do not know how to pray as we ought, but that very Spirit intercedes with sighs too deep for words. (Rom 8:26)

> And all of us, with unveiled faces, seeing the glory of the Lord as though reflected in a mirror, are being transformed into the same image from one degree of glory to another; for this comes from the Lord, the Spirit. (2 Cor 3:18)

We are led by these Scriptures, argues Cunningham, to the conclusion that "the biblical witness to the Spirit seems to underscore a stereoscopic vision of God and human beings as the agents of Christian practices. We act, but the Spirit acts through us—providing us with speech, prayer, and perhaps even the potential for deification."[33]

As a doctrine of salvation, Cunningham's statement that "we act, but the Spirit acts through us" is suspect, because it prioritizes human action over that of the Spirit and values human ingenuity over the grace that makes everything possible. But Cunningham's book is more about ethics and *practicing* trinitarian theology than it is about the salvation to which trinitarian theology bears a potent witness. Even so, had Cunningham highlighted that the Holy Spirit goes before human acts, which is one meaning of the phrase "prevenient grace," his theo-logic would be not only more modest but more in keeping with the firm lineaments of the Christian gospel.

---

[31]David S. Cunningham, *These Three Are One: The Practice of Trinitarian Theology* (Malden, Mass.: Blackwell, 1998), p. 234.

[32]Ibid., p. 305 n. 1.

[33]Ibid., p. 234.

When recently several professors from my alma mater retired, the alumni magazine featured a captioned "life statement" from each of them. Each statement was presumably not a teaser, not a "coming attraction," not a parting shot, but something closer to a distillation, a vantage point through which everything about that retiring professor's life could be more or less understood. For Cunningham the idea of participation is such a distillation, an ordering idea, that is not only a summit's peak but also at the same time a valley, a river, a plateau, a plain and everything else that gives texture and continuity to a life. Modeled on the perichoresis enjoyed among Father, Son and Holy Spirit, Cunningham believes "we too are called to live lives of mutual participation, in which our relationships are not just something that we 'have,' but are what constitute us as human beings."[34]

Cunningham is a theologian of culture who illustrates many of his theological points by drawing upon the works of great novelists such as Fyodor Dostoyevsky, Iris Murdoch and Toni Morrison.[35] In her novel *The Time of the Angels* Murdoch employs a copy of Andrei Rublev's renowned icon of the fifteenth century, "The Holy Trinity." For one who reads the novel with trinitarian eyes, Cunningham sees that "the icon becomes the central focus: not simply a scrap of wood being casually tossed about, but rather the only fixed point of reference in the story. It brings to presence pure mutual participation, willing donation, unbounded agapic love—everything that the novel's human characters lack."[36]

If Cunningham's assessment that "our culture is profoundly antitrinitarian"[37] is true, and sadly it is true, then Jean-Paul Sartre's one-act play *No Exit* is "Exhibit A" in the antitrinitarian gallery. Here the one fixed reference point is not, as in Murdoch's novel, a magnificent trinitarian icon but a bronze ornament on the mantelpiece of a drawing room done in the Second Empire style. Garcin, a pacifist journalist from Rio de Janeiro, calls it "a bronze atrocity.... A collector's piece. As in a nightmare."[38] Too heavy to be moved, the bronze ornament pres-

---

[34]Ibid., p. 169.

[35]For Dostoyevsky, see ibid., pp. 156-64, 322-25; for Murdoch see 190-95; for Morrison see 225-30.

[36]Ibid., p. 193.

[37]Ibid., p. 171.

[38]Jean-Paul Sartre, *No Exit and Three Other Plays*, trans. Stuart Gilbert and Lionel Abel (New

ages another immovable fact: that Garcin and his two codwellers, Inez and Estelle, each apportioned to his or her own sofa, are in this drawing room for life. As the three bite and scratch and gouge one another, and form unholy alliances they devolve into Sartre's indictment: "Hell is—other people!"[39]

Father, Son and Holy Spirit are from all eternity a happening of love and mutual regard. But Inez, Estelle and Garcin implode into rivalry, jealousy and hatred. While alive, Inez was a stolid postal clerk in contrast to the flighty Estelle, who married a man nearly three times her age and killed the baby she had conceived with an illicit lover, causing the lover to blow his brains out. Forgetting all shame in the presence of Inez, Garcin and Estelle become drawing-room lovers. Now in hell, Inez more easily falls to hatred than to love, and Garcin believes that in fact Inez's hatred of him could be his salvation. Inez declares herself to be "a dead thing, ready for the burning" and "rotten to the core," a sadness equally true of Estelle and palpably so of Garcin.[40]

The cocktail of choice for these drawing-room habitués is bile, and like a prison cell whose naked light bulb is never out, Garcin faces an eternity "with one's eyes open. Forever. Always broad daylight in my eyes—and in my head."[41] Inez's speech sounds like well-crafted philosophy, but in reality is only resignation: "One always dies too soon—or too late. And yet one's whole life is complete at that moment, with a line drawn neatly under it, ready for the summing up. You are—your life, and nothing else."[42]

As an atheist's credo, Inez's seven-word plaint, "you are—your life, and nothing else" is unsurpassed. None of Estelle, Garcin and Inez has any resources to draw upon except calculated bitterness. If ever they rise even to being three "persons in relation," it is only to perfect the foul act of recrimination. What a contrast to those who populate hell is the triune God, whom Cunningham describes as "pure mutual participation: relation without remainder."[43]

York: Vintage Books, 1955), pp. 4-5.

[39]Ibid., p. 47.

[40]Ibid., p. 30.

[41]Ibid., p. 7.

[42]Ibid., p. 45.

[43]Cunningham, *These Three Are One*, p. 189.

At its best, life in hell is degrees of conflict. There is no peace in hell. But Cunningham believes that "the doctrine of the Trinity establishes the theological priority of peace" and that, being three, God could have chosen strife over peace.[44] But God's "resulting potentiality for conflict is faced and negotiated by means of mutual love and abundant donation—not through coercion, strife, or violence."[45] Even at their human best Garcin, Inez and Estelle could have managed only a passing, blighted unity, and their devilish worst usually prevailed. But Father, Son and Holy Spirit indwell and promote peace.

MUST CHRISTIAN ETHICS BE TRINITARIAN?

The doctrine of the Trinity is both the beginning of all Christian theology as well as the ending toward which it strives. Not every theological pronouncement may be demonstrably trinitarian, in an obvious, overt way. Is a theology of the miraculous, for example, necessarily trinitarian? Must Christian eschatology, aside from dispensational schemes wherein the Age of the Father yields to that of the Son and finally to that of the Spirit, be trinitarian? Theological doctrines dealing with revelation, salvation and the church may be more naturally trinitarian than is every particular thrust of the theological enterprise. Christology, the study of the person and work of Jesus Christ, obviously has a profound interface with the doctrine of the Trinity, and this is equally true for pneumatology, which investigates who the Holy Spirit is and how the Spirit acts in the world.

Not every theological "letter," then, bears a trinitarian postmark as decisively as every other. But, to extend the metaphor, every theological letter passes through this mailing system and none other, because all Christian doctrine is finally accountable to the Christian doctrine of God, the Trinity, and is fully susceptible to a trinitarian examination. The Trinity cannot be irrelevant for any theological investigation or formulation.

Is Christian ethics under precisely this identical obligation of passing the ultimate muster of trinitarian scrutiny? At first glance it seems not. Every system of Christian ethics is responsible to some vision of God that centers and unifies the whole effort. Yet some of these anchoring

---

[44]Ibid., p. 243.
[45]Ibid.

visions, these conclusions about the nature of God, are not necessarily trinitarian. Too close of an alliance with this or that philosophy may dull the trinitarian mandate, especially if one follows the perspective of Karl Barth, who famously opposed the incursion of all philosophy into Christian doctrine. Roman Catholic moral philosophy has traditionally been constructed on the basis of natural law. However convincing such proposals may be, does a natural-law approach hinge on a three-in-one God, or only on a monotheistic God? Likewise, Christian ethics that have borrowed heavily from social scientific analysis, economic models or political ideals may not be inherently trinitarian. In fact such ethics may have no trinitarian imagination at all.

Into the land of Christian ethics there are many possible portals and, once inside, a terrain to explore that is truly infinite. And yet the point of entry into this land of Christian moral discourse, this indispensable passport, must be the triune character of God. Just as a well-traveled passport will bear many colorful stamps of coming or going, entering and exiting dozens of countries, so the doctrine of the Trinity, and the many varieties of trinitarian theology thereby spawned, is the requisite point of entry into Christian ethics, as well as the encouragement toward a deeper and richer exploration than a simple, unmodified monotheism can ever afford.

If we return once again to the two historical trinitarian analogies, the psychological and the social, we find there much that is ethically relevant in many ways. Intrapersonal or intrapsychic conflicts—the war of the self against the self—may be released and resolved by contemplating the psychological analogy. This analogy, to refresh our memory, asserts that though each personality is deeply and richly layered, each of the layers presupposes the functional support of the others. Thus each of memory, understanding and the will, to use Augustine's example, is reliant and even contingent on the other two. Augustine's discovery of these trinitarian dynamics within his very self is recommended for one and for all. In Anders Nygren's descriptive phrase, "by entering into himself and examining his own nature, Augustine thinks he can pierce the mystery of the Holy Trinity."[46]

---

[46]Anders Nygren, *Agape and Eros*, trans. Philip S. Watson (Chicago: University of Chicago Press, 1982), p. 517.

The social analogy moves the conversation outside of one human mind trying to make sense of its psychological dynamics and engages the relational world. To herself, a woman may be simply a woman (if a woman can ever be simple!) sharing in a universal essence of womanhood. But to those who know her, those among whom she lives, she may be a mother, a sister, an aunt, a grandmother, a business executive, a gardener, a tennis player or whatever vocational and avocational life she has chosen for herself. The social analogy plays upon the one and the many theme, and sees this theme as flowering in a trinitarian light. The woman is our example of one in identity, as universally woman, and yet many in her various expressions and involvements. The ancient example posited three men who shared together an irreducible humanity and yet were still differentiated according to personal identity. None could dispute that Peter, James and John shared humanhood together, and not dogness, but these three men were even so vigorously different from one another.

Of what relevance are the psychological and the social analogies for Christian ethics? The oneness of God emerges most expectedly at the close of the psychological analogy and God's threeness follows from the social analogy. Christian ethics does not divide every conceivable case or possible situation according to its propensity toward either the one or the many, and yet to have these tools of analysis available for use is helpful. For example, if the agonies which often accompany end-of-life medical decisions are seen in a trinitarian light, great care will be taken to balance the oneness and singularity of the patient, which is itself very complex, with the manyness of others such as family members, the medical community and even the greater public good. The contemplation of abortion may become more sobering still if the developing fetus is viewed not as an isolated entity but as the fruit of parental love, the bond of love between mother and father, not as some parasitic incursion.

I heartily agree with Gregory Jones that "the moral life, understood most adequately in terms of Christian life, is to be lived in the mystery of the Triune God."[47] For Stephen Webb the mystery of God is wrapped up in God's ability to give excessively, and in his book *The Gifting God*

---

[47]L. Gregory Jones, *Transformed Judgment* (Notre Dame, Ind.: University of Notre Dame Press, 1990), p. 74.

Webb proposes "a trinitarian ethics of excess." He finds that the dynamics of giving is at the center of "theo-economics" and that theology's very task "is to show how God enables an excessive giving that promotes equality and reciprocity without thereby diminishing the power of excess."[48]

Living in the consumer age as we do, we understand with perfect clarity what excess is. But Webb is not thinking of the sort of excess that caused the man in Jesus' story to build more barns to store more worldly goods (Lk 12:17-19). He is thinking of the excess of grace and the surplus of love which, in the phrase of the gospel song, God "giveth, and giveth, and giveth again."[49] These multiplied gifts are *from* the triune God and *for* humankind. The interplay between God's free offer and humanity's chance to respond is in fact where the discipline of Christian theology happens. One of the centering tenets of the "theo-economics" of God "is to show that the gifts of God—primarily creation and salvation—are simultaneously free and undeserved, yet binding and obliging."[50] Here the meaning of *simultaneously* must apply only to "free and underserved," because God's grace is certainly prior to our human response, and not at the same time. The *yet* of binding and obliging must refer to a human response that is after God's free offer of grace. Regardless of the coordinates of time, Webb's point rings true. God's gift to humanity, while free, is not cheap. God's gift does invite from us our grace-enabled giving back to God.

On the occasion of our medium-sized and not ostentatious wedding, my bride, Stephanie, and I greeted wedding guests so long— punctuated by cake-eating photographs—that when the receiving line ended the reception was essentially over. When we grabbed a wedding sandwich we were essentially eating alone, the church hall deserted by then. We tried to give the gifts of hospitality and gratitude to acknowledge those who had attended, to thank them for their efforts. Given the institution of the wedding ceremony and the reception to follow, any

---

[48]Stephen H. Webb, *The Gifting God: A Trinitarian Ethics of Excess* (New York: Oxford University Press, 1996), p. 16.

[49]Annie J. Flint, "He Giveth More Grace."

His love has no limits, His grace has no measure,
His power no boundary known unto men;
For out of His infinite riches in Jesus
He giveth, and giveth, and giveth again.

[50]Webb, *Gifting God*, p. 84.

couple would have done likewise. Our standing long in that reception line was after a fashion the continuing of the giving impulse. Marriage is itself of divine origin, a primal divine gift. When Stephanie's father walked her down the aisle and gave her to me he was perpetuating the trajectory of giving.

A wedding and its aftermath is only a small demonstration of Webb's point that "God's giving [is] sovereign but not dominating, free but involved."[51] God gives to humankind in such a way "that both exceeds and maintains our own, initiating but also entering into acts that involve an extravagant outpouring and a cooperative return."[52] As I said previously, God's grace is assuredly freely given to all, but grace's profusion is denigrated if we ignore the implied demand that grace extends to us. God's unconditional love yet has the condition of God's costly undertaking to make love unconditional. Webb's claim that God's giving is "free but involved" brings to mind that working parent whose many exertions—two or three menial jobs—situate the child for a college education and the better life the parent never had. The parent's "sweat equity" is freely given, yet the parent is very much involved in what the child accomplishes with the free gift.

The language of extravagance and excess long ago entered the mainstream American idiom. Next to the stuffed iguana enticing customers into a Mexican restaurant along New York City's Fifth Avenue is a slogan tattooed on a thousand biceps: "Too much ain't enough." But Webb stands the excess of consumerism on its head and reclaims the meaning of excess for Christian ethics:

> Christian excess is not simply at odds with ethics but implies or, better, is itself an ethics. To go too far in the name of the other is to wager that hyperbole makes sense, that too much, sometimes, is just right. The strange logic of this rhetoric of giving enables us to solicit excess not as an intoxicating experience or as a means to a moderate ethics of neighborliness but as a conjunction of style and praxis that conjures and creates the bold and vigorous desire that finds the self in the other.[53]

Webb's admonition toward "a conjunction of style and praxis" is far more than reaching deep into one's pocket and retrieving all the coins

---

[51]Ibid., p. 123.
[52]Ibid.
[53]Ibid., pp. 140-41.

to "keep the kettle boiling" for the Salvation Army at Christmas. Webb is proposing nothing less than a fundamentally new way of encountering the world and looking at reality: the way of excessive giving that frees one from miserly grasping and misbegotten holding.

Oskar Schindler, near the end of Steven Spielberg's Holocaust masterpiece *Schindler's List*, is being praised for all of the Jews he has saved, over one thousand. Without benefit of anesthesia, several gold-filled teeth were recently extracted from some of Schindler's Jews, the found gold melted into a presentation ring given to Herr Direktor. The ring is inscribed in Hebrew with the Talmudic saying that is the lifeblood of the film: "Whoever Saves One Life, Saves the World Entire." Yet for Oskar Schindler to save one life, to save eleven hundred Jewish lives, was not enough. Amid tears and bodily wrenching Oskar proclaims, "I could've got more out." "I didn't do enough," he wails. Approaching his German touring car he wails, "Why did I keep the car? Ten people right there, the car." As heroic as was this Roman Catholic capitalist, he is just beginning to learn the ethics of excess.

Through Stephen Webb's deft and lucid handling the idea of the gift becomes, if not quite the hinge of all reality, then at least the end point of his considered arguments. Giving endures, giving multiplies, the gift performs. It really is the case in gift-giving that the right hand may not know what the left hand is doing. Webb asserts that "the gift is not controlled by the intention of the individual; the gift has its own amorphous and fluid energy, which moves it along in unpredictable and even faceless directions."[54]

Webb's explication of the theo-economics of God may be nothing other than an extended meditation on the Doxology: "Praise God from whom all blessings flow," and a lengthy commentary on James 1:17: "Every generous act of giving, with every perfect gift, is from above, coming down from the Father of lights, with whom there is no variation or shadow due to change." This Scripture places the origin of the gift within God the Father. Webb completes the triunity of giving by naming God the Son as the Given and God the Spirit as the Giving. God is hence the Giver, the Given, the Giving.[55] Webb clarifies that

---

[54]Ibid., p. 128.
[55]Ibid., p. 90.

God gives excessively, to the point of the given, as a way of empowering relationships of mutuality and reciprocity. In the end, what God gives is the power of giving itself, the possibility that we can all participate in the movement of giving with the hope that such generosity will be enhanced, organized, and consummated in God's very own becoming. God is, then, the Giver, the Given, and the Giving, in such a way that God's giving is a form of receiving that creates even more giving in turn.[56]

A traditional trinitarian Webb is not. At times he seems to subject everything he finds within God to his idea of the gift, thereby subjecting God to the Gift. Webb imagines that "from the gifting perspective there is reason to think not only that God has always given but also that God will continue to grow and change along with the gift and share in its various expressions and manifold destinations."[57] In reality being a Giver is only one thing God does, and at times God's will is accomplished not by the gift but by the withholding.

To Webb's credit, however, his understanding of the gift is not one-dimensional. Tragedy, loss and ambiguity often accompany the gift and at times actually constitute the gift: "giving occurs in and through loss, the wound, the wasted, suffering."[58] Nowhere is this truer than in the cross, which illumines "the christological dimension of giving." Therein we see that "Jesus Christ preserves both the futility and the fecundity of the gift. In Jesus Christ, the giving of God is both sacrificed and revealed, hidden and made manifest, squandered and returned, denied and reborn."[59] Through the thousand-day vigil with our daughter Rebecca, every word in Webb's antinomies has hit the target at one time or other. Different seasons of her healing, tragic regressions nearly to the point of her death, eruption of hope that often dissipated, the long, slow grind of her recovery: all of these confirm that her postcrash life is a gift, if a gift immersed in loss.

Not all Christian ethics, to return to our section-opening question, will concern themselves directly with the doctrine of the Trinity. Even the examples discussed in this chapter, notably Barth's divine command ethics and Stephen Webb's fascinating ethics of giving, may be more indirectly trinitarian than obviously so. The revival of trinitar-

---

[56]Ibid., p. 91.
[57]Ibid., p. 147.
[58]Ibid., p. 144.
[59]Ibid.

ian theology has yet to provoke a similar revival of trinitarian ethics, although any strong trinitarian theology will necessarily have at least an implicit ethics. Indeed, for many and possibly most leading trinitarian theologians, there can be no sharp division between theology and ethics. Jürgen Moltmann's epigram that the holy Trinity is our social program is a necessary conclusion from his theology.[60] Anyone who claims that the doctrine of the Trinity is the most practical of all theological doctrines had better be prepared to bolster this assertion with attention to ethics.

"Christian ethics" is a time-honored and traditional phrase, and I am not looking to mothball it in favor of "trinitarian ethics." The Christian ethicist realizes that such an ethics is necessarily launched from the Christian doctrine of God. This is universally acknowledged as the Trinity, so that, yes, Christian ethics will at one level of engagement or other be a trinitarian ethics. The goal of Christian ethics is not for one interpretive vector to compete for supremacy against all others, but rather that what the triune God requires of humanity may be known and the contours of grace applied to particular human situations.

---

[60]Jürgen Moltmann, quoted in John J. O'Donnell, *The Mystery of the Triune God* (New York: Paulist, 1989), p. 108.

Afterword

Of the many paths one might walk in the exploration of trinitarian theology, none is as promising as the christological. In Jesus Christ the Father's eternal Word has come into flesh:

> Word of the Father
> Now in flesh appearing

This is the gospel, and anyone who lives the gospel life lives to adore the Christ:

> O come, let us adore him
> Christ the Lord[1]

But adoration is not a natural human inclination. The seeds of adoration and its flowering are wrought in us only by God the Spirit.

The implicit and yet palpably present trinitarianism to which I have made frequent reference is subtly displayed in a spare novel of great spiritual power. *The Short Day Dying*, a first novel from Peter Hobbs, is spoken by an itinerant Methodist preacher in late-nineteenth-century England, apprenticing as a blacksmith. Brother Wenmoth, not yet thirty, and in that day nearly middle-aged, is often perplexed about life's

---

[1]John F. Wade, "O Come, All Ye Faithful" *(Adeste Fideles)* (c. 1743), trans. Frederick Oakley (1841).

expectations and invitations. Should he marry? Should he follow the many of that day who sought their fortunes in Australia?

Nature cannot be trusted for an accurate rendering and reading of the Holy, in spite of Brother Wenmoth's traversing of wind-raked paths that hug the cliffs overlooking the crashing surf. And yet God the Holy Spirit might be seen even in the morning's kitchen dust:

> In the mornings I sit exhausted watching the dust that fills the kitchen become living sparks in sunlight's forge. I have stayed there a long while until my imagination had convinced me that the dust had come to life. Tiny insects born of light alone. In the past I have taken this apparition for a reminder of the Holy Spirit among us that *he* is all around us even in the smallest of things.[2]

Brother Wenmoth's faith is incarnational and even perichoretic. The healing hand of Jesus Christ, whom Wenmoth prefers to call the Master, descends and touches corrupted human flesh. He "touched earthly flesh and filled it with white fire and made that flesh whole again its afflictions stripped away."[3] In the company of the distraught and soon to die Harriet French, an invalid, the Brother is drawn ever closer to the Master to whom both have given their utmost allegiance. Harriet's reception and reflection of Christ's love "breaks the days" of Wenmoth's tedious and brutal life in the forge.[4] Miss French and Brother Wenmoth become one in spirit through the Spirit of Jesus Christ.

The Short Day Dying finds the Holy Spirit in the kitchen dust and in the hope for revival. Christ as Master suffuses the dying Harriet French, whose suffering throws her toward the wounded and healing Christ: "she who suffers most is given to have most faith in her Saviour I am brought to tears thinking on it."[5] Harriet's all-night battle with an evil spirit ends when "her Saviour came to the foot of the bed the rock of her Salvation and light shone around the room and she rejoiced."[6]

The Lord Jesus Christ as Master resounds throughout this understated but piercing novel. He appears in multiples of the number of times one meets the Father and the Holy Spirit. But trinitarian the-

---

[2]Peter Hobbs, *The Short Day Dying* (Orlando: Harcourt, 2005), p. 148.
[3]Ibid., p. 149.
[4]Ibid., p. 20.
[5]Ibid., p. 55.
[6]Ibid., p. 75.

ology is not a matter of tallying up which divine person puts in the most appearances, because even to think thus ends in tritheism, where each person's identity is self-defined and not triunely wrought. Robert Jenson's compact yet all-encompassing phrase "the triune identity" is exactly correct.[7] None of three is a self-determined entity. None has his own, separable identity; although as Augustine taught, each defines himself relationally in contrast to the other two. This must be "God according to the gospel" in Jenson's subtitle.

The fact that Peter Hobbs makes more particular mention of Christ the Master is not a suspension of trinitarian sensibilities but a call to dig deeper. When Brother Wenmoth is called to negotiate with a woman soliciting a reward for her son's Sunday school attendance, even though the son has long since transferred to another Sunday school, he ruminates: "Where is the Father going to have *his* fair play from?"[8]

However unfairly those under the Brother's pastoral care may treat God the Father, God does not withhold the love of his Son or the power of the Holy Spirit. For Brother Wenmoth the primary gift of the triune God is not fairness but truth that steels the mind and changes the heart. Human cleverness is deceiving. What really counts is "the pulse's steady beat where we feel the truth in the heat of our blood."[9] This is not the hot-bloodedness of sensual passion but the assurance of the Holy Spirit.

The theological progression from the centrality of Jesus Christ to the fullness of God's triunity is what makes Christian theology Christian. If there is a perennial theology, this is it. This theme, often articulated in the history of Christian thought, is well spoken by "Christ Is Made the Sure Foundation," a hymn originating in Latin in the seventh century:

> Christ is made the sure foundation,
> Christ the head and cornerstone,
> chosen of the Lord and precious,
> binding all the church in one;
> holy Zion's help forever
> and her confidence alone.

---

[7]Robert W. Jenson, *The Triune Identity: God According to the Gospel* (Philadelphia: Fortress, 1982).
[8]Hobbs, *Short Day Dying*, p. 32.
[9]Ibid., p. 65.

This ringing christological announcement is followed by the invitation for the Christ to visit, descend and indwell his holy temple. This visitation can only be started, never consummated, here below, so the singing pilgrims point ahead to glory in the penultimate stanza:

And hereafter in thy glory
Evermore with thee to reign.

All of this is only prologue to the fully endowed trinitarian reach of the final stanza:

Laud and honor to the Father,
laud and honor to the Son,
laud and honor to the Spirit,
ever Three and ever One,
consubstantial, co-eternal,
while unending ages run.[10]

The theologically sophisticated words, "consubstantial, co-eternal," chosen by translator John Mason Neale in 1851, are not widely understood today. To cast the God who is known as pure Spirit into the language of substance is today baffling, but it was well understood by the ancient mind for whom *substance* conveyed the sense of "spiritual essence."

Hymn singers of today may nearly always sing the modern "one in might and glory" instead of the archaic sounding "consubstantial, co-equal."[11] Regardless of the choice, whether the august and dignified "consubstantial, co-eternal" or the accessible, reassuring, yet challenging "one in might and glory," the finality of "while unending ages run" asserts itself. This is the truth of the God who is ever three and ever one.

---

[10]"Christ Is Made the Sure Foundation" *(Angularis fundamentum)*, trans. John M. Neal (1851).
[11]"Christ Is Made the Sure Foundation," *United Methodist Hymnal* (Nashville: United Methodist Publishing House, 1989), no. 559.

Index of Persons

Index of Subjects

Index of Scripture